THE

DIFFERENCE

"DIFFERENCE"

MAKES

THE
DIFFERENCE
"DIFFERENCE"
MAKES

women and leadership

EDITED BY

Deborah L. Rhode

STANFORD LAW AND POLITICS
An imprint of Stanford University Press
Stanford, California 2003

Stanford University Press
Stanford, California

Based on a leadership summit sponsored by the American
Bar Association Office of the President, the ABA Commission
on Women in the Profession, and the Center for Public
Leadership at the John F. Kennedy School of Government,
Harvard University.

The views expressed in this book are not necessarily those
of the ABA or its Commission on Women in the Profession.

Printed in the United States of America
on acid-free, archival-quality paper.

Library of Congress Cataloging-in-Publication Data

Rhode, Deborah L.
    The difference "difference" makes : women and leadership /
edited by Deborah L. Rhode.
        p.   cm.
    "Based on a leadership summit sponsored by the American
Bar Association Office of the President, the ABA Commission on
Women in the Profession, and the Center for Public Leadership
at the John F. Kennedy School of Government, Harvard
University"—Verso t.p.
    Includes bibliographical references and index.
    ISBN 0-8047-4634-6 (cloth : alk. paper) —
ISBN 0-8047-4635-4 (pbk. : alk. paper)
    1. Sex discrimination against women—United States.
2. Leadership in women—United States.   3. Women in the
professions—United States.   4. Equality—United States.
I. Rhode, Deborah L.
HQ1237.5.U6 D54   2003
303.3'4'0820973—dc21   2002015099

Original Printing 2003
Last figure below indicates year of this printing:
12   11   10   09   08   07   06   05   04   03

Designed by James P. Brommer
Typeset in 10/14 Sabon

for
MARTHA W. BARNETT
and
BARBARA KELLERMAN

Contents

III

WHEN DOES DIFFERENCE MAKE A DIFFERENCE?

IV

CHANGING THE CONTEXT AND CHANGING THE CAST:
BREAKING THE BARRIERS TO GENDER EQUALITY

V

WHAT ABOUT MEN?

VI

MEETING THE CHALLENGES

Acknowledgments

This publication grows out of a summit on women's leadership co-sponsored by the President's Office of the American Bar Association, the Association's Commission on Women in the Profession, and the Center for Public Leadership at the John F. Kennedy School of Government, Harvard University. As chair of the Commission and the planning committee for the summit, I owe many debts to those who joined me in the effort. I am especially grateful to Martha Barnett, then president of the ABA, who was the inspiration and guiding force for the summit, and to Barbara Kellerman, the executive director of the Center for Public Leadership at the John F. Kennedy School of Government, Harvard University, who embodies all the leadership qualities we discuss in this volume. I am also indebted to professors Herma Hill Kay and Linda C. McClain for their insightful comments and suggestions on an earlier draft. This publication was made possible by the superb research and manuscript preparation assistance of Paul Lomio, Shana Scarlett, Mary Tye, and Erica Wayne of Stanford Law School, and by the tireless dedication and exceptional talents of Pamela Krambuhl of the ABA Commission on Women in the Profession.

Contributors

TEVEIA R. BARNES is the executive director and general counsel of the Bar Association of San Francisco (BASF). Prior to her appointment at BASF, Ms. Barnes served as the executive director and general counsel of Lawyers for One America, as well as the associate general counsel and senior vice president for Bank of America. Ms. Barnes is the architect of various diversity initiatives and programs and is widely regarded as a national leader.

KIM CAMPBELL is known internationally as a preeminent woman leader and champion of women's rights. She is currently a visiting professor at Harvard University's John F. Kennedy School of Government. Ms. Campbell served as the nineteenth and first female prime minister of Canada in 1993. Prior to that service, she was the first woman to hold justice and defense cabinet portfolios, and was the first female defense minister of a NATO country. She is the chair of the Council of Women World Leaders and will assume the presidency of the International Women's Forum in 2003.

MARY B. CRANSTON is currently firm chair of the law firm Pillsbury Winthrop LLP. She is a former member of the American Bar Association's Commission on Women in the Profession and has received numerous honors for her work and accomplishments, including the Anti-Defamation League Distinguished Jurisprudence Award. Ms. Cranston has also been named to the National Law Journal's list of the hundred most influential lawyers in America.

ROBIN J. ELY teaches organizational behavior at Harvard University School of Business Administration. Prior to working at the business school, Dr. Ely was a professor of organizational behavior at Columbia University and Harvard University's John F. Kennedy School of Government, and a teaching fellow at Yale University. She is the author or coauthor of numerous publications and reports, and has served as a member and on the board of directors for the Feminist Institute.

JACOB H. HERRING is a management consultant who works with Fortune 100 companies in the area of diversity and affirmative action. He also works with law firms and corporate legal departments regarding the retention of minority attorneys. Mr. Herring has been a speaker at numerous conferences of the legal profession and women lawyer's associations. Prior to his career as a management consultant, Mr. Herring worked for the University of California at Berkeley as a staff psychologist in the Counseling Center, and practiced at Berkeley Therapy Institute.

LINDA A. HILL is the Wallace Brett Donham Professor of Business Administration and chair of Organizational Behavior Area and Leadership Initiative at Harvard Business School. Professor Hill's consulting and executive education activities have been in the areas of managing change, managing interfunctional relationships, globalization, career management, and leadership development. Organizations with which Professor Hill has worked include General Electric, IBM, PricewaterhouseCoopers, and Morgan Stanley Dean Witter.

MUZETTE HILL is the group leader for the Ford Motor Credit's Strategic Initiatives Practice. Prior to working at Ford, she was a partner at the Chicago law firm Lord, Bissell & Brook. Ms. Hill has received the Distinguished Service Award from the Black Women Lawyers Association, has been named to Crain's Chicago Business "40 Under 40" list, and is a member of the advisory board for the National Lawyer's Committee for Civil Rights.

PATRICIA IRELAND is the longest-serving president of the National Organization for Women (from 1991 through 2001). She currently lobbies on behalf of clients at the federal level and consults on equal employment and communication strategies. Ms. Ireland is of counsel to Katz Kutler Alderman Bryant & Yon and works in the Washington, D.C. office of that Florida-based firm. Ms. Ireland's publications include *What Women Want* (1986) and numerous articles and opinion pieces. Ms. Ireland's most recent work is a chapter opposing privatization of Social Security in *Controversial Issues in Social Policy* (2d ed. 2002).

ELAINE R. JONES is the president and director of the NAACP Legal Defense and Educational Fund. Prior to this position, Ms. Jones spent two decades as a litigator and civil rights activist. She became the first

African American elected to the American Bar Association Board of Governors, and is also a member of the executive committee of the Leadership Conference on Civil Rights and the board of the National Women's Law Center.

BARBARA KELLERMAN is the executive director of the Center for Public Leadership at Harvard's John F. Kennedy School of Government, where she is also a lecturer in public policy. Prior to this position, she served as a professor of political science at Fordham, Tufts, Fairleigh Dickinson, George Washington, and Uppsala universities. She has been awarded three Fulbright Fellowships and is the author or editor of many books and articles on leadership.

CHARISSE R. LILLIE is a partner at the law firm of Ballard Spahr Andrews & Ingersoll, LLP, in Philadelphia, where she is the chair of the litigation department. Her practice focuses on representing management in employment cases. She is the former city solicitor of the City of Philadelphia. She has defended major corporations, the City of Philadelphia, and the federal government in contract discrimination actions, as well as serving as an advisor to clients on diversity and antidiscrimination issues. She has received many awards and honors for her work regarding diversity and civil rights.

RUTH B. MANDEL is professor of politics and director of the Eagleton Institute of Politics at Rutgers University. Prior to her current position, Professor Mandel spent many years building and directing Eagleton's Center for American Women and Politics, where she remains affiliated as a senior scholar. Professor Mandel's teaching and publications focus on women and leadership with a particular emphasis on women in politics.

MICHELE COLEMAN MAYES is the vice president, legal and assistant secretary for the Colgate–Palmolive company. Ms. Mayes joined Colgate–Palmolive in 1992 after working for the Unisys Corporation as its staff vice president and associate general counsel for worldwide litigation. She is a former member of the American Bar Association's Commission on Women in the Profession and is currently the chair of the board for the NOW Legal Defense and Education Fund.

DEBRA E. MEYERSON is an associate professor at Stanford University's School of Education and a professor of management at the Center for Gender in Organizations at Simmons Graduate School. Her research interests include organizational change strategies directed at eradicating gender and race inequities, grass roots leadership practices in organizations, and men and women's strategies for constructing boundaries between work and other parts of their lives. She is the author of *Tempered Radicals: How People Use Difference to Inspire Change at Work* (2001) and more than thirty articles and chapters in popular and scholarly publications.

ELEANOR HOLMES NORTON is currently in her sixth term as the congresswoman for the District of Columbia. She has served as the Democratic chair of the Women's Caucus and was the first woman to chair the Equal Employment Opportunity Commission. Prior to her election to Congress, Ms. Norton served on the board of three Fortune 500 companies and as a tenured professor of law at Georgetown University, where she continues to teach a course each year. She has served as a member of the board of governors for the D.C. Bar Association and is on the boards of various civil rights and national organizations.

BARBARA RESKIN is a professor of sociology at the University of Washington and past president of the American Sociological Association. She has written six books and several dozen articles and chapters about gender and race inequality in the workplace, sex segregation, discrimination, and affirmative action. She has served as an expert witness in employment discrimination litigation. Ms. Reskin has lectured widely on her research both in the United States and abroad.

JUDITH RESNIK is the Arthur Liman Professor of Law at Yale Law School, where she teaches about federalism, feminism, and adjudication. Professor Resnik has chaired the Section on Women in Legal Education, as well as the Sections on Civil Procedure and on Federal Courts of the American Association of Law Schools. She is the recipient of the Margaret Brent Award from the American Bar Association Commission on Women in the Profession and is a member of the American Academy of Arts and Sciences and the American Philosophical Society. She is the author of several books and essays, including, as a coauthor, the monograph *The Effects of Gender: The Final Report of the Ninth Circuit Gender Bias Task Force* (July 1993), also reprinted in 67 *Southern California Law Review* 744–1081 (1994).

DEBORAH L. RHODE is the Ernest W. McFarland Professor of Law at Stanford Law School and director of the Keck Center on Legal Ethics. She has served as the chair of the American Bar Association's Commission on Women in the Profession, as president of the Association of American Law Schools, and as director of Stanford's Institute for Research on Women and Gender. She is vice chair of the board of the NOW Legal Defense and Education Fund, and a former board member of Equal Rights Advocates.

Professor Rhode is the author or coauthor of ten books and over a hundred articles on issues concerning gender or legal ethics and has been recognized by the *National Law Journal* as one of the country's fifty most influential women lawyers.

PATRICIA SCOTT SCHROEDER is the president and CEO of the Association of American Publishers. As a former member of the U.S. House of Representatives (Colorado) she has been dedicated to promoting human rights and equal opportunity throughout her career. She has been involved with numerous organizations and formerly served on the board of the NOW Legal Defense and Education Fund.

JEROME J. SHESTACK chairs the Litigation Department at Wolf, Block, Schorr & Solis-Cohen in Philadelphia. He served as the president of the American Bar Association from 1997 to 1998. Mr. Shestack has also served as the chair of the American Bar Association's section of Individual Rights and is the creator of the first ABA Committee on Human Rights. He is the author of some two hundred articles and op-ed pieces.

SHEILA WELLINGTON is the president of Catalyst, the nation's leading nonprofit agency focused on women's private sector leadership. Since her appointment as president of Catalyst in 1993, the organization has experienced unprecedented growth and expanded influence. Ms. Wellington is the author of *Be Your Own Mentor* (2001), which details the insights of top working women.

Foreword

MARTHA W. BARNETT

Some may say that it was predictable I would focus attention during the year I was president of the American Bar Association on issues related to women. In truth, I was in my mid-twenties before I really thought much about them or experienced my first taste of discrimination and learned about the stereotypes and prejudices facing women. By then it was too late, at least it was too late to intimidate me.

I wasn't naïve. I just had the good fortune to grow up in a family and a community where my gender was never a limiting factor. That same supportive and nurturing environment has followed me throughout my legal career. Women of my generation have benefited from a paradigm shift in the profession.

Women are the emerging majority in the legal profession and increasingly are called "Judge," "Dean," and "Madame Chair." They are managing law firms, running corporate legal departments—in some cases literally running the company—making rain, and changing attitudes. Women who are leaders in the profession have the opportunity to use those positions, and the power that comes with them, responsibly. We are obligated to finish the agenda started so many decades ago by true pioneers of our profession.

To explore these issues, the ABA office of the President and the ABA Commission on Women in the Profession, working with the Center for Public Leadership at the Kennedy School of Government, convened a Women's Leadership Summit. Participants addressed questions such as "what difference does difference make?" and "what about men?" Panels included some of the more remarkable and powerful women and men in the legal profession: leaders in government, law firms, bar associations, corporations, and academia.

The following pages provided the basis of discussion during this most interesting meeting. I hope they will spur further thinking on where women stand as leaders and where we can and indeed must go from here to continue to build a better future for all.

THE

DIFFERENCE

"DIFFERENCE"

MAKES

I

INTRODUCTION

DEBORAH L. RHODE

The Difference "Difference" Makes

INTRODUCTION

For most of recorded history, women were largely excluded from formal leadership positions. A comprehensive review of encyclopedia entries published just after the turn of the last century identified only about 850 eminent women, famous or infamous, throughout the preceding two thousand years. In rank order, they included queens, politicians, mothers, mistresses, wives, beauties, religious figures, and "women of tragic fate."[1] Few of these women had acquired leadership positions in their own right. Most exercised influence through relationships with men.

Since that publication, we have witnessed a transformation in gender roles. As Charlotte Bunche of the Women's Global Leadership Institute notes, "over the last three decades, women have taken a leadership role in redefining fundamental aspects of our lives—work, family, sexuality, equality, and justice."[2] Yet our progress is incomplete. Women remain dramatically underrepresented in formal leadership positions. The aim of this book, and the women's leadership summit on which it is based, is to explore the reasons for that underrepresentation and identify strategies for change.

This introductory chapter, which served as a background paper for the summit, examines "the difference difference makes" both in access to leadership and in its exercise. The chapters in Parts II and III address that same question from diverse perspectives. Barbara Reskin, Ruth Mandel, and Barbara Kellerman analyze the constraints and choices that women face, relying on research from sociology, psychology, political theory, leadership studies, and related fields. Jacob H. Herring, Patricia Scott Schroder, Sheila Wellington, Eleanor Holmes Norton, and Kim Campbell focus on the challenges that women face in particular contexts, such as law, business, and public service. Muzette Hill and Charisse R. Lillie pay special attention to the interaction of gender with race and ethnicity and to the additional obstacles confronting women of color. In Part IV, Debra E. Meyerson and Robin J. Ely, Linda A. Hill, Elaine R. Jones, Michele Coleman Mayes, and Mary B. Cranston offer perspectives on what works for individual women seeking to exercise leadership roles, and the organizational structures that can support that effort. In Part V, Teveia R. Barnes and Jerome J. Shestack look at what men can do to equalize leadership opportunities and how to enlist them as allies. A concluding section in this introductory chapter and the chapters by Patricia Ireland and Judith Resnik in Part VI suggest both institutional and individual strategies. The goal is to expand women's opportunities for leadership and to encourage its use in pursuit of the public interest in general and equality for women in particular.

Summarizing the relevant research is a daunting task. The last quarter century has witnessed a rapidly expanding volume of commentary on leadership, gender difference, and the relationship between the two. By the early 1990s, surveys identified over five thousand scholarly works on leadership and over five hundred programs in colleges and universities.[3] The market for leadership training, self-help publications, and popular commentary has been increasing as well, with a growing segment focused on women.[4] One emphasis of this work is on gender differences in opportunities—on the glass ceilings that exclude many women from leadership positions and on the subtle biases that confront women who attain such positions. A second area of emphasis involves gender differences in the exercise of leadership—differences in the styles, effectiveness, and priorities of men and women.

Yet despite this cottage industry of commentary, key concepts remain elusive. To begin with, there is no consensus on what accounts for effective leadership. At its core, leadership is generally viewed as the ability to influence and inspire others to act in pursuit of common goals, often beyond what their jobs or roles require.[5] The traditional assumption was that leaders had distinctive personal traits. However, most contemporary research suggests that effectiveness also depends heavily on context and on the relationship between the characteristics of leaders and the needs, goals, and circumstances of their followers.[6] Researchers have identified a broad range of qualities, behaviors, and processes that are conducive to effective leadership but have not provided widely accepted theories about the leadership techniques or training that are most successful in practice.[7]

The literature on gender difference is similarly expansive, and the concept is similarly elusive. No issue is more central, or more contested, among those concerned with equality for women. There is widespread agreement that gender difference does make a difference in virtually all aspects of social experience. But there is no corresponding consensus on the origins or implications of difference in many contexts, including leadership. Nor is there agreement on the extent to which gender differences are experienced differently by different groups in different contexts. As researchers have increasingly noted, there is no "generic woman," and too little work has explored the interrelationship between gender and situational forces or other characteristics such as race, class, ethnicity, age, and sexual orientation.[8]

Yet despite these limitations, recent research casts considerable light on the opportunities and obstacles for women leaders. This chapter explores key findings concerning the difference "difference" makes in leadership. The focus is on formal, high-level positions in law, politics, and business, because these are the contexts where the greatest public influence is exercised and the most systematic information is available.

This focus is not meant to understate the importance of women's leadership in other contexts or to assume that formal positions always carry the most power. For example, many women have had enormous influence through their roles in workplace, cultural, community and nonprofit organizations, religious institutions, professional associations, and social reform movements. Yet although such contributions should not be undervalued, neither should we overlook the effects of exclusion from formal policy positions. By gaining a better sense of what we know and what we only think we know about women's leadership opportunities, we may also find ways to expand their roles and responsibilities in the pursuit of public interests.

GENDER DIFFERENCES IN
LEADERSHIP OPPORTUNITIES

A central problem for American women is the lack of consensus that there is a significant problem.[9] Gender inequalities in leadership opportunities are pervasive; perceptions of inequality are not. A widespread assumption is that barriers have been coming down, women have been moving up, and equal treatment is an accomplished fact. Two-thirds of surveyed men and three-quarters of male business leaders do not believe that women encounter significant discrimination for top positions in business, the professions, or government.[10] In the most recent poll by the journal of the American Bar Association (ABA), over half of lawyers of both sexes agreed that women are treated equally in the profession. Only a quarter of female lawyers and 3 percent of male lawyers thought that prospects for advancement were greater for men than for women.[11] Although other surveys paint a somewhat less optimistic picture, many Americans agree with the statement by Hewlett Packard's first female CEO at the time of her appointment: "the accomplishments of women across industry demonstrate that there is not a glass ceiling."[12]

Such views are hard to square with the facts. Although women have made enormous progress over the last several decades, they remain underrepresented at the top and overrepresented at the bottom in both the public and private sectors. Women now account for about half of managerial and professional positions but only 12 percent of corporate officers, 4 percent of top corporate earners, and about 1 percent of the Fortune 500 CEOs.[13] Almost 30 percent of lawyers are women, but they represent only about 15 percent of federal judges and law firm partners, 10 percent of law school deans and general counsels at Fortune 500 companies, and 5 percent of managing partners at major law firms.[14] Women constitute over half of American voters but only 25 percent of senior executive branch officials, 22 percent of state legislators, 16 percent of the mayors of large cities, 15 percent of congressional representatives, 6 percent of state governors, and no congressional committee chairs.[15] The United States ranks fiftieth in the percentage of women elected to legislative offices.[16] The underrepresentation of women of color is even greater. They account for only about 3 percent of state legislators, 3 percent of congressional representatives, 1 percent of corporate officers, and under 1 percent of law firm partners. Only two women of color serve as mayors of large cities, and only two as general counsel or chief executive of a Fortune 500 corporation. None serve as chief executives or state governors.[17]

What explains these disparities is a matter of dispute. One common assumption is that they are the product of cultural lag; current inequalities are the legacy of discriminatory practices that are no longer legal, and it is only a matter of time until women catch up. About two-thirds of male chief executive officers attribute women's low representation in leadership positions to the fact that they have not been in the pipeline long enough.[18] Such assumptions are equally common in gender bias studies on the legal profession.[19] However, this pipeline theory cannot explain the underrepresentation of women leaders in fields such as law or management, where they have long constituted between a third and half of new entrants.[20] Nor can cultural lag explain the disparities in advancement among male and female candidates with comparable qualifications.[21] For example, studies involving thousands of lawyers with similar entry-level credentials have found that men are at least twice as likely as women to obtain partnership.[22] As the discussion below indicates, many female professionals still do not receive the same opportunities to develop leadership qualifications as their male colleagues. In short, the pipeline leaks, and if we wait for time to correct the problem, we will be waiting a very long time. At current rates of change, it will be almost three centuries before women are as likely as men to become top managers in major corporations or to achieve equal representation in Congress.[23]

In accounting for gender disparities, a wide array of research reveals certain persistent and pervasive patterns. Women's opportunities for leadership are constrained by traditional gender stereotypes, inadequate access to mentors and informal networks of support, and inflexible workplace structures.

Gender Stereotypes

In order to make sense of a complex social world, individuals rely on a variety of techniques to categorize information. One strategy involves stereotypes, which associate certain socially defined characteristics with identifiable groups. In virtually every society, gender is a fundamental aspect of human identity, and gender stereotypes influence beliefs, behaviors, and self-concepts at both conscious and unconscious levels.[24] Perceptions of leadership ability are inescapably affected by these stereotypes, which work against women's advancement in several respects.

First, and most fundamentally, the characteristics traditionally associated with women are at odds with the characteristics traditionally associated with leadership.[25] It is scarcely surprising that positions of greatest power should be identified with men, since men have historically dominated those positions. The "great man" theories of leadership that once dominated the field were not using the term generically.[26] Most qualities traditionally linked with leaders have been masculine: forceful, assertive, authoritative, and so forth.

Although recent theories of leadership have stressed the need for interpersonal qualities more commonly associated with women, such as cooperation and collaboration, women aspiring to leadership still face double standards and double binds. They risk appearing too "soft" or too "strident," too aggressive or not aggressive enough.[27] And what is assertive in a man often seems abrasive in a woman. An overview of more than a hundred studies involving evaluations of leaders indicates that women are rated lower when they adopt "masculine," authoritative styles, particularly when the evaluators are men or the role is one typically occupied by men.[28] Since other research suggests that individuals with masculine styles are more likely to emerge as leaders than those with feminine styles, women face tradeoffs that men do not.[29]

The dilemma is not, however, insolvable. As subsequent discussion in this chapter notes, many women leaders have developed approaches that effectively combine masculine and feminine traits. But most researchers agree that the range of appropriate behavior is narrower for women than for men, especially in traditionally male-dominated fields such as law, management, and politics. Women who take strong positions risk being stereotyped as "bitchy," "difficult," or "manly."[30] Women who try to avoid those assessments risk losing ground to men who are more assertive.

A related obstacle for female leaders is that they often lack the presumption of competence accorded to their male counterparts. Despite a broad array of evidence summarized below finding that women perform at least as effectively as men in leadership roles, an equally substantial body of research indicates that women face greater difficulty in establishing their capability and credibility.[31] Surveys of women professionals find that the vast majority believe that they are held to higher standards than their male counterparts.[32] Political polling data indicate that male candidates generally start with a significant advantage over female opponents; men are seen as more decisive and better leaders than women.[33] Where the number of women is small, as is often the case in leadership contexts, their performance is subject to special scrutiny and more demanding requirements.[34] The devaluation of women and the influence of gender stereotypes is especially likely in organizations that have few women in leadership positions.[35] Even in experimental situations where male and female performance is objectively equal, women are held to higher standards, and their competence is rated lower.[36]

A wide array of research similarly finds that many women internalize these stereotypes. They see themselves as less deserving of rewards for the same performance and often lack confidence to take the risks or seek the challenges that would equip them for leadership roles.[37] Preconceptions about women's lesser competence or experience then become self-fulfilling prophesies. Such patterns also help explain why women are less likely to be viewed as leaders as similarly situated men.[38] For example, when individuals see a man seated at the head of a table for a meeting, they typically assume that he is the leader; they do not make the same assumption about a woman.[39] Nor do they accord her the same deference. And when women do seek to exercise control or authority, they have more difficulty than men in doing so effectively. Behavior that is acceptable for male leaders is often considered "bossy" and "domineering" in their female counterparts.[40] Indeed, executive training programs are now available to reeducate "bully broads" whose "toughness" is perceived to be a liability.[41]

Autobiographical accounts and opinion polls reveal repeated patterns of such double standards and demeaning stereotypes. Accomplished attorneys still face questions such as whether they can "really understand all the economics involved in this case."[42] Women seeking public office are still considered less able to manage conflict or financial affairs.[43] Only half of surveyed Americans believe that people are comfortable with the idea of a woman president.[44] Traditional gender biases are particularly common when evaluators have little accountability for their assessments and when those evaluated are women of color.[45] Disfavored groups find that their mistakes are more readily noticed and their achievements more often attributed to luck or special treatment.[46] Adverse stereotypes are most problematic for women of color who are frequently assumed to owe their positions to affirmative action rather than professional qualifications.[47]

Women with children face additional double standards and double binds. Working mothers are held to higher standards than working fathers and are often criticized for being insufficiently committed, either as parents or professionals. Those who seem willing to sacrifice family needs to workplace demands appear lacking as mothers. Those who take extended leaves or reduced schedules appear lacking as lawyers. These mixed messages leave many women with the uncomfortable sense that whatever they are doing, they should be doing something else.[48] Assumptions about the inadequate commitment of working mothers adversely influence performance evaluations, promotion decisions, and opportunities for challenging assignments that are prerequisites for leadership roles.[49] After maternity leaves, some women lawyers report being given such routine work that they are tempted to offer responses such as, "Look, I had a baby not a lobotomy."[50] Former Congresswoman Pat Schroeder encountered so many questions about her ability to balance family and work responsibilities that she finally pointed out that she had both a "brain and a uterus, and they both work."[51]

The double bind comes through clearly in public opinion polls. Voters are skeptical of both women who are childless and women who have children at home.[52] A recent case in point involves Massachusetts Lieutenant Governor Jane Swift, who was elevated to the governor's office while she was pregnant with twins. Her husband's willingness to serve as a full-time primary caretaker did little to allay public concerns. Who would provide the backup for child care and "the backup for the backup?" How could a governor adequately juggle lactation and legislation? As columnist Ellen Goodman summarized the situation, "Jane Swift is expecting and [the voters] are expecting. A lot."[53]

Any resolution of these challenges is problematic. Many women who wait to seek leadership positions until their children are grown never catch up with male competitors. Other women who attempt to juggle demanding work and family obligations simultaneously may lack sufficient "face time" to allay colleagues' or voters' concerns. Politicians who miss "too many pancake breakfasts" have been thought "insufficiently committed" to justify party support for higher office.[54] And women lawyers who "cook and tell," by acknowledging the need to be home for dinner, frequently find themselves off the track for advancement.[55] The irony is that it generally takes exceptional career commitment for women to juggle competing work and family responsibilities in unsupportive working environments. As one lawyer told a Boston Bar Association task force: "On most days I am taking care of children or commuting or working from the moment I get up until I fall in bed at night. No one would choose this if they weren't very committed."[56]

The force of traditional stereotypes is compounded by other biases. People are more likely to notice and recall information that confirms prior assumptions than information that contradicts them.[57] Since many lawyers assume that a working mother is unlikely to be fully committed to her career, they more easily remember the times when she left early than the times when she stayed late. So, too, attorneys who assume that women of color are beneficiaries of preferential treatment, not meritocratic selection, will recall their errors more readily than their insights. A related problem is that people share what psychologists label a "just world" bias.[58] They want to believe that in the absence of special treatment, individuals generally get what they deserve and deserve what they get. Perceptions of performance frequently are adjusted to match observed outcomes. If women, particularly women of color, are underrepresented in positions of greatest prominence, the most psychologically convenient explanation is that they lack the necessary qualifications or commitment.

These assumptions can again become self-fulfilling prophecies. Expectations affect evaluations, work assignments, and other career development opportunities. In effect, biased assumptions adversely affect performance, which reinforces the initial assumptions. Those in leadership positions are less likely to support and mentor women who appear unlikely to succeed. Women who are not supported are less likely to succeed and are more likely to leave. Their disproportionate attrition then reduces the pool of women mentors and role models and further perpetuates the assumptions that perpetuate the problem.[59]

The problem is compounded by the disincentives to raise it. A common response is to "shoot the messenger." Women who express gender-related concerns may learn that they are "overreacting" or exercising "bad judgment."[60] For example, one African American attorney serving on her corporate employer's equal opportunity task force made the mistake of candidly reporting problems in her own department. As she learned, many colleagues are "not really comfortable" with complaints about discrimination and they do not want to work with people "who make [them] uncomfortable."[61] The result is to stifle candid discussions of diversity-related issues. Targets of bias are reluctant to appear confrontational, and decision makers are reluctant to air concerns about performance that could make them appear biased.[62] Moreover, because stereotypes operate at unconscious levels and selections for leadership positions involve subjective and confidential judgments, the extent of bias is hard to assess. It is, however, instructive that in large-scale surveys of senior executive women, the most frequently cited obstacle to advancement is "male stereotyping and preconceptions."[63] In organizations where women are unprepared for leadership positions, the reason is often that too many men are unprepared to have female colleagues in such positions or to provide the career development opportunities that would get them there.

Unconscious bias is a problem not only for the individual women who encounter leadership barriers, but also for their employers, who are failing to take full advantage of the talent pool available. Limited opportunities for career development adversely affect female employees' morale, performance, and retention. For example, in the most recent study by the National Association for Law Placement, the top two reasons that women lawyers leave their firms are desires for more challenging work and better advancement potential.[64] For many employers, women's high rates of attrition impose substantial costs in recruitment, training, and disruption of working relationships.[65]

Mentoring and Support Networks

Another common obstacle for women leaders is the difficulty in obtaining mentors and access to informal networks of advice, contacts, and support. In surveys of upper-level management, between about a third to a half of women cite the lack of influential mentors as a major barrier to advancement.[66] Women lawyers and politicians experience similar problems.[67] Many men who endorse equal opportunity in principle fall short in practice; their efforts focus on other men who seem most similar in backgrounds, experiences, and values.[68] As one participant in the Department of Labor's Glass Ceiling survey explained, "What's important [in organizations] is comfort, chemistry . . . and collaborations," which are harder to sustain among those who seem "different."[69] Concerns about sexual harassment or the appearance of impropriety can heighten that discomfort. Some men are reluctant to mentor or be seen alone with a female colleague because of "how it might be perceived."[70] Others enjoy the bonding that occurs in all-male social or sporting events.

Surveys of professional women offer repeated refrains of exclusion from "boys clubs" or "old boys' networks."[71] Participation in informal networks is particularly difficult for women with demanding family commitments, who lack time for the social activities that could generate collegial support and client contacts. As Catalyst President Sheila Wellington notes, at the end of the day, many "men head for drinks. Women for the dry cleaners."[72] Men pick up career tips; women pick up laundry, kids, dinner, and the house.

The result is that many women remain out of the loop of career development. They are not adequately educated in their organization's unstated practices and politics. They are not given enough challenging, high-visibility assignments. They are not included in social and marketing events that yield professional opportunities. And they are not helped to plan a career progression that will groom them for leadership. Even when they obtain senior positions, many women often lack the support from influential clients and colleagues that would confer significant power.[73]

Problems of exclusion are greatest for those who appear "different" on other grounds as well as gender, such as race, ethnicity, disability, or sexual orientation. Many women of color report being treated as outsiders by white colleagues and as potential competitors by minority men.[74] In one recent ABA survey, less than 10 percent of black attorneys believed that law firms had a genuine commitment to diversity, and other studies reflect similar skepticism about corporate legal departments.[75] Despite growing tolerance toward gay and lesbian attorneys, those who are open about their sexual orientation too often risk isolation and denial of access to clients who might be "uncomfortable" working closely with them.[76] Even in jurisdictions that prohibit discrimination on the basis of sexual orientation, some professionals are quite explicit about their prejudices. As one anonymous participant in a Los Angeles bar survey described his firm's attitude: "Don't have any, don't want any."[77]

Men are, of course, not the only group responsible for patterns of exclusion. Recent research chronicles lingering difficulties with what sociologists once labeled "Queen Bees:" women who believe that they managed without special help, so why can't everyone else?[78] These women enjoy the special status that comes with being one of the few females at the top of the pecking order and are willing to serve as proof that gender is no barrier to those who are qualified. Although the vast majority of women leaders are more sensitive to gender-related problems, they are not always actively involved in the solution. Some women are hesitant to become "typed as a woman" by frequently raising "women's issues," by appearing to favor other women, or by participating in women's networking groups.[79] Other senior women, particularly women of color, do what they can but are too overcommitted to provide sufficient mentoring for all the junior colleagues who need assistance.[80] Given the demographics of upper-level positions, women will remain at a disadvantage unless and until adequate support networks are seen as both individual and institutional priorities.

Workplace Structures

A similar point can be made about workplace practices that fail to accommodate family commitments. A wide gap persists between formal policies and actual practices. Although most women in law and upper-level management are in businesses or partnerships that offer part-time work or flexible schedules, few of these women feel able to take advantage of such options. For example, over 90 percent of surveyed law firms report policies permitting part-time schedules, yet only about 3 percent of lawyers actually use them.[81] Most women surveyed believe, with good reason, that any reduction in hours or availability would jeopardize their prospects for advancement and could put them "permanently out to pasture."[82] They doubt, as do senior women in other contexts, that their organizations truly support workplace flexibility.[83] That doubt is reinforced by a wide variety of research, which finds that even short-term adjustments in working schedules, such as leaves or part-term status for under a year, result in long-term reductions in earnings and advancement.[84]

The problem is compounded by the sweatshop schedules routinely expected of those who seek or occupy leadership positions. Hourly requirements have increased dramatically over the last two decades, and what has not changed is the number of hours in the day.[85] For senior executives, top government officials, and partners in law firms, all work and no play is fast becoming the norm rather than the exception; fifty to seventy hour workweeks are typical.[86] Unsurprisingly, most surveyed female executives and lawyers feel that they do not have sufficient time for themselves or their families.[87] Few supervisors are as blunt as the partner who informed one junior colleague, "Law is no place for a woman with a child."[88] But surveys on work and family issues consistently report that leadership positions are incompatible with involved parenting.[89] That same message is sent by resistance to "special" treatment for women seeking to accommodate family obligations without compromising opportunities for advancement. As one observer wryly put it, "Can a woman have a high-powered professional career and still have children? Sure, just as long as she doesn't plan on ever seeing them."[90] And women who do not have a family often lack time for relationships that might lead to one. Unmarried law firm associates routinely end up with disproportionate work because they have no acceptable reason for refusing it.[91]

Although the inadequacy of family-friendly policies is not just a "women's issue," women pay a disproportionate price. Part of the problem involves women's biological clocks. The demands of bearing and caring for young children generally are most intense during the same period in which the foundations for career development are laid. Moreover, despite a significant increase in men's domestic work over the last two decades, women continue to shoulder the major burden.[92] Most male leaders in business and professional positions have spouses who are full-time homemakers or who are working part-time. The same is not true of female leaders, who, with few exceptions, are either single or have partners with full-time jobs.[93]

Underlying these inequalities are longstanding socialization patterns and workplace practices. Only about 13 percent of Fortune 1000 companies and 10 percent of surveyed law firms offer the same paid parental leave to fathers as well as mothers, and few men actually take them.[94] Although involved fathers are receiving somewhat greater support, most research suggests that the special leeway extends only so far. As a male lawyer explained to a Boston Bar Association work-family task force, it may be "okay [for men] to say that they would like to spend more time with the kids, but it is not okay to do it, except once in a while."[95]

In short, many workplace structures leave both men and women feeling unfairly treated. Men feel that they have fewer acceptable justifications than women do for seeking reduced schedules. Women feel that their justifications will never be seen as truly acceptable as long as their concerns are viewed as "women's issues." In short, men cannot readily get on the "mommy track." Women cannot readily get off it.

The resistance to flexible or reduced schedules stems from multiple causes. Part of the problem involves the long-standing devaluation of "women's work" in the home and many decision makers' failure to appreciate the conflicts it presents in workplaces designed by and for men. The problems are exacerbated by recent increases in competition and technological innovations, which have accelerated the pace of commercial life and created expectations of instant responsiveness.[96] Many lawyers also blame the escalation of hours on excessive salary demands by associates and unrealistic assumptions of total availability by powerful clients.[97] In some fields, unpredictable deadlines, uneven workloads, or frequent travel pose particular difficulties. In other contexts, a willingness to work long hours is viewed as a proxy for harder to measure qualities such as commitment, ambition, and reliability under pressure.[98] The result is a "rat race equilibrium" in which most individuals feel that they would be better off with shorter or more flexible schedules but find themselves in workplaces that offer no such alternatives.[99]

Those with substantial family commitments often drop off the promotion track, leaving behind a decision-making structure insulated from their concerns. Many professional and business leaders who have made substantial personal sacrifices to reach their positions resent the burdens imposed by colleagues with different priorities. Law firm surveys repeatedly find senior women as well as men whose attitude is, "I had to give up a lot. You [should] too."[100] If women want to be "players," the message is that they have to play by the existing rules.[101]

Yet these rules make little sense, even from a narrow economic calculus. A wide array of research from both professional and business settings indicates that part-time employees are more efficient than their full-time counterparts, particularly those working sweatshop schedules.[102] Bleary burned-out workers seldom provide cost-effective services and they are more susceptible to stress-related health disorders.[103] Nor are these full-time employees necessarily more accessible than those on reduced or flexible schedules. An attorney at a deposition for another client is less available than an attorney with a cell phone on the playground. What little research is available finds no negative impact on client relations from reduced or flexible schedules.[104] And considerable data indicate that such arrangements save money in the long run by reducing absenteeism, attrition, stress-related dysfunctions, and corresponding recruitment and training costs.[105]

That is not to discount the challenges posed in crafting accommodations that will be truly fair to all concerned. In some contexts, the nature of the work or the unavailability of other qualified employees may sabotage good faith efforts to reduce workplace demands. But those efforts are lacking in too many organizations, and too many women pay the price. What they lose is not only time for families but also opportunities for community involvement and public service that could enrich their capacities for leadership.

The Adverse Effects of Unequal Opportunities

Law has been of limited effectiveness in addressing these dynamics of gender disadvantages. Unlike previous, more overt forms of discrimination, current inequalities are typically a function of unconscious bias and workplace structures. These consequences are often difficult to trace to discrete intentional actions of identifiable individuals.[106] Legal claims of discrimination are therefore hard to prove and expensive to pursue, financially and psychologically. Plaintiffs are putting their performance on trial and the portraits that emerge are seldom entirely flattering. Even the rare complainant who wins in court may lose in life. Backlash, blackballing, and informal retaliation are common problems.[107] Moreover, the risk of discrimination claims often discourages employers from collecting data that would reveal systemic problems.[108]

This absence of information masks the true costs of gender inequality in leadership. Most obviously, the barriers to women's advancement compromise fundamental principles of equal opportunity and social justice. These barriers carry an organizational price as well. Workplaces that are preoccupied with short-term measures of productivity and bottom-line costs of family policies may fail to calculate the longer-term costs in recruitment and retention that the absence of such policies impose. As management experts have increasingly recognized, the "business case for diversity" is clear. A wide array of research indicates that the representation of women in leadership positions has a positive correlation with economic performance, measured in tangible terms such as organizational growth, increased market share, and return on investment.[109] Although correlation does not always imply causation, there are strong reasons to believe that greater diversity in fact promotes effective leadership.

The most obvious reason is demographic. Women represent a substantial and growing share of the pool of talent available for leadership. Organizations that create a culture of equal opportunity are better able to attract, retain, and motivate the most qualified individuals.[110] Reducing the obstacles to women's success also reduces the costs of attrition. It increases employees' morale, commitment, and retention and decreases the expenses associated with recruiting, training, and mentoring replacements.

A further rationale for ensuring equal access to leadership positions is that women have distinct perspectives to contribute. In order to perform effectively in an increasingly competitive and multicultural environment, organizations need a workforce with diverse backgrounds, experiences, and styles of leadership.[111] The point is not that there is some single "woman's point of view." But as the following discussion indicates, gender differences do make some difference, and they need to be registered in leadership positions.

GENDER DIFFERENCES IN LEADERSHIP STYLES AND PRIORITIES

Leadership Styles

The last two decades have witnessed the growth of a cottage industry of commentary on gender differences in leadership. Over two hundred empirical studies and a still greater volume of journalistic and pop psychological accounts have attempted to assess such differences in leadership styles and effectiveness.[112] These analyses reflect quite different views of women's "different voice," in part because their methodologies and quality vary considerably. Many claims of a distinctive female leadership style are based on anecdotal evidence, small samples, or highly artificial laboratory studies. Adequate information on women lawyers in leadership roles is particularly thin, as is research on the interaction of gender with other characteristics, such as race, ethnicity, age, class, and sexual orientation. As noted earlier, sweeping generalizations about women's experience risk overclaiming and oversimplifying.

However, some experts have helped make sense of the data on difference through sophisticated meta-analytic techniques, which cumulate findings from multiple studies after controlling for their quality.[113] Other researchers have also achieved greater reliability by examining large samples of leaders in organizational settings and by collecting evaluations from observers as well as self-reports from participants. Taken together, these studies challenge certain conventional assumptions about women's leadership.

First, perceptions of gender differences in style or effectiveness remain common, although the evidence for such differences is weaker than commonly supposed. For example, a survey of senior executives by the Economic Group and Korn Ferry International identified five top traits in female managers that reflect widely accepted stereotypes: effective women leaders were thought to be empathetic, supportive, nurturing, relation-building, and sharing.[114] In a recent ABA poll, only 8 percent of women lawyers believed that male and female lawyers had the same strengths, and only 18 percent believed that they had the same weaknesses.[115] Women lawyers were thought to have greater empathy and "better people skills" but insufficient assertiveness and aggressiveness.[116] Public opinion polls reveal similar assumptions about female politicians.[117]

The factual basis for such assumptions is thin. It comes largely from self-reports and laboratory studies, which often indicate that women leaders display greater interpersonal skills and adopt more participatory, democratic styles, while men rely on more directive and task-oriented approaches.[118] Yet other large-scale studies based on self-reports find no such gender differences.[119] Nor do these differences emerge in most research involving evaluations of leaders by supervisors, subordinates, and peers in real-world settings.[120] Most of these studies also fail to reveal significant gender differences in the effectiveness of leaders, although, as noted earlier, there are some contexts in which women are rated more poorly than men.[121] These tend to involve predominantly male evaluators and male-dominated roles, such as military service. But in some contexts, women are rated as more effective. One recent study by the Foundation for Future Leadership involving some six thousand evaluations of nine hundred managers found that women scored better than men on all but three of thirty-one measures; female managers did worse only in coping with pressure and their own frustrations, and scored the same in delegating authority.[122] Three other recent large-scale studies involving a total of

over sixty-five thousand managers similarly found that women outper-
formed men on all but a few measures.[123]

In accounting for such divergent results, leadership experts offer several
explanations. One involves socialization. Conventional gender roles encourage women to develop interpersonal skills and sensitivities, which increase their comfort level with participatory styles.[124] A second explanation involves gender stereotypes, which are particularly likely to influence
lab studies and self-reports. In experimental situations, where participants
have relatively little information about each other, they are more likely to
fall back on these conventional assumptions about appropriate masculine
and feminine behavior. Such stereotypical assumptions may also discour-
age individuals from behaving or describing their behavior in ways that
deviate from traditional norms.[125] Since women do not enjoy the same
presumption of competence or the same latitude for assertiveness as their
male colleagues, a less autocratic leadership style may seem necessary.[126] A
third explanation is that few studies on effectiveness adequately control
for variations in perceived power, so some gender-linked differences may
have more to do with variations in authority than in performance.[127]

It is not surprising that the force of conventional stereotypes is weaker
in actual organizational settings than in lab studies or self-assessments.
Women who have achieved leadership positions generally have been selected and socialized to conform to accepted organizational norms.[128] It
stands to reason that their styles are similar to those of male counterparts, particularly since recent trends in leadership education have encouraged both sexes to adopt more collaborative, interpersonally sensitive approaches.[129] Nor is it surprising that some studies find superior
performance by women leaders, given the hurdles that they have had to
surmount to reach upper-level positions and the pressures that they have
faced to exceed expectations.

Leadership Priorities

An equally important, but far less studied, cluster of issues involves the
extent to which women use their leadership differently than men, the reasons for such differences, and the conditions under which they emerge.
Of particular significance are the circumstances and motivations that encourage women leaders to support women's issues.

On the relatively infrequent occasions when researchers ask whether women have different leadership priorities than men, the answer generally is "some women some of the time." The most systematic studies involve judges and politicians. With respect to judicial behavior, the findings are mixed, and their reliability is sometimes limited by small sample sizes and inadequate controls for factors other than gender. Early studies tended not to find significant gender differences in judges' voting behavior, even in cases involving women's rights.[130] By contrast, some of the more recent studies have found differences at least on certain issues, although not always on women's rights or on sentencing matters traditionally thought to inspire feminine compassion.[131]

An equally critical question is the extent to which women judges have used their leadership to press for changes in the legal process that would make it more responsive to the needs of women. Here again, the evidence is mixed. In some respects, as Judge Gladys Kessler notes, "there has truly been a 'revolutionary reform' of the justice system's response to women's concerns" in areas such as domestic violence, child support, and gender bias.[132] Much of this reform has resulted from efforts by female judges, not only through their rulings but also through their work in organizations such as the National Association of Women Judges.[133] Yet as Kessler also observes, many women leaders have "become the victims of [their] own success." They have so many personal opportunities and claims on their time that their collective reform efforts are suffering from a "fading sense of urgency, diminishing energy, and a loss of commitment."[134] To take only one example, women leaders of the legal profession have often failed to take a leadership role on issues involving access to justice. Over four-fifths of the legal needs of the poor are unmet, and most courts have no formal services to assist underrepresented parties.[135] Since two-thirds of those living in poverty are women, they bear a disproportionate cost for these policy failures. And women judges and bar leaders bear at least some of the responsibility.

A similarly mixed picture emerges for political leaders. Without question, women in public office have made an enormous difference on issues of particular concern to women. Research on state and federal legislatures and high-ranking political appointees consistently finds that female representatives are more likely than their male colleagues to support and sponsor initiatives dealing with the interests of women and families and to rank such initiatives among their highest priorities.[136] In one study of congres sional behavior, women accounted for over 90 percent of the sponsors and two-thirds of the cosponsors of bills involving women's issues.[137] As the Center for American Women in Politics concludes, women policymakers have reformulated the agenda, redefined the debate, and reshaped the results on causes of particular concern to women.[138]

Yet while the distinctive contributions of women leaders should not be undervalued, neither should they be overstated. Political party affiliation is more important than sex in predicting votes supporting women's issues, and political ideology is more important in predicting sponsorship of legislation on these issues.[139] In one representative survey, congresswomen on average cast only one more vote advancing women's interests than their male counterparts.[140] Some of the worst voting records on women's rights belonged to women.[141] Less than half of surveyed female state legislators identify themselves as feminists, and relatively few make feminist concerns a top priority.[142] Some still run campaigns with the strategy that Barbara Boxer wryly described as the traditional wisdom for female candidates: "You never mentioned being a woman . . . you hoped nobody noticed."[143] World leaders also provide ample reminders that putting women in power is not the same as empowering women. To address women's interests, we need leaders of both sexes who have that commitment.

The same point could be made about other leadership contexts. What limited information is available about women lawyers and senior managers provides a similarly mixed record. Many of these women have made a crucial difference in promoting women's issues and in creating institutional structures that will do the same. The ABA Commission on Women in the Profession is a reflection of those efforts, as are women's bar associations, women's management and leadership organizations, and women's networks in law firms and corporations. These institutions have both provided support for individual members and pressed for policy changes on issues such as family leaves, sexual harassment, flexible or reduced schedules, performance evaluations, mentoring programs, and other diversity initiatives.[144]

Yet surveys of lawyers, politicians, and managers also reveal large numbers of senior women who do not actively advocate women's interests. One of the most common complaints by female associates in law firms is that some powerful female partners have not "played a role in promoting the opportunities and quality of life" for junior colleagues.[145] Many female leaders in business and politics have been similarly reluctant to press gender issues openly.[146] Underlying these different priorities are differences in personal experience and commitments, personal rewards and risks, and personal influence and self-confidence.

Personal Experience and Commitment

The most obvious factor accounting for different levels of support for women's issues among women leaders is their personal investment in those issues. For some women, their own experiences of discrimination, marginalization, or work-family conflicts leave them with a desire to make life better for their successors.[147] Other women, who do not initially see themselves as advocates for women's issues, take on that role when they realize that others are unwilling to do so.[148] Many female politicians report that their priorities shifted when they found themselves one of a small minority of women in a legislature indifferent to some of women's key interests.[149] As Republican Congresswoman Marge Roukema explained, "When I first came to Congress, . . . I really didn't want to be stereotyped as the woman legislator. . . . But I learned very quickly that if the women like me in Congress were not going to attend to some of these family concerns, . . . then they weren't going to be attended to."[150] Many senior women in business and professional contexts similarly end up representing the "woman's point of view" largely by default. They are often asked to serve as the "token woman" to ensure the fact (or at least the appearance) of diversity, or are enlisted by other female colleagues to raise their concerns. In these circumstances, women leaders generally feel a responsibility to speak out on gender issues that would otherwise remain unacknowledged and unaddressed.[151]

However, as noted earlier, not all women who experience bias or token status become committed to reform. Some of these leaders have internalized the values of the culture in which they have succeeded. As their colleagues note, these women have "gotten there the hard way," "given up a lot," and "conformed to the system."[152] Their assumption is that if they managed, so can anyone else.

Rewards and Risks

What lessons women draw from their own struggle may in part depend on what consequences they anticipate from continuing the struggle on behalf of other women. The costs and benefits of raising gender-related concerns vary considerably across contexts. For some women, the rewards from pressing such concerns outweigh the risks. Either they are "not high enough" in leadership circles to worry that their advocacy will seem threatening, or they are high enough that their own career will not be threatened.[153] So too, some women work in organizations or represent political constituencies that make it safe to raise women's issues, and to "stan[d] up for what [they] believe."[154] Other, more tangible benefits can also result from becoming a "squeaky wheel."[155] For lawyers and senior managers, these benefits may include more equitable compensation structures, greater flexibility in workplace schedules, increased career or client development opportunities, and a larger critical mass of supportive female colleagues.[156] For legislators, important political advantages may flow from addressing concerns of the women voters and the women's organizations that helped get them into office.[157] Even where career-related rewards are absent, many women take substantial personal satisfaction from helping to ensure that the next generation has opportunities that they did not.

Yet for other women, any such benefits come at too great a cost. Surveys of female lawyers, politicians, and corporate executives reflect common concerns. The first involves becoming "pigeonholed" as a "feminist" or "women's libber."[158] Female politicians from conservative districts generally want to avoid any "politically charged" women's issues; it is better for them to be known simply "as representatives, not women representatives."[159] And women working within conservative organizations similarly worry about taking positions that will brand them as "extremist," "militant," "strident," "oversensitive," "abrasive," "disruptive," or "difficult to work with."[160] Even when they express gender-related concerns in gentle, non-confrontational terms, women may risk being dismissed as "self-serving" "whiners" who are "unable to compete without special treatment."[161]

Such reputational risks leave women leaders in a double bind. Those who "rock the boat" on women's issues may lose the collegial support and career development opportunities that would provide a power base within their organizations and make their advocacy effective.[162] But those who obtain influence by becoming one of the "good old boys" cannot easily defect when gender-related controversies arise.[163] So too, some women who made substantial sacrifices in their own family lives in order to obtain leadership positions have difficulty supporting junior colleagues who want similar status without making similar sacrifices. As one of those colleagues put it, the attitude of these senior women is "I don't have what you have and therefore you can't have what I have."[164]

Personal Influence

How women leaders balance the rewards and risks of pressing women's issues also depends on their position within an organization. Most obviously, as former *New York Times* columnist Anna Quindlin notes, women who feel confident that they are "not going to get busted down to private any time soon" have the greatest opportunity to help other women who lack that security.[165] Judges with life appointments, elected officials with "safe seats," law firm partners with a large client base, or senior executives with outstanding profit records often can afford to deliver unwelcome tidings without serious risks.

Whether they are willing to do so may depend in part on their confidence that such advocacy will prove effective. Can they convince senior colleagues that there *is* a serious "woman problem" in their workplace? Can they make a persuasive business case for reform? Can they minimize the backlash that claims of "special treatment" often generate? And can they avoid the "battle fatigue" that comes from persistently raising concerns that others find inconvenient to acknowledge, let alone address?[166] Helping more women leaders reach better answers to these questions must be part of any reform agenda.

AN AGENDA FOR CHANGE

An effective agenda for women's leadership confronts two central challenges. The first is to ensure that women have equal access to leadership opportunities. A second challenge is to enlist and empower women in using their leadership to advance the public interest in general and women's equality in particular. With opportunities come obligations, and the point of this publication is to help identify promising individual and institutional strategies for change.

When asked what would be different if women ran the world, Harvard Professor Rosabeth Moss Kanter responds that the world would already have changed if it were possible for women to run it.[167] Bringing us closer to this goal will require more leaders who can envision the strategies that will make equal opportunity possible.

Institutional Strategies

Commitment and Accountability

The most important factor in ensuring equal access to leadership opportunities is a commitment to that objective, which is reflected in institutional priorities, policies, and reward structures.[168] Organizations must be prepared to translate principles into practice and to hold individuals accountable for the results. In law firm and corporate settings, managers need to build a business case for diversity, to incorporate diversity goals into their organizational plans, and to make progress toward those goals a factor in performance evaluations.[169] Individuals need to be rewarded for recruiting, retaining, mentoring, and promoting women. To make that possible, organizations need to monitor the effects of workplace practices on equal opportunity goals. Diversity-related initiatives also must be structured in ways that do not cause undue backlash. For example, one company that attempted to provide financial incentives for employing women at senior levels found that male employees' resentment made the "grab a girly" approach counterproductive.[170]

Organizations vary in their need for, and responses to, particular diversity-related strategies. The most successful equal opportunity initiatives are those that are responsive to the gender dynamics of different workplace cultures.

Assessment of Problems and Responses

To promote equal opportunity in practice as well as principle, it is often helpful to conduct formal or informal surveys. Their objective should be to assess gender-related issues in areas such as leadership positions, promotion patterns, and quality of life.[171] Organizations need to know whether men and women are advancing in equal numbers, whether they feel able to take advantage of alternative schedule policies, and whether they feel equally well supported in career development. A related strategy is to enlist diversity consultants or task forces in identifying barriers to equal opportunity and in designing educational programs and other appropriate responses.[172] Where an organization's leadership fails to acknowledge a significant "woman problem," survey findings or recommendations by outside experts and advisory groups can sometimes prove persuasive. And where colleagues fail to perceive the stereotypical assumptions and structural barriers that limit women's opportunities, diversity training can be similarly effective.[173] However, such initiatives need to be seen as a catalyst, not as a substitute, for change, and they must be part of a systematic, sustained strategy. Many women, particularly women of color, support diversity training but doubt the effectiveness of current efforts. As one disillusioned associate noted, law firms can hire consultants or "put on programs until the cows come home," but significant progress will also require leaders to act on the recommendations they hear.[174]

That, in turn, will require benchmarks for measuring progress and procedures for monitoring performance. Comparisons with similar institutions and guidance from best practice standards by bar associations and management organizations can often help in developing realistic strategies. However, the effectiveness of these strategies may depend less on their specific content than on the process by which they are adopted and implemented.[175] Although that process will vary across organizations, its basic objective should be the same: to ensure that women's concerns are fully understood and systematically addressed.

Leadership Evaluation, Selection, and Structures

Research by organizations such as Catalyst and the ABA Commission on Women in the Profession suggest a number of specific practices concerning leadership opportunities that should be subject to scrutiny. One set of practices involves the processes by which individuals are evaluated for promotion and selected for leadership positions. For example, the Commission has recommended various strategies that can help eliminate gender bias in performance assessments, which can in turn diversify the pool from which leaders are chosen. Such strategies include formalizing personnel processes and expectations; monitoring evaluations for adverse stereotypes; placing greater reliance on objective, outcome-related criteria; reviewing assignments to ensure equal opportunities for career development; and educating attorneys about how to give and receive effective performance assessments.[176] Having associates evaluate their supervisors can also help identify gender-related concerns and provide some measure of accountability for addressing them.[177]

Reexamining leadership selection systems, criteria, and structures can be equally important. More democratic, participatory processes generally increase women's access to decision-making roles. For example, in law firms, elections of managers from a slate chosen by a nominating committee usually ensures more diversity than systems relying on appointments by senior partners or incumbents.[178] More democratic procedures also enable coalitions to rally behind candidates who are responsive to gender-related concerns. Rotation systems can similarly help women gain leadership experience and expertise, while preventing entrenchment of senior attorneys who may not view diversity as a central priority. Selection criteria that do not give excessive weight to business development are also critical. Both women and firms can benefit from adequate consideration of other leadership capabilities, such as interpersonal and human resources skills.

Organizations can also help equalize leadership opportunities by providing adequate support for women who assume them. Many individuals, especially those with significant family responsibilities, have seen too little to gain from accepting a senior management position. Others have dropped off the leadership track after being "worn down and worn out" by serving as token women with insufficient influence to compensate for the burdens.[179] Ensuring adequate recognition, respect, and credit for leadership obligations could encourage more women to seek them and could provide the critical mass necessary for reform.

Quality of Life and Work-Family Initiatives

Any serious commitment to equalize leadership opportunities requires a similarly serious commitment to address work-family conflicts and related issues involving quality of life. Promising proposals are not in short supply. The ABA Commission on Women in the Profession, Catalyst, local bar associations, and experts in the field have identified best practices concerning matters such as flexible or reduced schedules, telecommuting, leave policies, and child-care assistance.[180] Although the details of effective policies vary across organizations, the key factors are mutual commitment and flexibility. Both the individual and the institution have to be committed to adjustments that will work effectively for all concerned. Employees on reduced schedules should be prepared to increase their hours when short-term needs emerge. Their colleagues should avoid taking advantage of that availability and should make reasonable accommodations of scheduling constraints. Technological innovations that blur the boundary between home and work can both assist and sabotage these efforts. With e-mails, cell phones, beepers, and faxes, individuals may become perpetually tethered to their offices. Organizations need to prevent employees who seek to demonstrate their commitment and accessibility from ending up with part-time status but full-time work.

Organizations also need to ensure that employees who seek temporary accommodations do not pay a permanent price. "Stepping out" should not necessarily mean "stepping down"; individuals on reduced or flexible schedules should not lose opportunities for challenging assignments or eventual promotion. Nor should other employees bear undue burdens to compensate for their colleagues' restricted availability. Peer resentment can sabotage the most family-friendly policies.

Finally, and most important, quality of life concerns need to be seen not just as "women's issues" but also as organizational responsibilities. Employers who want to ensure the most able and diverse pool of leadership candidates must also ensure a working environment that will attract, support, and retain them. At a minimum, that will often require adjustments in workplace schedules and reward structures. Organizations need to encourage the broad-gauge experience that comes from family, community, and pro bono pursuits.

Mentoring Programs and Women's Networks

Although the importance of mentors has long been recognized, the institutionalization of mentoring has lagged behind. For many women, the support of an influential senior colleague is critical in securing leadership opportunities. Mentors can sponsor women for challenging assignments and prestigious positions, as well as refer clients and provide business development opportunities. Mentoring relationships can also help prepare women to become leaders and to take full advantage of the opportunities that come their way. Senior colleagues can provide career advice, serve as role models, and offer personal support.[181] In many mentoring relationships, the rewards run in both directions. Quite apart from the satisfaction that comes from assisting those who need assistance, senior colleagues may receive more tangible benefits from the loyalty and influence that their efforts secure. Talented junior colleagues generally want to work for effective mentors and to support them in seeking and exercising leadership.

Yet as earlier discussion indicated, these benefits have not been sufficient to ensure that all women, particularly women of color, have adequate assistance. Part of the problem is that leadership levels in law, business, and politics are dominated by white men who bond most easily with other men, or who worry about the appearance of forming close relationships with women. So, too, some senior women worry about the appearance of favoritism if they focus their support on female colleagues. In any event, the number of senior women is too small and their schedules are too crowded to provide support for all the junior colleagues who need it.

Formal mentoring programs can help fill the gap. Of course, relationships that are assigned are seldom as effective as those that are chosen.[182] But some access to advice and support is better than none, and formal programs at least reduce men's concerns about appearances that inhibit mentoring relationships. Well-designed programs that evaluate, monitor, and reward mentoring activities can make a significant difference; the benefits show up in participants' skills, satisfaction, and retention rates.[183]

Another strategy is to encourage voluntary mentoring through women's networks and related activities. A growing number of initiatives have emerged both within and across organizations. At least a third of Fortune 100 companies have women's groups, and such associations are becoming increasingly common in law, politics, and other fields.[184] Many individuals on the leadership track also belong to women's business or professional organizations outside their workplace. These networks sponsor a variety of activities, such as workshops, seminars, speaker series, talent banks, and informal social events. Some groups link professionals with potential clients; some help individuals develop marketing, leadership, media, and other career-advancement skills; and some focus on representing women's shared concerns in their professions or workplaces. Many of these networks play a crucial role in addressing the sources and symptoms of gender inequality. They expand aspirations, expose obstacles, and identify solutions. By bringing women together around common interests, these networks can encourage informal mentoring, forge coalitions on gender-related issues, and enhance individuals' reputations within the broader community.

Building effective networks does, however, present its own share of challenges. Not all women—or men—see the value of separatism. Some women are concerned about being "branded" with women's issues or appearing to want special favors.[185] Other women view particular networks as too inclusive or not inclusive enough. Groups with broad memberships often encounter difficulties in building cohesiveness and in responding effectively to diverse needs. By contrast, groups that restrict their size and focus may be viewed as elitist and insensitive to concerns of those most in need of assistance, such as women of color or women in lower-level positions.[186] Many men express further concerns. Some senior managers worry that exposure of gender-related problems may build demand for expensive solutions or create liability issues if the organization is ever sued for sex discrimination. Other men resent having their employer subsidize career development opportunities that are not available to them.[187]

How best to respond to these concerns varies across organizations. Some networks have attempted to reduce resentment by including men as members or by inviting their participation in certain events. Other groups have built a business case for all-female memberships by demonstrating substantial profits from their marketing initiatives.[188] Proactive recruiting and inclusive programming efforts have also helped networks increase their responsiveness to underrepresented groups, especially women of color. Although the activities of successful networks differ, they generally rely on similar processes. After systematically assessing women's needs, these groups establish attainable goals and monitor progress. The "small wins" that such efforts can secure often lay the foundations for fundamental change.[189]

The Role of Education, Professional Associations, and Public Policy

Equalizing leadership opportunities is the responsibility not only of employers but also of other public and private institutions. Educators at all levels should make greater efforts to inspire and equip women to assume leadership positions. Business, professional, and public policy schools are especially likely to prepare future leaders and therefore have a special obligation to convey the importance of diversity and exemplify the strategies necessary to achieve it. At a minimum, that will require far more schools to integrate diversity-related issues in their core curricula; to respond effectively to problems of bias and intolerance; and to address the underrepresentation of women students, faculty, and administrators in leadership roles.[190]

Professional associations have comparable opportunities and obligations. They can actively promote and prepare women for leadership in their own ranks and encourage employers to do the same. State and local

associations can follow the lead of national organizations such as Catalyst and the ABA Commission on Women in the Profession and adopt
model policies and best practices. They can monitor employers' progress
and work together with professional schools and women's groups to provide training, mentoring, and educational programs on diversity-related
issues. Professional associations can also actively work for structural reforms concerning workplace schedules and reward structures that affect
women's access to leadership.

A similar role is possible for those in public office. Women's access to
leadership is affected by a broad range of social policies, such as those
concerning affirmative action, child care, family leave, and equal opportunity enforcement. Women's ability to influence those policies depends
partly on access to public office and the structure of campaign financing.
Experience in many European countries suggests that electoral reforms
could make a major difference in opening opportunities for women. As
many politicians at the ABA-Harvard leadership summit made clear, one
of the best ways to equalize access to power is for more individuals to
make that a priority and provide financial support for candidates and
causes that advance this objective.

Social Responsibility

Organizations that are truly committed to equal opportunity must also
assume some obligation to promote it in the world outside their workplace. Although pro bono and social responsibility initiatives are not dis-
tinctively "women's issues," they hold particular importance for women
in several respects. First, many women enter fields such as law and politics with a commitment to social justice and social welfare.[191] Support
from these women and their employers has been crucial to the struggle
for gender equality. To take only the most obvious examples, the ABA
Commission on Women in the Profession and the women's rights organizations represented at the ABA-Harvard leadership summit have all de-
pended on pro bono support from the private sector. Public interest initiatives are an essential vehicle for women of influence to use that
influence for the common good and to speak on behalf of those who cannot speak effectively for themselves.[192]

Greater support from a greater number of individuals and institutions
is needed. Too few law firms and businesses that are readily able to make
substantial contributions have actually done so. For example, over the

last decade, although the revenues of the nation's one hundred most profitable law firms have more than doubled, pro bono contributions have dropped by a third; lawyers at these firms average only about eight minutes a day on public interest work.[193] The average contribution for the profession as a whole is less than half an hour a week.[194] Too many women work in organizations where bottom-line concerns have discouraged the public interest pursuits that traditionally have ranked among professionals' most satisfying experiences. According to ABA surveys, lawyers' greatest sense of disappointment in their careers is lack of connection to "the common good."[195] For many business and professional leaders, public service also provides opportunities for valuable training, experience, and community contacts. It is a way for women to connect their ideals and institutions and to develop the vision necessary for effective leadership in any context.

Individual Strategies

Similar points can be made about leadership strategies for individuals. Most obviously, women need to press for institutional changes that will help equalize leadership opportunities and promote socially responsible exercises of leadership. Women who have gained leadership positions need to mentor junior women and to support women's networks, women's causes, and women candidates. Women who are seeking such positions need to take advantage of the opportunities that are available. Demonstrating leadership abilities is the clearest path to greater leadership responsibilities. To that end, women should understand and communicate their own strengths, seek mentors and challenging assignments, develop informal relationships with influential colleagues and clients, and cultivate a reputation for effectiveness within professional and business communities.[196] These efforts should include attention to areas where women's performance has traditionally been thought weak, such as on-line positions for managers or foreign policy positions for politicians.[197] Individual career development plans and formal leadership training may also enhance interpersonal capabilities. Common areas of focus include risk-taking, conflict resolution, and strategic vision.[198]

The greatest challenge lies in adapting sufficiently to succeed within an organization without losing the capacity or commitment to change it. Part of that challenge, according to surveyed women managers and professional consultants, lies in finding a "style that men are comfortable with."[199] Projecting a decisive and forceful manner without seeming arrogant or confrontational is an important skill. But as many participants in the ABA-Harvard leadership summit also emphasized, women also need to find a style that *they* are comfortable with, and respectful confrontation is sometimes a necessary catalyst for change. There is no single style that is most successful; different approaches will be appropriate for different settings at different times. The key is for women to be strategic in choosing their battles. That means keeping a focus on long-term goals and determining what public or private actions are most likely to be effective in reaching those objectives.

Although what works best depends heavily on context, most research underscores one generalizable strategy. In order to retain both an insider's influence and an outsider's critical perspective, women need allies.[200] Support from respected colleagues, both men and women, is crucial for gaining leadership positions and leverage. Support from women's groups, both inside and outside the organization, can be equally critical. Leaders need to be reminded of progress yet to be made and their own responsibility for its achievement.

The importance of such reminders is brought home by a popular women's history exhibit. At museums like the one at Seneca Falls commemorating the birth of the American women's movement, visitors are invited to write their responses on a display asking what the world would be like if men and women were truly equal. Suggestions have included "homophobia will be unnecessary"; "Revlon will go bankrupt"; and "everything will be pretty much the same, except men and women will be equally responsible for the condition." The point of publications like this collection is to suggest an alternative vision in which gender difference makes a difference and to support leadership opportunities that will make this vision a reality.

NOTES

1. Karin Klenke, *Women and Leadership: A Contextual Perspective* 27 (1996).

2. Charlotte Bunch, quoted in Helen S. Astin and Carole Leland, *Women of*

Influence, Women of Vision: A Cross-Generational Study of Leaders and Social Change xi (1991).

3. Klenke, *Women and Leadership*, at 12, 241; *Talking Leadership: Conversations with Powerful Women* 7–8 (Mary S. Hartman, ed. 1995).

4. Barbara Kellerman, *Reinventing Leadership: Making the Connection Between Politics and Business* 177 (1999).

5. Jeanette N. Cleveland, Margaret Stockdale, and Kevin R. Murphy, *Women and Men in Organizations: Sex and Gender Issues at Work* 287, 319 (2000); Sumru Erkut, *Inside Women's Power: Learning from Leaders* 2 (2001).

6. Klenke, *Women and Leadership*, at 61; Cleveland, Stockdale, and Murphy, *Women and Men in Organizations*, at 288–292.

7. Klenke, *Women and Leadership*, at 12; Kellerman, *Reinventing Leadership*, at 149, 175–179.

8. Elizabeth V. Spelman, *Inessential Woman: Problems of Exclusion in Feminist Thought* 114–117 (1988); Deborah L. Rhode, *Speaking of Sex* 22, 41 (1997).

9. Rhode, *Speaking of Sex*, at 1–19.

10. Federal Glass Ceiling Commission, *Good for Business: Making Full Use of the Nation's Human Capital* 145 (1995).

11. Hope Viner Samborn, "Higher Hurdles for Women," *ABA J.*, Sept. 2000, at 30, 33.

12. John Markoff, "Hewlett-Packard Picks Rising Star at Lucent as Its Chief Executive," *N.Y. Times*, July 20, 1999, at C1 (Quoting Carly Fiorina); for more pessimistic assessments see text at note 32 infra; Catalyst, *Women in Law: Making the Case* 22 (2001); Abbie F. Willard and Paula A. Patton, National Association for Law Placement (NALP) Foundation, *Perceptions of Partnership: The Allure and Accessibility of the Brass Ring* (1999).

13. Catalyst, *Catalyst Facts: Women in Business* (2000), and *2000 Census of Women Corporate Officers and Top Earners* (2000); U.S. General Accounting Office, *A New Look Through the Glass Ceiling: Where Are the Women?* 2 (Jan. 2002). See also Tamar Lewin, "Women Profit Less Than Men in the Nonprofit World, Too," *N.Y. Times*, June 3, 2001, at A26 (reporting gender disparities in the nonprofit sector).

14. ABA Commission on Women in the Profession, *A Snapshot of Women in the Law in the Year* 2000; ABA Commission on Women in the Profession, *The Unfinished Agenda: Women and the Legal Profession* 14 (2001).

15. Marjorie E. Kornhauser, "A Legislator Named Sue: Re-Imagining the Income Tax," 5 *Journal of Gender, Race, and Justice* 289, n. 2 (2002); Marie Tessier, "Washington Lookout: Women's Appointments Plummet Under Bush," *Women's ENews*, July 1, 2001, at [www.womensenews.org]; Center for American Women in Politics, *Women in Elected Office, 2000 Fact Sheet Summaries* (May 2000); Ruth B. Mandel, "Women's Leadership in American Politics: The Legacy and the

Promise," in *The American Woman 2001–2002: Getting to the Top* 43, 45 (Cynthia B. Costello and Ann J. Stone, eds. 2001); Associated Press, "No Women Chair House Panels," *Houston Chronicle*, Jan. 6, 2001, at A1; Mary Hawkesworth, "Gender Gap: American Women Still Trail in Elected Office," *Dallas Morning News*, Mar. 8, 2000, at A17.

16. Kornhauser, "A Legislator Named Sue," at 289 n. 2.

17. Catalyst, 2000 *Census*; Catalyst, *Women of Color in Corporate Management: Three Years Later* (2002); ABA Commission on Opportunities for Minorities in the Profession, *Miles to Go: Progress of Minorities in the Legal Profession* 3–5 (2000).

18. Catalyst, *Women in Corporate Leadership: Progress and Prospects* 37 (1996).

19. Rhode, *Speaking of Sex*, at 3–4, 140; *Report of the Ninth Circuit Gender Bias Task Force, The Effects of Gender in the Federal Courts* 60 (discussion draft, 1992) (quoting male attorney's suggestion that women should "relax and let time take care of the problem").

20. ABA Commission on Women in the Profession, *Unfinished Agenda*, at 14.

21. Virginia Valian, *Why So Slow? The Advancement of Women* 214–16 (1998); Rhode, *Speaking of Sex*, at 141–146; Virginia Valian, "The Cognitive Basis of Gender Bias," 65 *Brook. L. Rev.* 1037 (1999); Cherryl Simrell King, "Sex Role Identity and Decision Styles: How Gender Helps Explain the Paucity of Women at the Top," in *Gender Power, Leadership, and Governance* 67, 71 (Georgia Duerst-Lahti and Rita Mae Kelly, eds. 1995).

22. ABA, Young Lawyers Division, *The State of the Legal Profession* (1991); Cynthia Fuchs Epstein et al., "Glass Ceilings and Open Doors: Women's Advancement in the Legal Profession," 64 *Fordham L. Rev.* 291 (1995) (noting that in the period of study, men's chances of making partnership were 17 percent and women's 5 percent); Cynthia Grant Bowman, "Bibliographical Essay: Women and the Legal Profession," 7 *Am. U. J. Gender, Soc. Pol'y & L.* 149, 164 (1999) (citing studies).

23. Gail Collins, "A Social Glacier Roars," *N.Y. Times Magazine*, May 16, 1999, at 77; Eleanor Clift and Tom Brazaitis, *Madame President: Shattering the Last Glass Ceiling* 18 (2000); Marcia Lynn Whicker and Lois Duke Whitaker, "Women in Congress," in *Women in Politics: Outsiders or Insiders?* 171 (Lois Duke Whitaker, ed. 1999).

24. For general discussion of gender stereotypes and schema, see Valian, *Why So Slow?* at 16–17; Rhode, *Speaking of Sex*, at 145–147; Mark R. Poirier, "Gender Stereotypes at Work," 65 *Brook. L. Rev.* 1073, 1086–1089 (1999).

25. International Labour Organization, *Breaking the Glass Ceiling: Women in Management* 4 (1997). See sources cited in Marilyn J. Davidson and Ronald J. Burke, *Women in Management: Current Research Issues* 3 (1994); Georgia

Duerst-Lahti and Rita Mae Kelly, "On Governance, Leadership, and Gender," in *Gender Power, Leadership, and Governance* 12, 24–26 (1995); Mary Anne C. Case, "Disaggregating Gender From Sex and Sexual Orientation: The Effeminate Man in the Law and Feminist Jurisprudence," 105 *Yale L. J.* 1, 72–73 (1995); Judith A. Kolb, "The Effect of Gender Role, Attitude Toward Leadership, and Self-Confidence on Leader Emergence: Implications for Leadership Development," 4 *Hum. Resource Dev. Q.* 305, 307 (1999); Richard F. Martell, "Sex Stereotyping in the Executive Suite: 'Much Ado About Something,'" 13 *J. Soc. Behav. and Personality* 127 (1998).

26. Lahti and Kelly, "On Governance," at 24. For a compilation of "great man" approaches, see *Political Leadership: A Source Book* (Barbara Kellerman, ed. 1986).

27. See Joan Brockman, *Gender in the Legal Profession* 154–158 (2001); Kathleen Hall Jamieson, *Beyond the Double Bind: Women and Leadership* 4, 129 (1995) (quoting Barbara Boxer and Jean Kirkpatrick); Joyce K. Fletcher, *Disappearing Acts: Gender, Power, and Relational Practice at Work* 118 (1999); Peggy Ornstein, *Flux: Women, Sex, Work, Kids, Love, and Life in a Half Changed World* 51 (2000); *Nine and Counting: The Women of the Senate* 181 (Barbara Mikulski et al., eds. 2000); Ann M. Morrison et al., *Breaking the Glass Ceiling: Can Women Reach the Top of America's Largest Corportions?* 54, 61–62 (1994); Deborah L. Rhode, "Gender and Professional Roles," 63 *Fordham L. Rev.* 39, 67 (1994); Alice H. Eagly, Mona G. Makhijani, and Bruce G. Klonsky, "Gender and the Evaluation of Leaders: A Meta-Analysis," 111 *Psychol. Bull.* 3, 17 (1992).

28. Eagly, Makhijani, and Klonsky, "Gender and The Evaluation of Leaders," at 17; Cleveland, Stockdale, and Murphy, *Women and Men in Organizations*, at 106, 307; Rochelle Sharpe, "New Studies Find that Female Managers Outshine Their Male Counterparts in Almost Every Measure," *Businessweek Online*, Nov. 20, 2000, [www.businessweek.com].

29. Judith A. Kolb, "Are We Still Stereotyping Leadership? A Look at Gender and Other Predictors of Leader Emergence," 28 *Small Group Research* 370 (1997): Russell L. Kent and Sherry E. Moss, "Effects of Sex and Gender Role on Leader Emergence," 37 *Acad. of Mgmt. J.* 1335 (1994).

30. Suzanne Nossel and Elizabeth Westfall, *Presumed Equal: What America's Top Lawyers Really Think About Their Firms* xii, 214, 222, 269, 279 (2d ed. 1998); Rhona Rapoport, Lotte Bailyn, Joyce K. Fletcher, and Bettye H. Pruitt, *Beyond Work-Family Balance: Advancing Gender Equity and Workplace Performance* 33 (2002); Maureen Dowd, "A Man and a Woman," *N.Y. Times*, Sept. 20, 2000, at A27; Barbara Lee Family Foundation, *Keys to the Governor's Office* 24 (2001); Judy Percy Martinez, "Professionalism: One and Only One Woman's Perspective," 75 *Tulane L. Rev.* 1713, 1724 (2001). See also International Labour Organization, *Breaking the Glass Ceiling* 59 (discussing narrower range of acceptable behavior for women than men).

31. See studies cited in Kay Deaux and Marianne La France, "Gender," in *The Handbook of Social Psychology* 788 (Daniel T. Gilbert et al., 4th ed. 1998); Erkut, *Inside Women's Power*, at 25–26; Rhode, *Speaking of Sex*, at 145; Federal Glass Ceiling Commission, *Good for Business*, at 26–28, 64–72, 93–96, 104–106; Valian, "Cognitive Basis," at 1046–49; Cecilia J. Ridgeway and Shelly J. Correl, "Limiting Inequality Through Interaction: The End(s) of Gender," 29 *Contemp. Sociol.* 110, 113 (2000); Diana L. Bridge, "The Glass Ceiling and Sexual Stereotyping: Historical and Legal Perspectives of Women in the Workplace," 4 *Va. J. of Soc. Pol'y & L.* 581, 605–606 (1997).

32. Catalyst, *Women in Financial Services: The Word on the Street* (2001); Catalyst, Center for the Education of Women, University of Michigan and University of Michigan Business School, *Women and the MBA: Gateway to Opportunity* 22–29 (2000); ABA Commission on Women in the Profession, *Fair Measure: Toward Effective Attorney Evaluations* 14 (1997).

33. Clift and Brazaitis, *Madame President*, at 23; Kim Freidkin Kahn, *The Political Consequences of Being a Woman* 8–13 (1996); Barbara Lee Family Foundation, *Keys to the Governor's Office*, at 13; Senator Patty Murray was accordingly advised to run as "Pat." Mikulski et al., eds., *Nine and Counting*, at 45.

34. Susan Estrich, "The Gender Trap," *San Jose Mercury News*, Dec. 9, 2001, at D1; Thomas F. Pettigrew and Joanne Martin, "Shaping the Organizational Context for Black American Inclusion," 43 *J. Soc. Issues* 36–57 (1987). For the classic description of the problem, see Rosabeth Moss Kanter, *Men and Women of the Corporation* (1977).

35. Robin J. Ely, "The Power in Demography: Women's Social Construction of Gender Identity at Work," 38 *Acad. Management J.* 589, 614, 619 (1995).

36. Martha Foschi, "Double Standards in the Evaluation of Men and Women," 59 *Soc. Psychol.* 237 (1996); Jacqueline Landau, "The Relationship of Race and Gender to Managers' Rating of Promotion Potential," 16 *J. Organizational Behav.* 391 (1995).

37. See studies cited in Rhode, *Speaking of Sex*, at 145; Valian, "Cognitive Basis," at 1050.

38. Ridgeway and Correl, "Limiting Inequality," at 116.

39. Valian, "Cognitive Basis," at 1048–1049.

40. Valian, *Why So Slow?* at 131.

41. Viela Banerjee, "Some 'Bullies' Seek Ways to Soften Up; Toughness Has Risks For Women Executives," *N.Y. Times*, Aug. 10, 2001, at C1.

42. Rhode, "Gender and Professional Roles," at 66.

43. Barbara Lee Family Foundation, *Keys to the Governor's Office*, at 13; Maria Braden, *Women Politicians and the Media* 131 (1996).

44. National Women's Leadership Summit, Roper ASW Poll, Apr. 2002.

45. Catalyst, *Women of Color in Corporate Management* 27–29; Ella L.J. Ed-

mondson Bell and Stella M. Nkomo, *Our Separate Ways: Black and White Women and the Struggle for Professional Identity* 138–146 (2001); Sheila Wellington and Katherine Giscombe, "Women and Leadership in Corporate America," in *The American Woman* 90; Foschi, "Double Standards"; Federal Glass Ceiling Commission, *Good for Business*, at 26–28, 64–72, 93–96, 104–106; ABA Commission on Minorities, *Miles to Go*, at 3–5; Multicultural Women Attorneys' Network of the ABA, *The Burdens of Both, the Privileges of Neither: A Report* 23–24 (1994).

46. See sources cited in Rhode, *Speaking of Sex*, at 145; Bridge, "The Glass Ceiling," at 605–606. Jacob Herring, "The Everyday Realities of Minority Professional Life in the Majority Workplace," discussed in Bar Association of San Francisco Committee on Minority Employment, *Interim Report: Goals and Timetables for Minority Hiring and Recruitment* 28 (2000).

47. See Paul M. Barrett, *The Good Black: A True Story of Race in America* 55–56, 279–280 (1999); Orenstein, *Flux*, at 76; Rhode, *Speaking of Sex*, at 163–171; Ridgeway and Correl, "Limiting Inequality," at 114; Wellington and Giscombe, "Women and Leadership in Corporate America," at 87, 102; T. Shawn Taylor, "Executive Strategies: Women of Color Must Confront Unique Obstacles," *Chi. Tribune*, June 24, 2001, at C3; Bell and Nkomo, *Our Separate Ways* 147.

48. Cameron Stracher, "All Aboard the Mommy Track," *Am. Law.*, Mar. 1999, at 126; Deborah L. Rhode, "Myths of Meritocracy," 65 *Fordham L. Rev.* 585, 592–593 (1996); Meredith K. Wadman, "Family and Work," *Washington Lawyer*, Nov.–Dec. 1998, 33; Willard and Patton, *Perceptions of Partnership*, at 99; Epstein et al., "Glass Ceilings and Open Doors," at 391–399.

49. Epstein et al., "Glass Ceilings and Open Doors," at 298; Harvard Women's Law Association, *Presumed Equal: What America's Top Lawyers Really Think About Their Firms* 72 (1995); Rhode, "Myths of Meritocracy," at 588; International Labour Organization, *Breaking the Glass Ceiling*, at 61.

50. Harvard Women's Law Association, *Presumed Equal*, at 72.

51. Pat Schroeder, *24 Years of House Work . . . and the Place Is Still a Mess* 128 (1998).

52. Barbara Lee Family Foundation, *Keys to the Governor's Office*, at 35; Mikulski et al., *Nine and Counting*, at 181.

53. Ellen Goodman, "Huge Juggling Act Ahead for 'Gov. Mom,'" *San Francisco Chronicle*, Feb. 22, 2001, at A25.

54. Amy H. Handlin, *Whatever Happened to the Year of the Woman? Why Women Still Aren't Making It to the Top in Politics* 29 (1998). See also Mikulski et al., *Nine and Counting*, at 181; Catherine Cowan, "Women Find a Home in State Government," *State Government News*, Mar. 2001, at 10, 11.

55. Rhode, "Gender and Professional Roles," at 62–63; Deborah L. Rhode, "Balanced Lives for Lawyers," 70 *Fordham Law Review* 2207, 2213 (2002).

56. Boston Bar Association Task Force on Professional Challenges and Family Needs, *Facing the Grail: Confronting the Cost of Work-Family Imbalance* 25 (1999); Laura Gatland, "The Top 5 Myths About Part-Time Partners," *Perspectives*, spring 1997, at 11.

57. Linda Hamilton Krieger, "The Content of Our Categories: A Cognitive Bias Approach to Discrimination and Equal Employment Opportunity," 47 *Stan. L. Rev.* 1161, 1207–1209 (1995); Federal Glass Ceiling Commission, *Good for Business*, at 26–28, 64–72, 93–96, 104–106, 123–125.

58. Melvin J. Lerner, *The Belief in a Just World: A Fundamental Delusion* vii–viii (1980); Valian, "Cognitive Basis," at 1059.

59. Epstein et al., "Glass Ceilings and Open Doors," at 28; ABA Commission on Minorities, *Miles to Go*, at 6–7, 14–15; Bar Association of San Francisco, *Goals '95 Report: Goals and Timetables for Minority Hiring and Advancement* 17, 25 (1996); David B. Wilkins and G. Mitu Gulati, "Why Are There So Few Black Lawyers in Corporate Law Firms? An Institutional Analysis," 84 *Calif. L. Rev.* 493, 570 (1996); David A. Thomas and Karen L. Proudford, "Making Sense of Race Relations in Organizations," in *Addressing Cultural Issues in Organizations: Theory for Practice* 51 (Robert T. Carter, ed. 2000).

60. "Green Pastures," *Perspectives*, summer 1995, at 3; Barrett, *The Good Black*, at 59; Martinez, "Professionalism," at 1724.

61. "Green Pastures," at 3.

62. Thomas and Proudford, "Making Sense of Race."

63. Catalyst, *Women in Corporate Leadership: Progress and Prospects* 37 (1996). See also International Labour Organization, *Breaking the Glass Ceiling*, at 4 (discussing role of stereotypes).

64. National Association for Law Placement (NALP) Foundation, *The Lateral Lawyer: Why They Leave and What Makes Them Stay* (2000).

65. National Association for Law Placement (NALP) Foundation, *Keeping the Keepers: Strategies for Associate Retention in Times of Attrition* (1998); Rhode, "Balanced Lives for Lawyers," at 2209, 2218.

66. Catalyst, *Women of Color*, at 13; Catalyst, *Women in Corporate Leadership*, at 37. See also Catalyst, *Women and the MBA*, at 53; Catalyst, *Women in Financial Services.*

67. Cowan, "Women in State Government," at 11; Rhode, "Myths of Meritocracy," at 589; Nossel and Westfall, *Presumed Equal*; Ida O. Abbott, *The Lawyer's Guide to Mentoring* (2000); Catalyst, *Women in Law*, at 4–6; and NALP Foundation, *The Lateral Lawyer* (finding that 40 percent of surveyed women wanted better training and mentoring).

68. Mats Alvesson and Yvonne Due Billing, *Understanding Gender and Organizations* 194 (1997); Michael Roper, "'Seduction and Succession': Circuits of Homosocial Desire in Management," in *Men as Managers, Managers as Men: Criti-*

cal Perspectives on Men, Masculinities, and Managements 210 (David L. Collinson and Jeff Hearn, eds. 1996); Judith Lorber, *Paradoxes of Gender* 237–238 (1994).

69. Federal Glass Ceiling Commission, *Good for Business*, at 28; Wellington and Giscombe, "Women and Leadership in Corporate America," at 92.

70. Epstein et al., "Glass Ceilings and Open Doors," at 356; Klenke, *Women in Leadership*, at 185.

71. A striking number of women volunteered these descriptions in a recent survey of large law firms. Nossel and Westfall, *Presumed Equal*, at 68, 99, 113, 129, 144, 173, 179, 187, 194, 200, 203, 204, 224, 228, 259, 264, 274, 356, 361, 366, 374, 379. See also Catalyst, *Women in Corporate Leadership*, at 37; Orenstein, *Flux*, at 21; Mikulski et al., *Nine and Counting*; Whicker and Whitaker, "Women in Congress"; Linda Witt, *Running as a Woman: Gender and Power in American Politics* (1994).

72. Sheila Wellington and Catalyst, *Be Your Own Mentor* 110 (2001).

73. Nossel and Westfall, *Presumed Equal*, at 9, 45, 101, 176, 211–212, 291.

74. Report of the Ninth Circuit Gender Bias Task Force, at 171. See also Bell and Nkomo, *Our Separate Ways* 150; Catalyst, *Women of Color in Corporate Management: Dynamics of Career Advancement* 15 (1999); Ella L. Bell, Toni Denton, and Stella Nkomo, "Women of Color in Management, Toward an Inclusive Approach," in *Women in Management: Trends, Issues, and Challenges in Managerial Diversity* 114 (Ellen A. Fagenson, ed. 1993).

75. Wendell LaGrand, "Getting There, Staying There," *ABA J.*, Feb. 1999, at 54; Cliff Hacker, "Making the Majors," *ABA J.*, Feb. 1997, at 58.

76. Los Angeles County Bar Association Ad Hoc Committee on Sexual Orientation Bias, "The Los Angeles County Bar Association Report on Sexual Orientation Bias," reprinted in 4 *S. Cal. L. & Women's Stud.* 295, 444–449, 471 (1995). See also Nossel and Westfall, *Presumed Equal*, at 256, 266, 297; William B. Rubenstein, "Queer Studies II: Some Reflections on the Study of Sexual Orientation Bias in the Legal Profession," 8 *UCLA Women's L. J.* 379, 394 (1998). Some evidence suggests that these patterns are changing, especially in the large firms. For comments suggesting supportive attitudes toward gay and lesbian attorneys, see Nossel and Westfall, *Presumed Equal*, at 76, 90–91, 138, 144, 168, 175, 251, 288–291, 319.

77. "Los Angeles Report on Sexual Orientation Bias," at 312.

78. Klenke, *Women in Management*, at 185; Epstein et al., "Glass Ceilings and Open Doors," at 408; Harvard Women's Law Association, *Presumed Equal*, at 18; Orenstein, *Flux*, at 52; Rhode, "Myths of Meritocracy," at 590; Nossel and Westfall, *Presumed Equal*, at 126, 187, 266, 277, 297.

79. *Talking Leadership: Conversations with Powerful Women*, at 128; Nossel and Westfall, *Presumed Equal*, at 50, 59, 176; Handlin, *Whatever Happened to the Year of the Woman*, at 52–58; Amy Saltzman, "Woman versus Woman: Why

Aren't More Female Executives Mentoring Their Junior Counterparts?" *U.S. News & World Rep.*, Mar. 25, 1996 (citing survey findings that women are less likely than men to mentor).

80. Saltzman, "Women versus Women;" Catalyst, *Women of Color*, at 13, 22; Nossel and Westfall, *Presumed Equal*, at xii, 131, 266, 299; Cynthia Fuchs Epstein, Carroll Seron, Bonnie Oglensky, and Robert Saute, *The Part-Time Paradox: Time Norms, Professional Lives, Family, and Gender* 5 (1999); Handlin, *Whatever Happened to the Year of the Woman*, at 49–50.

81. Epstein et al., *The Part-Time Paradox*, at 5; Willard and Patton, *Perceptions of Partnership*, at 99; Catalyst, *A New Approach to Flexibility: Managing the Work/Time Equation* 16, 25–27 (1997).

82. Nossel and Westfall, *Presumed Equal*, at 168; see also 3, 14, 59, 71, 180–181, 194, 199, 255, 358, 362, 366, 375; Women's Bar Association of Massachusetts, *More Than Part Time* (2000); Michael D. Goldhaber, "'Part Time Never Works' Discuss," *Nat'l L. J.*, Dec. 4, 2000, at A51. In a recent study of part-time lawyers, only 1 percent had become partners. Epstein et al., *The Part-Time Paradox*, at 56.

83. Catalyst, *A New Approach*, at 37–38.

84. Ann Crittendon, *The Price of Motherhood* 96 (2000); U.S. General Accounting Office, *A New Look Through the Glass Ceiling*. See also Epstein et al., *Part-Time Paradox*.

85. Juliet B. Schor, *The Overworked American: The Unexpected Decline of Leisure* 1–5, 79–82 (1993); Rhode, "Balanced Lives for Lawyers," at 2210.

86. Joan Williams, *Unbending Gender: Why Family and Work Conflict and What to Do About It* 671 (2000); Arlie Russell Hochschild, *The Time Bind: When Work Becomes Home and Home Becomes Work* 70 (1997); Carl T. Bogus, "The Death of an Honorable Profession," 71 *Ind. L. J.* 911, 925–926 (1996).

87. Betsy Morris, "Executive Women Confront Midlife Crisis," *Fortune*, Sept. 18, 1995; Bogus, "The Death of an Honorable Profession," at 926.

88. Marilyn Tucker, "Will Women Lawyers Ever Be Happy?" *Law Practice Management*, Jan.–Feb. 1998, at 45.

89. Williams, *Unbending Gender*, at 71; Catalyst, *A New Approach to Flexibility*, at 33.

90. Lorraine T. Zappert, *Getting It Right*, 85 (2000).

91. Nossel and Westfall, *Presumed Equal*, at 90, 259, 270.

92. The extent of the inequality is estimated differently by researchers using different methodologies. Compare studies cited in Williams, *Unbending Gender*, at 71 (citing studies suggesting that women perform about 70 percent of the tasks); Rhode, *Speaking of Sex*, at 7–8, 149 (citing studies suggesting that employed women spend about twice as much time on family matters as employed men); with Tamar Lewin, "Men Assuming Bigger Role at Home," citing James T. Bond et al., *The 1997 National Study of the Changing Workforce* (1998); Mark Williams Walsh, "So Where Are the Corporate Husbands?" *N.Y. Times*, June 24, 2001, at

1, 13; Deborah L. Rhode, "Balanced Lives," 102 *Columbia University Law Review* 834, 841–842 (2002).

93. Williams, *Unbending Gender*, at 71; Rhode, "Balanced Lives for Lawyers," at 2213.

94. Families and Work Institute, *Business Work-Life Study* (1998); John Turrettini, "Mommie Dearest," *Am. Law.*, Apr. 2000, at 19; *Final Report and Recommendations of the Eighth Circuit Gender Fairness Task Force*, 31 *Creighton L. Rev.* 7, 54 (1997); Linda B. Chanow, *Results of Lawyers, Work, and Family: A Study of Alternative Schedule Programs at Law Firms in the District of Columbia* (May 2000).

95. Boston Bar Association, *Facing the Grail*, at 17. See also Catalyst, *A New Approach to Flexibility*, at 25–26; Catalyst, *Women and the MBA*, at 63; Rhode, "Balanced Lives," at 842–843.

96. Epstein et al., *The Part-Time Paradox*, at 5; Deborah L. Rhode, *In the Interests of Justice: Reforming the Legal Profession* 41 (2000); ABA Commission on Women in the Profession, *Balanced Lives: Changing the Culture of Legal Practice* (prepared for the Commission by Deborah L. Rhode 2001).

97. Epstein et al., *The Part-Time Paradox*; Gatland, "The Myths of Part Time."

98. Renee M. Landers, James B. Rebitzer, and Lowell J. Taylor, "Rat Race Redux: Adverse Selection in the Determination of Work Hours in Law Firms," 86 *Am. Econ. Rev.* 329 (1996); Epstein et al., *The Part-Time Paradox*, at 56; Rhode, "Balanced Lives for Lawyers," at 2211.

99. Landers, Rebitzer, and Taylor, "Rat Race Redux."

100. Nossel and Westfall, *Presumed Equal*, at 126 (quoting lawyer at Fried Frank). See id., at 9, 44, 187, 266, 277, 297.

101. Nossel and Westfall, *Presumed Equal*, at 21, 24, 261, 277.

102. ABA Commission on Women, *Balanced Lives*, at 23.

103. Rapoport, Bailyn, Fletcher, and Pruitt, *Beyond Work-Family Balance*, at 7; ABA Commission on Women, *Balanced Lives*, at 21; Rhode, "Balanced Lives," at 840; Rhode, "Balanced Lives for Lawyers," at 2218.

104. "Firm Feedback on Part-Time Lawyering," *Mass. Lawyers Weekly*, Apr. 22, 1996, at B4 (reporting findings of Boston Bar Association study indicating little impact on client relations); *New Models for Part-Time or Flex-Time Partnerships, Compensation and Benefits for Law Offices*, Jan., 1997, at 12; "Part-Time Partners," *Am. Law.*, Apr. 1997, at 82.

105. Williams, *Unbending Gender*, at 71–73; Boston Bar Associaiton, *Facing the Grail*, at 39; Catalyst, *A New Approach to Flexibility*, at 20–21; Rhode, "Balanced Lives for Lawyers," at 2217–2219.

106. Susan Sturm, "Second Generation Employment Discrimination: A Structural Approach," 101 *Colum. L. Rev.* 458 (2001).

107. Id.; Rhode, *Speaking of Sex*, at 161–162; Patrick McGeehan, "Wall Street Highflier to Outcast: A Woman's Story," *N.Y. Times*, Feb. 10, 2002, Section 3 at 1.

108. Sturm, "Second Generation," at 476.

109. Cleveland, Stockdale, and Murphy, *Women and Men in Organizations*, at 363; Business and Professional Women Foundation and American Management Association, *Compensation and Benefits: A Focus on Gender* (1999); Theresa M. Welbourne, "Wall Street Likes Its Women: An Examination of Women in the Top Management Teams of Initial Public Offerings" (working paper, 2001); Susan Stites-Doe and James J. Cordiro, "The Impact of Women Managers on Firm Performance: Evidence from Large U.S. Firms," *Int'l Rev. of Women and Leadership*, July 1997.

110. Catalyst, *Women in Corporate Leadership*, at 70 (reporting survey in which 98 percent of senior executive women cited demographic reasons to support initiatives aimed at women's advancement). National Association of Law Placement (NALP) Foundation, *Beyond the Bidding Wars: A Survey of Associate Attrition, Departure, Destinations, and Workplace Initiatives* (2000); Catalyst, *Women in Corporate Management*; Robin Ely and David Thomas, "Making Differences Matter: A New Paradigm for Managing Diversity," *Harvard Business Review*, Sept.–Oct. 1996, at 79.

111. Catalyst, *Women in Corporate Management*; Thomas and Ely, "Making Differences Matter," at 79.

112. See Robert I. Kabacoff, *Management Research Group, Gender Differences in Organizational Leadership: A Large Sample Study* 1 (1998).

113. Alice H. Eagly and Wendy Wood, "Explaining Sex Differences in Social Behavior: A Meta-Analytic Perspective," 17 *Personality and Social Psychol. Bull.* 306 (1991); Alice H. Eagly and Blair T. Johnson, "Gender and Leadership Style: A Meta-Analysis," 108 *Psychol. Bull.* 233 (1990); Eagly, Makhijani, and Klonsky, "Gender and the Evaluation of Leaders"; Eagly, Karau, and Makhijani, "Gender and the Effectiveness of Leaders."

114. Betsy Wangensteen, "Managing Style: What's Gender Got to Do with It?" *Crain's N.Y. Bus.*, Sept. 29, 1997, at 23. See also Judy Wajcman, *Managing Like a Man: Women and Men in Corporate Management* 66 (1998).

115. Terry Carter, "Paths Need Paving," *ABA J.*, Sept. 2000, at 34. It is interesting that men were less likely to hold such views: 40 percent thought that the strengths of male and female lawyers were the same, and 49 percent thought that they had the same weaknesses. See also Brockman, *Gender in the Legal Profession*, at 137 (finding that about 40 percent of men and over 65 percent of women saw themselves as more conciliatory than adversarial).

116. Carter, "Paths Need Paving," at 37.

117. Barbara Lee Family Foundation, *Keys to the Governor's Office*, at 24; Klein, *The Political Consequences of Being a Woman*, at 8–11.

118. Cleveland, Stockdale, and Murphy, "Gender and Leadership," at 307; Eagly and Johnson, "Gender and Leadership Style," at 233–256; Eagly, Karau,

and Makhijani, "Gender and the Effectiveness of Leaders," at 125–145; Kaba-coff, "Gender Differences in Organizational Leadership." See also Jean Lipman-Blumen, "Connective Leadership: Female Leadership Styles in the 21st Century Workplace," 35 *Soc. Perspectives* 183, 200–201 (1992).

119. Radcliffe Public Policy Institute and The Boston Club, *Suiting Themselves: Women's Leadership Styles in Today's Workplace* (1999).

120. Gary N. Powell, *Women and Men in Management* 45–49, 105–109 (1988); Klenke, *Women and Leadership*, at 160; Rosalind Chait Barnett and Janet Shibley Hyde, "Women, Men, Work, and Family: An Expansionist Theory," 56 *American Psychol.* 781, 790–791 (2001); Gary N. Powell, "One More Time: Do Female and Male Managers Differ?" 4 *Acad. of Mgmt. Executive* 68 (1990); Eagly and Johnson, "Gender and Leadership Style," at 246–247; King, "Sex Role Identity and Decision Style," at 66. See Alvesonn and Due Billing, *Understanding Gender in Organizations*, at 146, 151; Linda Molm and Mark Hedley, "Gender, Power, and Social Exchange," in *Gender, Interaction, and Inequality* 8 (Cecilia L. Ridgeway, ed. 1992); Burke and Davidson, "Women in Management."

121. For studies finding no difference, see S. B. Shimanoff and M. M. Jenkins, "Leadership and Gender: Challenging Assumptions and Recognizing Resources," in *Small Group Communication* (R. S. Cathcart and L. A. Samovar, eds. 1996); Barnett and Hyde, *Women, Men, Work, and Family*, at 791; Sue Platz, "Sex Differences in Leadership: How Real Are They," *Acad. of Mgmt. Rev.* 118 (1986). For studies finding some differences, see Eagly, Karau, and Makhijani, "Gender and the Effectiveness of Leaders," at 126–140; Eagly, Makhijani, and Klonsky, "Gender and the Evaluation of Leaders," at 16–18.

122. Brian S. Moskal, "Women Make Better Managers," *Industry Wk.*, Feb. 3, 1997, at 17.

123. Sharpe, "New Studies."

124. Eagly and Wood, "Explaining Sex Differences," at 314; Eagly, Makhijani, and Klonsky, "Gender and the Evaluation of Leaders," at 18.

125. Klenke, *Women and Leadership*, at 151; Cleveland, Stockdale, and Murphy, *Gender and Leadership*, at 307; Eagly, Makhijani, and Klonsky, "Gender and the Evaluation of Leaders," at 18; Eagly and Wood, "Explaining Sex Differences," at 314 (1991).

126. Eagly and Johnson, "Gender and Leadership Style," at 247–248.

127. Klenke, *Women and Leadership*, at 154; Deaux and La France, "Gender."

128. Joanne Martin and Debra Meyerson, "Women and Power: Confronting Resistance and Disorganized Action," in *Power and Influence in Organizations* 311, 313 (Roderick M. Kramer and Margaret A. Neale, eds. 1998); Cynthia Fuchs Epstein, *Deceptive Distinctions: Sex, Gender, and the Social Order* 173–84 (1988). See also Brockman, *Gender in the Legal Profession*, at 158 (describing some women's felt need to prove themselves).

129. Cleveland, Stockdale, and Murphy, *Women and Men in Organizations*, at 293–299; Kellerman, *Reinventing Leadership*, at 149. See also Lipman-Blumen, "Connective Leadership," at 183–201.

130. Michael E. Solimine and Susan E. Wheatley, "Rethinking Feminist Judging," 70 *Ind. L. J.* 891 (1995); Thomas G. Walker and Deborah J. Barrow, "Diversification of the Federal Bench: Policy and Process Ramifications," 47 *J. Pol.* 596, 607 (1985); John Gruhl et al., "Women as Policymakers: The Case of Trial Judges," 25 *Am. J. Pol. Science* 308, 319–320 (1981).

131. Daniel R. Pinello, *Gay Rights and American Law* Table 6.2 (forthcoming, 2003) (finding women judges substantially more likely to rule in favor of gay rights but not controlling for other potentially relevant characteristics); Theresa M. Beiner, "What Will Diversity on the Bench Mean for Justice?" 6 *Mich. J. Gender and L.* 113 (1999) (suggesting some differences on civil rights suits); Sue Davis, Susan Haire, and Donald R. Songer, "Voting Behavior and Gender on the U.S. Court of Appeals," 77 *Judicature* 129 (1993) (finding some differences in employment discrimination and search and seizure cases but not obscenity cases); Jennifer A. Segal, "The Decision Making of Clinton's Nontraditional Judicial Appointees," 80 *Judicature* 279 (1997) (finding differences on individual liberties and criminal procedure but not on women's issues); Jeffrey Toobin, "Women in Black," *New Yorker*, Oct. 30, 2000, at 48 (finding greater severity in enforcement of the criminal laws in general and the death penalty in particular by Texas' female judges than male judges).

132. Gladys Kessler, "Women, Justice, and Authority Conference," unpublished paper for Women Justice and Authority Conference, Yale University, 2000, at 4.

133. Carolyn Heilbrun and Judith Resnik, "Convergences: Law, Literature, and Feminism," 99 *Yale L. J.* 1913, 1948–1950 (1990).

134. Kessler, "Women, Justice, and Authority," at 4.

135. Deborah L. Rhode, "Access To Justice," 69 *Fordham L. Rev.* 1785 (2001); Jona Goldschmidt, "How Are Courts Handling Pro Se Litigation?" 83 *Judicature* 13, 14 (July–Aug. 1998).

136. Kahn, *The Political Consequences of Being a Woman*, at 41, 137; Sue Thomas, *How Women Legislate* 92 (1994); Michele Swers and Amy Caizza, "Transforming the Political Agenda: Gender Differences in Bill Sponsorship on Women's Issues," reprinted in Institute for Women's Policy Research, *Research-in-Brief*, Oct. 2000, at 1; Mandel, "Women's Leadership in American Politics," at 54; Julie Dolan, "Support for Women's Interests in the 103rd Congress: The Distinct Impact of Congressional Women," 18 *Women and Politics* 81 (1997); Susan J. Carroll, "The Politics of Difference: Women Public Officials as Agents of Change," 5 *Stan. L. & Pol'y Rev.* 11 (1994); Ruth B. Mandel and Debra L. Dodson, "Do Women Officeholders Make a Difference?" in *The American Women* 1992–1993 (Paula Ries and Ann J. Stone, eds. 1992); Sue Thomas, "Women in State Legisla-

tures: One Step at a Time," in *The Year of the Woman: Myths and Realities* 141–160 (Elizabeth Adell Cook, Sue Thomas, and Clyde Wilcox, eds. 1994).

137. Karen L. Tamerius, "Sex, Gender, and Leadership in the Representation of Women," in *Gender Power, Leadership, and Governance* 93, 108 (Georgia Duerst-Lahti, Rita Mae Kelly, eds. 1995).

138. Center for American Women in Politics, *Voices, Views, and Votes: Women in the 103rd Congress* 4 (1995).

139. Dolan, "Support for Women's Interests, at 86–89; Swers and Caizza, "Transforming the Political Agenda," at 4; Susan Gluck Mezey, "Increasing the Numbers of Women in Office: Does It Matter?" in *The Year of the Woman*, at 255–270.

140. Tamerius, "Sex, Gender, and Leadership," at 107.

141. Id.; Katha Pollitt, "Where are the Women We Voted For," in *Subject to Debate* 77 (2001).

142. Center for American Women in Politics, *The Impact of Women in Public Office*, at 14; Keith T. Poole and L. Harmon Zeigler, *Women, Public Opinion, and Politics: The Changing Political Opinions of American Women* 8, 16–17 (1985).

143. Mikulski et al., *Nine and Counting*, at 102, (quoting Boxer).

144. Catalyst, *Creating Women's Networks* (1999); ABA Commission on Women, *Unfinished Agenda*; ABA Commission on Women, *Balanced Lives*.

145. Nossel and Westfall, *Presumed Equal*, at 349. See also id., at 30, 187, 261, 266–267, 365.

146. Martin and Meyerson, "Women and Power," at 340; Susan J. Ashford, "Championing Charged Issues: The Case of Gender Equity Within Organizations," in *Power and Influence in Organizations* 349, 375–376 (Roderick M. Kramer and Margaret A. Neale, eds. 1998).

147. Tamerius, "Sex, Gender, and Leadership," at 99 (recounting politicians' lack of maternity leave); Hartmann, *Talking Leadership*, at 229–230 (quoting Patricia Schroeder).

148. Susan J. Carroll, Center for American Women in Politics, *Representing Women: Congresswomen's Perceptions of Their Representational Roles* 4 (2000) (quoting Leslie Byrne).

149. Carroll, *Representing Women*, at 4–7; Center for American Women in Politics, *Voices, Views, and Votes*, at 15–16.

150. Carroll, *Representing Women*, at 4 (quoting Marge Roukema). See also Swers and Caizza, "Transforming the Political Agenda" (quoting Roukema).

151. See Ashford, "Championing Charged Issues," at 366; *Dear Sisters, Dear Daughters: Words of Wisdom from Multicultural Women Attorneys Who've Been There and Done That* (Karen Clanton, ed. 2000); Deborah L. Rhode, "The 'Woman's Point of View,'" 38 *J. Leg. Educ.* 39 (1988).

152. Nossel and Westfall, *Presumed Equal*, at 126, 261, 277. See also id., at 187, 251, 266, 277.

153. Ashford, "Championing Charged Issues," at 365.

154. Id., at 365–366, 370.

155. Id., at 365.

156. Id., at 365–366.

157. Carroll, *Representing Women*, at 10 (quoting Deborah Pryce); see also Mandel, "Women's Leadership in American Politics," at 53.

158. Ashford, "Championing Charged Issues," at 369–370; Carroll, *Representing Women*, at 9–10; see also Carroll, "The Politics of Difference," at 18 (noting that less than half of surveyed politicians identify as feminists).

159. Carroll, *Representing Women*, at 9–10 (quoting Karen Shephard and Deborah Pryce). See also Handlin, *Whatever Happened to the Year of the Woman*, at 51–52.

160. Ashford, "Championing Charged Issues," at 369–370, 375. See also Nossel and Westfall, *Presumed Equal*, at 105, 108; Handlin, *Whatever Happened to the Year of the Woman*, at 52.

161. Ashford, "Championing Charged Issues," at 370, 375; see also Jennifer L. Pierce, *Gender Trials: Emotional Lives in Contemporary Law Firms* 176–177 (1995); Nossel and Westfall, *Presumed Equal*, at 50, 59, 105; Peter Glick and Susan T. Fiske, "Hostile and Benevolent Sexism," 21 *Psychol. of Women* 119, 129 (1997).

162. Nossel and Westfall, *Presumed Equal*, at 50; Catalyst, *Advancing Women in Business*, at 23.

163. The terms come from Carroll, *Representing Women*, at 9 (quoting Cynthia McKinney).

164. Epstein et al., *The Part-Time Paradox*, at 67.

165. Hartman, *Talking Leadership*, at 186 (quoting Quindlin).

166. Nossel and Westfall, *Presumed Equal*, at 180. See also Debra E. Meyerson and Maureen A. Scully, "Tempered Radicalism and the Politics of Ambivalence and Change," 6 *Org. Science* 585, 598 (1995).

167. Rosabeth Moss Kanter, *Comments, Leadership 2002: Bridging the Gap between Theory and Practice*, Kennedy School, Harvard University (2002).

168. Klenke, *Women and Leadership*, 173; International Labour Organization, *Breaking Through the Glass Ceiling*, at 77; Catalyst, *Advancing Women in Business*, at 6, 12–13; Catalyst, *Women of Color in Corporate Management* 69 (1999); Mary C. Mattis, "Organizational Initiatives in the USA for Advancing Managerial Women," in *Women in Management: Current Research Issues* 275 (Marilyn J. Davidson and Ronald J. Burke, eds. 1994); Klein and Thomas, "Difference"; Rapoport, Bailyn, Fletcher, and Pruitt, *Beyond Work-Family Balance*, at 52 and 160.

169. Catalyst, *Advancing Women in Business*, at 5–6, 11–12; Catalyst, *Women of Color in Corporate Management*, at 69–74; Bar Association of San Francisco, *Goals and Timetables*, 34–37 ; Ridgeway and Correll, "Limiting Inequality," at 118.

170. Wajcman, *Managing Like a Man*, at 99.

171. Catalyst, *Women of Color in Corporate Management*, at 32–33, 66; Mattis, "Organizational Initiatives," at 275.

172. Rapoport, Bailyn, Fletcher, and Pruitt, *Beyond Work-Family Balance*, at 82–89; Ely and Thomas, "Making Differences Matter"; Susan Sturm, "Second Generation," at 494.

173. John F. Davidio et al., *On the Nature of Prejudice: Automatic and Controlled Processes*, 33 J. Experimental Soc. Psychol. 510, 535–536 (1997); Valian, "Cognitive Bases," at 1058; E. Ashby Plant and Patricia G. Divine, "Internal and External Motivation to Respond Without Prejudice," 75 *J. Personality and Soc. Psychol.* 811 (1998). See also Catalyst, *Women and the MBA*, at 58 (finding that 41 percent of African American women compared with only about a third of white women and a fifth of white men rate gender and/or racial awareness training as important).

174. Stephanie Francis Cahill and Pearl J. Platt, "Bringing Diversity to Partnerships Continues to Be an Elusive Goal," *San Francisco Daily J.*, July 28, 1997, 1–2; Wellington and Giscombe, "Women and Leadership in Corporate America," at 88 (half of surveyed women of color believe diversity programs are ineffective).

175. Mattis, "Organizational Initiatives," at 275. For general discussion of benchmarks, see Catalyst, *Advancing Women in Business*, at 39–57; Catalyst, *Women of Color*, at 31–32.

176. ABA Commission on Women, *Fair Measure*, at 9–24.

177. Id., at 21. See also Jill Schachner Chanen, "You Rang, Sir?" *ABA J.*, Oct., 2000, at 82, 83.

178. Deborah Graham, "Second to None: Best Practices for Women Lawyers and Their Employers" (ABA Commission on Women in the Profession, unpublished discussion draft, 2001).

179. Id. For general discussion of tokens, see Klenke, *Women and Leadership*, at 176; and Kanter, *Men and Women of the Corporation*.

180. ABA Commission on Women, *Balanced Lives*; Catalyst, *A New Approach to Flexibility*; Boston Bar Association Task Force, *Facing the Grail*; Catalyst, *Women and the MBA*, at 63; Williams, *Unbending Gender*; Rhode, "Balanced Lives for Lawyers."

181. Klenke, *Women and Leadership*, at 183–184; Catalyst, *Women of Color*, at 27; Catalyst, *Advancing Women in Business*, at 62–63; Ronald J. Burke and Carol A. McKeen, "Career Development Among Managerial and Professional Women," in *Women in Management: Current Research Issues* 65, 73 (Marilyn J. Davidson and Ronald J. Burke, eds. 1994); Kelly L. Griffin, "Mentoring Program Trumps Old Boy Network," *Women's ENews*, Feb. 26, 2002.

182. Cleveland, Stockdale, and Murphy, *Women and Men in Organizations*, at 374; Catalyst, *Women in Corporate Leadership*, at 29.

183. Catalyst, *Women in Corporate Leadership*, at 29; Abbott, *The Lawyer's Guide to Mentoring*, at 25, 32–33.

184. Catalyst, *Creating Women's Networks: A How-to Guide for Women and Companies* 5 (1999); Griffin, "Mentoring Program Trumps Old Boy Network"; Darryl McGrath, "Campaign Trail," *Women's ENews*, Aug. 19, 2002.

185. Graham, *Second to None*; Pat Terry, "Marketing Groups Shape New Rainmakers," *Perspectives*, fall 2000, at 7, 8.

186. Catalyst, *Creating Women's Networks*, at 31.

187. Id.; Graham, "Second to None."

188. Catalyst, *Creating Women's Networks*, at 31; Terry, "Marketing Groups," at 8.

189. For discussion of small wins, see Debra E. Meyerson, "A Modest Manifesto for Shattering the Glass Ceiling," 78 *Harv. Bus. Rev.* 1, Jan. 1, 2000.

190. See ABA Commission on Women, *Unfinished Agenda*, at 27–28; Lani Guinier, Michelle Fine, and Jane Balkin, *Becoming Gentlemen* (1997); Rhode, *In the Interests of Justice*, at 192; Deborah L. Rhode, "Whistling Vivaldi: Legal Education and the Politics of Progress," 23 *N.Y.U. Rev. Law & Soc. Change* 217 (1997).

191. Rhode, "Gender and Professional Roles," at 41; Handlin, *Whatever Happened to the Year of the Woman*, at 15–16.

192. Judy Perry Martinez, Speech Before the Women's Caucus of the ABA Forum on Franchising Law, Oct. 21, 2000. Women's rights organizations represented at the summit included Catalyst, Equal Rights Advocates, NOW, the NOW Legal Defense Fund, the National Women's Law Center, and the National Partnership for Women & Families.

193. Aric Press, "Eight Minutes," *Am. Law.*, July 2000, at 18.

194. Rhode, *In the Interests of Justice*, at 37; Rhode, "Access to Justice," at 1810.

195. ABA Young Lawyers Survey (2000); Rhode, *In the Interests of Justice*, at 38.

196. Catalyst, *Women in Corporate Leadership*, at 15; Erkut, *Inside Women's Power*, 54–56, 69; Wellington and Giscombe, "Women and Leadership in Corporate America"; Catalyst, *Be Your Own Mentor*, at 166–167.

197. Catalyst, *Women in Corporate Leadership*; Catalyst, *Women and the MBA*; Catalyst, *Women in Financial Services*; Klein, *The Political Consequences of Being a Woman*, at 135–137.

198. Klenke, *Women and Leadership*, at 242–249; see Kellerman, *Reinventing Leadership*, at 175–178; Minority Corporate Counsel Association 2000 Survey.

199. Catalyst, *Women in Corporate Leadership*, at 15, 21; Clift and Brazaitis, *Madame President*, at 321, 324.

200. Meyerson and Scully, "Tempered Radicalism"; Graham, "Second to None."

II

WHAT DIFFERENCE

DOES DIFFERENCE MAKE?

2

BARBARA KELLERMAN

You've Come a Long Way, Baby— and You've Got Miles to Go

It has been my lot to spend my entire academic career tilling soil in a new field of intellectual inquiry: Leadership Studies. Of course, working fresh ground has its advantages. There are few rules. No great body of literature constrains the discussion. Self-important experts are few and far between. And the field is, as it were, wide open. But there is a downside as well. Scholars in traditional academic disciplines are often suspicious of work that is, by nature, multidisciplinary. The absence of parameters can work against researchers, who are generally more comfortable digging deep than scanning wide. And ostensibly simple tasks—such as defining key words and establishing common frames of reference—can be difficult and even contentious.

Consider, for example, the first line of Professor Deborah L. Rhode's exceptionally useful chapter, "The Difference 'Difference' Makes": "For most of recorded history, women were largely excluded from formal leadership positions." To a leadership scholar, this line demands deconstruction. In particular, how is Rhode using "leadership" and "position"? The first paragraph of the chapter goes on to state that women in "leadership positions" include "queens, politicians, mothers, mistresses, wives, beauties, religious figures, and 'women of tragic fate.'" Although these categories are derived from a period piece, from century-old encyclopedia entries, we can't help but wonder: Does every queen exercise leadership? And how exactly is being beautiful positional? Although leadership scholars are too obsessed with semantics, it is nevertheless fair to say that on issues pertaining to women and leadership in particular, words matter. This is not to deny the truth of the initial assertion—women have been "largely excluded from formal leadership positions." It is, however, to suggest the statement is incomplete. It is to point out that recent scholarship yields a subtler picture of the range of leadership roles that women have played in human history.

Put simply, a growing body of evidence demonstrates that although women have not generally held formal positions of authority, this is not tantamount to saying they did not exercise power or exert influence. The leader-follower dynamic can be played out in many different ways and contexts. To the degree that women persist in equating leadership with position, they diminish their role—both historical and contemporaneous—and belittle their accomplishments. But let us for the sake of this discussion stay with issues pertaining to women in positions of authority. Professor Rhode's paper raises several interesting questions in this regard, three of which I will extract and explore.

QUESTION I
WHAT DO WOMEN WANT?

Rhode writes, "a central problem for American women is the lack of consensus that there is a significant problem." What underlies the widespread impression that equity between women and men is no longer an issue? Not, as Rhode makes clear, the facts. There is no arguing that "women remain underrepresented at the top and overrepresented at the bottom in both the public and private sectors." How, then, to explain why the majority of female lawyers as well as male lawyers believe that women are treated equally in the profession? Given statistics that belie this optimistic view, we must assume another dynamic altogether.

Let me propose an alternative explanation, one that grows out of leadership and management patterns more generally, but is not, for what I would argue are reasons of political correctness, widely considered. It grows out of the proposition that there are differences in the ways women and men make meaning. It is at least plausible that many women do not see inequities in the legal profession (to stay with this example) as a "significant problem" because they do not want, or at least they do not badly want, what men have. To be a federal judge, to be a partner in a law firm, or to be a law school dean is demanding business. Work at the top of the greasy pole takes time, saps energy, and is usually all-consuming. Maybe women's values are different from men's values. Maybe the trade-offs high positions entail are ones that many women do not want to make. Maybe when deciding what matters most, gender matters. One of the least talked about aspects of leadership, of holding a position of considerable authority, is the toll taken. Leading is working. Leading is stressful. Leading is time-consuming. Leading is limiting. Leading is isolating. Leading is tiring.

Well, if leading is tiring for women, leading must be tiring for men. What's the difference? Well, the difference may be that more women than men have children whom they badly want, and often need, to spend time with. The difference may be that women are less motivated than men to limit the number of family tasks they undertake and interests they pursue. In short, the difference may be that women are less willing than men to incur the costs of leadership, particularly if the benefits, such as money and power, are less valued. All of this is not to take issue with Professor Rhode's assertion that "women's opportunities for leadership are constrained by traditional gender stereotypes, inadequate access to mentors and informal networks of support, and inflexible workplace structures." Nor is it to deny the possibility that women are less willing to incur costs because they are less likely to believe their investment will pay off. Rather it is to argue that the picture is almost certainly more complex than many conventional explanations would suggest; and it is to claim that research in the area of women and leadership does not adequately consider alternative explanations for gender differences such as those I suggest here.

QUESTION 2
WHAT, IF ANY, HAS BEEN THE EFFECT OF TIME ON GENDER STEREOTYPES THAT PARTICULARLY AFFECT LEADERSHIP?

This question divides into two parts: Has the modern women's movement effected changes that might be relevant? And has the American leadership culture evolved in ways that might also play a role? The movement that began with Betty Friedan's book about the "problem that [had] no name" did not trigger a revolution, but it was the genesis of an evolution. Although statistics regarding women in positions of authority in both the public and private sectors are still disheartening, and although the anecdotal evidence on discrimination against women still startles, the culture has undeniably changed.

Women are expected to be the majority of students entering law school this fall. And women are in the workplace in numbers and in ways that differ enormously from those of a generation or two ago. In particular, access to positions of leadership and management, while still less than what it should be, is nevertheless considerably greater than it was even in the recent past. Moreover the often-derided term "political correctness" has made it less acceptable, legally and culturally, to be biased against women. Laws have changed; and lines like the one that was directed at Senator Dianne Feinstein—"The gentle lady from California needs to become a little bit more familiar with firearms and their deadly characteristics"—are simply less palatable now than they were just a few years ago. Once again, this is not to argue that the struggle is over. In fact, those in the trenches know full well that although it is no longer politically correct to be sexist in pubic, private asides along these lines are alive and well. Still, the modern women's movement has made a difference. And in this changing social context, the relevant research findings become quickly dated.

Similarly, the American leadership culture has changed in ways that, on paper at least, make it more amenable to women. As Rhode points out, "recent theories of leadership have stressed the need for interpersonal qualities more commonly associated with women, such as cooperation and collaboration. . . . " The issue is obviously a complex one, for leadership is always contingent on context. In other words, although virtues such as cooperation and collaboration do now permeate the leadership literature, we also know that when the going gets tough, the tough tend to revert to command and control. The 9,600 men and women laid off in spring 2001 by Procter & Gamble are just some of the bodies testifying to the fact that virtuous leadership, leadership based on "teams" and "empowerment," can fly out the window when the occasion seems to demand. Still, it matters that the value that dominates the ideology of leadership at the beginning of the twenty-first century is equality—that leaders and followers are presumed to be of similar status. The leadership literature now takes it for granted that those who lead depend on those who follow. This presumed parity, which is based on the implicit assumption that, given another task to fill, leaders and followers could as easily switch roles, makes a difference to women who lead, and, as important, it makes a difference to the women who follow. As Joseph Rost framed the contemporaneous mentality, "Followers do not do followership, they do leadership. Both leaders and followers form one relationship that is leadership."

QUESTION 3
WHICH CONTEXTS MATTER MOST?

Although the leadership dynamic consists of three key components, our tendency is to fixate on only one—the leader. For all the democratization of the leadership culture, it is in the nature of things that we remain in thrall to even the blandest of those in positions of authority. Followers— or constituents, or stakeholders, for those who incline to language more politically correct—are still usually given short shrift. And context, which is of inestimable importance to understanding leadership, is often ignored altogether.

Professor Rhode does not make this mistake. One section of her paper, the one devoted to "institutional strategies," looks carefully at the ways in which organizations, "law firm and corporate settings" in particular, matter to "ensuring equal access to leadership opportunities." Once again, my point here is not to take issue with Professor Rhode; rather it is to expand her frame of reference. If the organizational context matters, so do the other contexts within which organizations are necessarily embedded. Indeed the American Bar Association's Commission on Women in the Profession is testimony to the recognition that that there is a larger professional context in which law firms operate—one that, it is hoped, has at least a modest impact on how they conduct their business insofar as it relates to women's issues. Of course, like those Russian dolls within dolls within dolls, the law firm is in the profession and the profession is in the —in the what? Well, for starters the profession is in the nation. To say the conversation about "the difference 'difference' makes" is taking place in early twenty-first century America is to say something of consequence with regard to women in positions of leadership. We know that in many ways the United States is a good place for women to be at this moment in human history. We also know that the United States lags far behind many other countries when it comes to matters that matter, such as providing for the care of children.

The phenomena of globalization and information technology push context to yet another level. The discussion about women being "dramatically underrepresented in leadership positions" is now worldwide. Inevitably, twenty-first century women from one country compare their situations to twenty-first century women in other countries. Just as inevitably, all women's issues, for example equal access to education, in one or another fashion now pertain to who has power, authority, and influence—to who can and does exercise leadership.

Professor Rhode's chapter assumes the conventional wisdom: that having more women in positions of leadership would be, ipso facto, good. I bring this comment to a close by injecting a few cautionary notes.

First, real change is often generated by women and men outside, rather than inside, the system.

Second, too many women in positions of leadership—in the law, for example—might produce unintended consequences. Think "pink-collar ghetto." Think of professions such as nursing and teaching in which high numbers of women seem to have diminished coins of the realm—coins like money and prestige.

Third, "leadership positions" do not, by definition, always come with the power and influence we typically associate with them. As I suggested at the outset, holding a position of authority, and having the capacity to exercise leadership, are not one and the same.

Fourth, that which holds for white women does not necessarily hold for women of other racial and ethnic groups. We need to shy away from overarching assumptions that take account of the gaps between women and men but ignore the gaps between white women and women of color.

Finally, we may just be entering an era in which leadership is less important than it once was. To be sure, leaders will always emerge from the pack, they will always have an effect on the organizations within which we work, and they will always play a part in shaping the course of human history. But overarching trends, such as the decline of authority, equal access to information, and flattened organizational hierarchies, do make a difference. Women should therefore be leery of simple assumptions—of assuming that gaining a "leadership position" is all it's cracked up to be.

3

BARBARA RESKIN

What's the Difference?
A Comment on Deborah Rhode's
"The Difference 'Difference' Makes"

Deborah L. Rhode's superb assessment of gender and leadership emphasized two kinds of gender difference: the difference between women's and
men's opportunities to hold positions of leadership, and the difference in
their leadership styles and priorities. Based on her comprehensive review of
research, Rhode reaffirmed what most of us observe in the world around
us: One's sex is strongly associated with whether one occupies a position
of leadership. On the matter of leadership styles and priorities, it's a different story. Rhode concluded that *some of the time, some* women differ
from *some* men. In other words, sex is sometimes linked to leadership
styles and priorities, but more often it is not.

Both of these conclusions mirror what we know about women and
men in the general population. That sex makes a major difference in access to employment opportunities and rewards is well known. The world
of work continues to be segregated by sex across occupations, industries,
and firms. Men outearned women at the turn of the twenty-first century
in all but one occupation, and in some occupations the annual earning
bonus for being male amounts to thousands or even tens of thousands of
dollars. As a result, employed women are more likely than employed men
to live in poverty. In addition, men have more flexible jobs, higher rates
of promotion, and more authority on the job.[1]

Turning to leadership style, the fact that sex differences are neither large nor pervasive is not surprising. Meta-analyses of women and men in the general population show very few reliable sex differences. Nonetheless, many Americans believe that the sexes significantly differ in interests, skills, dispositions, and values. Although these perceptions are unfounded, they linger because people's expectations distort what they perceive and recall about the world around them. As a result, we recall perceptions that appear to be consistent with stereotype-based expectations and neglect, misremember, or treat as exceptional stereotype-disconfirming evidence. Thus, a friend's description of a meeting in which a high-ranking government leader had banged the table with his fist eighteen times supported my stereotype of male leaders, despite the fact that I have attended countless meetings in which no one of either sex slammed a fist on the table. Similarly, a provocative essay that decried female professors' tendency to play nurturing roles in business schools rang true to me even though I know any number of academic women who are no more nurturing than their male colleagues.[2]

In short, the presumption that the sexes differ in style and goals is often off the mark, but it survives partly because of biases in the way that we process information and because it implicitly supports a status quo from which the current (mostly male) leaders benefit.

WHERE DO GENDER DIFFERENCES COME FROM?

Because our society attaches so much importance to sex differences, it is worth briefly considering what accounts for these differences. In the case of differences in access to leadership, the acknowledgement of glass ceilings has helped us recognize the barriers to advancement that exist in work organizations and other institutions.

What about gender differences in leadership style and goals? Bearing in mind that the sexes are more alike than they are different, it is nonetheless useful to consider possible sources of any differences. The most popular answer to this question is the socialization of children. This explanation has immediate appeal because our culture is ripe with examples of ways that boys and girls are treated differently. All those pink and blue baby clothes, sex-differentiated Pampers, trucks, and dolls come to mind. And the adult world provides plenty of examples—such as the table-banging man or a caring female boss—that could have plausibly resulted from gender-role socialization.

I have revisited the question of the impact of gender-role socialization several times in the past two decades, and I have never been able to find any credible research that has demonstrated an impact of pre-adult gender-role socialization on adult behavior. But I have encountered some very good reasons to question its impact.

Sociologists' primary objections to the socialization approach are (1) that it assumes that all boys are socialized to customarily male gender roles and all girls are socialized to customarily female roles, when in fact there is wide variability in how children are socialized, and (2) that it focuses on the rewards and punishments we experienced as children, when what our adult behavior is shaped by is the rewards and punishments we encounter on a daily basis as adults.[3] Whether we are rewarded for conforming to traditional or nontraditional gender roles as adults depends on the setting. Some settings reward gender-role traditional behavior and punish nontraditional behavior in both sexes, others reward behavior that is not sex typed, and still others—such as careers in legal practice or politics—reward both women and men for customarily male behavior. Sociologists term these rewards and punishments "social control systems" because they control our actions by rewarding and punishing behavior depending on its acceptability in a particular context. Because culturally acceptable male behavior differs from culturally acceptable female behavior, the same action that is rewarded in women may be punished in men. And vice versa. Thus, women may be punished for assertiveness or the failure to be nurturing, just as men may be punished for being nurturing and failing to be assertive. And we are far more likely to continue to exhibit traits and values that relevant others reward than those they punish. So to the extent that others around us reward different traits and values in men and women, men and women will tend to differ on those traits.

Note, however, that pursuit of behaviors for which we have been rewarded gives us the opportunity to acquire skills. Caregivers, for example, become accomplished at noting others' needs and at nurturing and communication skills. To the extent that more women than men are rewarded for assuming caregiving roles and punished for evading them, women are more likely to polish these skills and discover their value at work and in other public spheres.

Our work style and values also depend on the opportunities available to us. As Rosabeth Kanter observed in *Men and Women of the Corporation*, when we occupy positions from which advancement is possible, we aspire to and work toward advancement.[4] When opportunities to advance are blocked, we cool ourselves out. Thus, when employers segregate the sexes into different managerial roles, with women overrepresented in staff positions and men overrepresented in line positions, they expose fewer women than men to opportunity-enhancing positions. And in curtailing women's advancement opportunities, employers reduce the importance women attach to being promoted relative to men.[5] People who see little chance of advancement tend to disinvest in their careers, and sex segregation means that such people are more likely to be female than male.[6] As Alexander Hamilton observed, "The expectation of promotion . . . is a great stimulus to virtuous exertion, while examples of *unrewarded* exertion, . . . talent and qualification, are proportional discouragements."[7] Thus, sex segregation within institutions not only depresses women's chance for mobility, it also reduces their commitment to advancement.

Also contributing to women's exclusion from leadership roles are ways that we *automatically* process information about others. Rhode's essay discussed one of these processes, sex stereotyping. In addition, we automatically categorize the people we encounter as either members of our in-group or as out-group members. This is consequential because categorization is accompanied by an automatic preference for in-group members. We are more comfortable with members of our in-group than out-group members, have more trust in them, hold more positive views of them, feel more obligated to them, and prefer to cooperate with them rather than compete with them.[8] In-group membership also shapes with whom we seek equal treatment and who serves as our reference group.[9] Moreover, we tend to make biased inferences about why people succeed and fail, assuming that in-group members succeed because of their internal predispositions, such as skill or drive, and fail because of external events, such as bad luck, whereas we tend to make the opposite attributions for the out-group members' success and failure.[10] These attributions affect how we evaluate others for leadership roles. The phenomena associated with in-group preference are especially marked in members of high-status in-groups.[11]

Given the complex and sometimes dangerous world in which we live, automatically categorizing others is adaptive. But automatic in-group preference works against outsiders, and because in-group membership is often based on sex and since most incumbents of institutions' upper echelons are male, in-group favoritism disadvantages women.

This is not inevitably the case, however. The occasional positive effect of mentorship on women's access to leadership may reflect the fact that powerful mentors help women win in-group status. And the positive effects of women's presence in top jobs on the employment of midlevel women managers may reflect in-group preference.[12] But in general, in-group preference in high-level posts tends to limit women's representation. Thus, in-group preference—and sex stereotyping—by employers, supervisors, and even one's peers can lead to women's exclusion from crucial networks and prevent their socialization to organizational goals, outcomes that their "perpetrators" neither intend nor recognize.

Employers can check the negative consequences of automatic stereotyping and automatic in-group favoritism by some of the methods that Rhode suggested. Accountability is particularly important, as is interdependence between in- and out-group members and the sex makeup of the workplace or institutional sphere.

Marginality ("token status") may also contribute to differences in leadership style by enhancing women's visibility and by lowering the likelihood that they will be members of the in-group, a combination that fosters sex stereotyping.[13] Insofar as women's values challenge traditional organizational norms, a critical mass of women may help women retain those values. But this is a double-edged sword, because it simultaneously reduces women's chance to learn mainstream organizational values by interacting with male peers. (Although we may question mainstream organizational values, few can become effective leaders without knowing what they are.)

In sum, men continue to dominate leadership positions, but when it comes to leadership styles and values, gender is less important. In generating and maintaining both of these differences, the actions of organizational leaders and, sometimes, women's peers are more important than women's—and men's—pre-adult socialization to gender roles. By and large, people engage in behaviors for which they are rewarded and pursue socially valued opportunities that are open to them. Thus, in creating reward structures (including deciding what traits and activities to reward, such as long hours, unquestioning loyalty, or concern for colleagues), in placing the sexes within these structures, and in rewarding the same or different traits and behaviors for women and men, employers and leaders of other institutions can generate or minimize gender differences.

We all agree that institutions should minimize gender difference in access to positions of leadership. At least in the employment context, Rhode reviewed some of the ways to do this. The sociological research supports her conclusions. Organizational leaders must be committed to equal opportunity, they must use formalized personnel practices and avoid hiring through networks, and they must make gatekeepers accountable for both the decision-making processes they use and the outcomes of those processes.[14] They will do well to follow the practices that have been shown to be effective in affirmative action programs for federal contractors—namely, monitoring departures from proportional representation, identifying its causes, altering personnel practices accordingly, using goals and timetables to measure progress, and making existing leaders accountable for the results.[15]

Whether organizational leaders should maintain or minimize gender differences in leadership style and values is another matter. I question whether rewarding men and women for different traits or values serves justice. In the first place, doing so reifies sex stereotypes and creates obstacles for women who do not conform to them. In the second place, male-dominated settings rarely value stereotypically female interests. And rewarding women for stereotypically female behavior diverts them from pursuing their own talents and acquiring the expertise necessary for advancement to leadership positions. For organizational and institutional leaders to foster more just and caring societies, they must reward *both* female and male workers for mentoring, communicating effectively, and other stereotypically female nurturing behavior. As Rhode has shown us, some women, some of the time, may be more inclined than the average man to push to make the public sphere better for everyone. But we all know and work with men who are similarly inclined. Of the many challenges before us, one of the hardest is in getting institutions to value and reward nurturance in both sexes. An especially important difference that women bring to this endeavor is our second-class status that gives us a personal incentive to work for fairness and justice. If we are fortunate enough to have retained empathy for others, we are able to generalize that desire beyond our immediate self-interest and seek fairness and justice for all groups.

NOTES

1. Barbara F. Reskin and Irene Padavic, "Sex, Race, and Ethnic Inequality in United States Workplaces," in *Handbook of Gender Research* 343–374 (Janet S. Chafetz, ed. 2001); Barbara F. Reskin and Irene Padavic, *Women and Men at Work* (1994).

2. Ann Huff, *Wives of the Organization* (unpublished manuscript, 1991).

3. Cynthina Fuchs Epstein, *Deceptive Distinctions: Sex, Gender and the Social Order* (1988); Jerry A. Jacobs, *The Revolving Door* (1989).

4. Rosabeth Moss Kanter, *Men and Women of the Corporation* (1977).

5. Naomi Cassirer and Barbara Reskin, "High Hopes: Organizational Location, Employment Experiences, and Women's and Men's Promotion Aspirations," 27 *Work and Occupations* 438, 463 (2000).

6. Kanter, *Men and Women of the Corporation.*

7. *The Works of Alexander Hamilton* (Henry Cabot Lodge, ed., 1904).

8. Marilyn B. Brewer and Rupert J. Brown, "Intergroup Relations," in *Handbook of Social Psychology* 554 (D. T. Gilbert et al., eds. 1998).

9. James Baron and Jeffrey Pfeffer, "The Social Psychology of Organizations and Inequality," 57 *Social Psychology Quarterly* 190, 209 (1994).

10. Susan T. Fiske, "Stereotyping Prejudice and Discrimination," in *Handbook of Social Psychology* 357 (D. T. Gilbert et al., eds. 1998).

11. Brewer and Brown, "Intergroup Realations," at 554.

12. Joseph Broschak, Lisa Cohen, and Heather Haveman, "And Then There Were More? The Effects of Organizational Sex Composition on Hiring and Promotion," 64 *American Sociological Rev.* 711, 727 (1998).

13. Kanter, *Men and Women of the Corporation.*

14. Debra McBrier and Barbara F. Reskin, "Why Not Ascription? Organizations' Employment of Male and Female Managers," 65 *American Sociological Rev.* 210, 233 (2000).

15. Barbara F. Reskin, "The Realities of Affirmative Action," *American Sociological Rev.* (1999).

4

RUTH B. MANDEL

A Question About Women
and the Leadership Option

Deborah L. Rhode's "The Difference 'Difference' Makes" presents a valuable overview of current knowledge about women and leadership. Both accurate and cogent in raising questions about the status of women's leadership and the obstacles to its advancement, the chapter points to issues requiring attention and identifies targets for change. It offers a useful outline for discussion about a subject that poses difficult and persistent conundrums while simultaneously challenging us to think strategically about how to achieve realistic goals.

In this response, my primary attention will be on adding to our discussion a question that is outside the chapter's central focus but essential to take up if we are considering the future of women's leadership. Namely, is there reason to ask whether women today—especially young women— might be opting not to move in traditional leadership directions? In a world with many options now available to highly educated young women, is leadership an appealing choice? I raise this question mainly because more than thirty years after the new feminism, women have made very limited advances in positions of leadership and power. At the same time, we see many examples of highly educated young women shaping professional and family lives that do not include dreams of becoming leaders. Have today's young women seen previews of the leadership life, not found it particularly appealing, and decided to skip the full feature? Are other scripts more enticing?

In the political arena, for example, recent evidence shows the movement of women into elective office as sluggish at best. The crucial state legislative level warrants special attention. Beginning in the late 1960s, each election cycle has resulted in a small but measurable increase in the number of women serving in state legislatures, one that has gradually lifted women's representation from a minuscule 4.0 percent in 1969 to 22.5 percent in 2000. The elections of 2000 marked the first setback in that progress, with women lawmakers in 2001 representing 22.4 percent of the total.[1] In statewide elective office, the proportion of women also dropped slightly after the elections of 2000, falling from 28.5 percent to 27.6 percent.[2] Although these hardly significant declines make it premature for loud alarms, there is reason for concern if this pattern continues and is replicated in other offices. In this regard, it should be noted that many women candidates for statewide and congressional offices have climbed the political ladder from state legislatures. Were that pipeline to begin drying up, we could see fewer and fewer women ready to run for higher-level offices.

A small number of aspiring public leaders even win high office at a young age without spending years in the political trenches at local or mid-levels. Yet of the six members of the 107th Congress (2000–2002) who are age thirty-five or younger, none is a woman.

More worrisome is preliminary information gathered in early 2002 by the Eagleton Institute of Politics for a study of young elected officials revealing that of the total population of 7,424 legislators across the country, 320 are age thirty-five or younger, and only thirty-six of them are women. Thus in 2002, after thirty years of activism on behalf of increasing women's participation in politics, women are 22 percent of all state legislators but only 11 percent of the young legislators.[3] It is also striking that the age of women in state legislatures is increasing at the same time that their numbers appear to be flattening. In a 2001 national study comparing women and men in state legislatures, the Center for American Women and Politics reported:

> There is a widespread perception that more young women are running for office nowadays; yet women legislators are older on average than they were in 1988. Significantly more women legislators in 2001 (74%) than in 1988 (58%) are 50 years of age or older. The women are also older than

the men. Only about a quarter (24%) of the women legislators are under the age of 50, in contrast to 39 percent of male legislators.[4]

Inside Women's Power: Learning from Leaders, an analysis of in-depth interviews conducted in 2000 with sixty prominent women leaders in a variety of professional arenas, notes that there is a "continued scarcity of women in top leadership positions" and concludes that "the passage of time [i.e. three decades of social change] alone cannot solve the problem of professional women's advancement; rather, it may exacerbate the problem."[5] Commenting on the sluggishness of progress, the report notes,

> Women's scarcity in the pipeline may have been a plausible explanation for low numbers of women in top leadership positions in the 1960s and 1970s. On the other hand, the slow pace of progress since 1980, when women already held 40.9% of the managerial professional specialty positions, has eroded this theory's credibility. If the lack of diversity in top leadership were due *only*, or even primarily, to the small numbers in the pipeline, there would have been more progress by now.[6]

If these patterns can be documented in a number of leadership arenas, discussions of the kinds of difference "difference" makes will be shaped by an apparent challenge to what many of us have considered a relatively predictable trajectory of change.

In pondering why so few women have risen to top leadership over recent decades, *Inside Women's Power* concludes that, "external barriers, although diminishing in strength and becoming more subtle than overt, continue to carry the blame for the slow pace of progress in increasing women's representation in top leadership" and emphasizes that "external barriers continue to be severe especially for leaders of color."[7] Granted that "external barriers" is a viable—perhaps the most viable—explanation for women's continuing absence from top leadership, theoretically the parameters of "external" can extend to the structure of society itself and all its cultural patterns. Specifying precisely what we mean by "external barriers" seems critical for understanding the adequacy of that explanation for women's leadership status and prospects. Are women opting not to challenge existing "external barriers" and thereby widen access to leadership positions? It is uncomfortable and unpopular to raise the issue, especially among those of us who have spent our adult lives battling the notion that women themselves have accepted their historical status outside leadership because they inherently favor a list toward nurture over a pull to power.

As a consequence of vast changes in laws and attitudes about gender roles as well as in access to virtually all the institutions of our society, today we ought to view the situations in which women make choices as shaped by considerations beyond historically inbred sexist barriers. The question of how many women find the new leadership options appealing and whether significantly more women can be expected to choose the leadership life is in itself mired in conflicting views about achieving a traditional leadership position and whether that should be a desirable goal. Although the justice of the goal escapes challenge, there is a concern about the kinds of women who would want formal roles of power and prestige. Who besides the individual beneficiaries themselves would gain from opening "the system" at its top to women if the system itself is the problem? As has often been expressed, this would simply be an "add women and stir" approach; the old soup would still be the old soup. This would be women's leadership without change.

The lack of enthusiasm in this attitude embodies a profound and understandable distrust of traditional institutions, those structures built by and for powerful men in a culture of second-class citizenship for women. Making room for women within relatively unaltered structures would leave intact the overall system that historically has denied leadership opportunities to women and other powerless groups. Skepticism about incremental gains inside traditional systems is a familiar and understandable stance for those who believe that real, progressive change requires a radical restructuring of society that cannot take place by numbers alone. Dreams and visions have been articulated, but the practical blueprint for achieving a radically restructured, equitable, and just society has yet to emerge.

For those who are less committed to radical restructuring and more concerned with equalizing opportunities inside traditional systems, the daunting challenge remains of how to increase change in the composition of leadership and speed up its pace.[8] Opportunities for women who manage to "fit" into the old molds will be likely to produce relatively meager, painfully slow results. Policies of accommodation such as flex time, onsite child care, job sharing, divided household chores, and the like are desirable and even necessary options in the twenty-first century, making work and family life more manageable for more women and men. Positive adjustments in workplaces and in homes notwithstanding, these benefits do not represent fundamental change; their effect is more likely to support established patterns of power. It is a near certainty that presidents of major universities, corporate CEOs, United States senators, and partners in prestigious law, accounting, or public affairs firms will not arise from job-sharing or flex-time positions. Recruitment and career patterns, selection standards, and job performance requirements would be unlikely to allow for it.

Although women's patterns of life and work look dramatically different in twenty-first century America, the routes to leadership look unchanged. For women, old questions continue to nag. Will the few winners of the traditional race make a significant difference simply by entering executive suites and joining clubs of power? Will anything noteworthy change simply because of women's presence even if their numbers grow ever larger? To stretch the awkward culinary metaphor, would not the addition of large amounts of new ingredients in fact change a soup? If so, what proportion of it must be women for the soup to take on a different texture and flavor even if the women do nothing more than add themselves to the old mix? If women do not deliberately promote changes in policy or process, will they not still have been the agents for progressive change simply by being there and thus pushing the society into meeting its democratic ideal and obligation to provide opportunity for all? That may not be everything, but it is something.

Take the case of politics. In elective office, the thirteen women (and growing) in the U.S. Senate, the sixty women (as of January 2002) who vote in the U.S. House, and the five women governors will matter in more ways than to illustrate that opportunity for women does exist in politics. Male colleagues (logically or illogically) will defer to their presumed expertise on certain issues.[9] Female constituents and women who live beyond geographic constituency areas will turn to elected women assuming that their lives have given them an understanding of issues outside of most men's experiences. Children will grow up having assimilated images of both women and men as decision makers. Women in office will continue to enlarge and diversify the pool of talent in public life by drawing staff and making appointments from networks familiar to them. For the foreseeable future, women will likely continue to promote public policies and rank policy priorities somewhat differently from their male colleagues, bringing new emphases into the political arena and placing new issues on the public agenda.[10]

Many political women will be conscious that gender has an impact on how they are viewed, what is expected of them, and how they do their jobs in politics and government.[11] For an individual political woman, this consciousness will be a part of daily life and arise in many ways. A few typical examples include understanding that she must speak out on particular issues or no one will; accepting her role as presumed expert on certain topics deemed as "female" by her colleagues, the media, or the public; agreeing to take on assignments as a party spokesperson to advance party messages and attract women's votes for the party's candidates; lending herself to efforts aimed at increasing women's participation in public leadership; making herself widely available as a role model and educator for young women. Still part of a small minority of visible women leaders, she will be viewed as representative of her gender, a perception that will thrust on her the stress of proving women's capabilities and will impose on her schedule the burden of filling slots on committees, delegations, negotiating teams, panels, programs—wherever it seems necessary to have a woman in the room.

Among the very few women who hold power in public and professional arenas, a considerable number have used their "difference" to make a difference. These differences, positive and progressive as many of them are, have been made *inside* traditional institutions and systems. They have helped make them function better or be more sensitive and responsive to the needs of broad segments of the population. However, they cannot properly be viewed as bringing about permanent, systemic change or social transformation.

Faced with the likelihood that by virtually anyone's progressive definition, society will remain fundamentally "untransformed" but that the presence of women leaders will continue to result in social betterment, the question remains: Given the vast array of new options for women's lives in the twenty-first century, what will women choose? Will large numbers of women want a track to the top, or will they want flex time, part-time work, telecommuting, or small business ownership? To state the obvious—different women want different things, and individual women want different things at different points in their lives. In the first instance, the women who aspire to leadership in the traditional ways have more opportunity than ever before to achieve such a goal. To do so, they confront daunting challenges and sometimes brutal choices regarding family life and personal priorities. (In fairness, the same is true for many men, but often not to the same extent or at the same cost.) However, women who choose not to enter the proverbial "rat race" also make choices reflecting their priorities and life preferences, both personal and professional. Notwithstanding the fact that thirty years of change have eroded or even removed historic barriers to traditional leadership opportunities for women, we must recognize that although only a small corps of highly ambitious professional women take the track to the top, proportionately many more women than men choose other options.

There is a continuing conundrum here. Nothing will change the picture of leadership and perhaps the practices of leadership unless women themselves choose to pursue leadership. In the United States, far and away, this matter of women's choices stands as the single greatest remaining challenge to achieving parity for women in leadership. Pioneers over the last thirty years have led the way and often did make a difference by their very presence as well as by their actions. Let me state emphatically that I am not saying that women at one time were choosing to lead and now are not. I am saying that today women can enter a path to leadership that has been cleared of many old impediments. They confront more opportunities and options than ever before. Nonetheless, women must choose to walk the path. If few women today are opting for positions of top leadership, perhaps it is even because young women who have been schooled in a world of feminist consciousness are not enticed by joining what they perceive to be a type of life they want to shun—an alien, high pressured, brutally competitive lifestyle with unappealing rewards. Without denying the importance of knowing the *reasons* for the choices today's woman makes, it is unavoidable to notice that the *results* look like the same old male-dominated world.

Entertaining this as an accurate observation about current reality is not the same as believing that the pages of history have been turned back and women are choosing to retreat into outmoded versions of domesticity. Although some polls have reported that many mothers of young children would like to stay home or hold part-time jobs, there is as yet no body of hard evidence that large proportions of women aspire to stay-at-home lives for the long run. Given the history of the last fifty years, this life plan would be unlikely. Irreversible changes in education, labor force participation, control of reproduction, life expectancy, marital patterns—these and virtually all other areas of everyday life have profoundly and permanently altered both the choices available to women and the context in which both women and men shape their lives. A World Wide Web, CNN, dot-com, multinational corporate world to which women's lives are fundamentally connected makes it unrealistic to envision a return to a mythically tranquil private home separated from the public sphere.[12] Nonetheless, we must not deny the possibility that given the choice, many women who can afford to "stay home" might opt to do so, and many mothers whose economic circumstances compel them to work full-time outside the home might choose differently if they could afford it. As one former CEO who left behind corporate life and decided instead to become a full-time wife and mother explained, "I personally came to the conclusion that being a CEO is hell. . . . It wasn't what I wanted to do with the rest of my life. . . . My generation went out of the gate full tilt, propelled to have a career, and for some number maybe that choice didn't reflect who we were."[13]

Yet the women who set out on a road to top leadership will still travel in domains designed by and for men, replete with the residues of men's leadership for centuries. The fit may not be comfortable. Perhaps it can become so if women wish to redesign the space and language of leadership to make it friendly to both sexes.[14] But realistically, what does that mean? I am not sure that anyone knows. I am sure that we must face and tell the truth about what we see. Achieving women's leadership may be a process in progress; and so is our thinking about it. We must entertain the explanation that if women's presence in leadership does not grow, women are making other choices and that many kinds of choices are important and valuable, indeed emerge from the garden of many options planted by feminists thirty years ago. The biggest hurdle at the moment—the choice itself—appears to be in women's power. Although we can acknowledge that for women the leadership route poses far greater obstacles than for men, in a practical sense there is little to be gained in 2001 from concluding that women's ambitions are thwarted by forces largely outside of their control. The most profound (and uncomfortable) questions at the moment may not be so much about the obstacles to women's leadership as about the appeal of leadership to women.

Relative to others in a group, organization, or community, if the leader is the person who takes on more responsibility, gives more time and energy, withstands more pressure and (when necessary) controversy, is publicly accountable for more consequences or results, is ultimately accountable for the success or failure of the enterprise, women must have the appetite for such a leadership life. Frankly, no matter how much those who believe that the future of societal betterment depends on the leadership that women and other groups of new leaders will bring, its appeal may be questionable. Could it be that a life of micro richness beckons with more allure than the appeal of macro power? Though the two are not mutually exclusive, they are hard to reconcile at any single point in time. My point is simply that a full, forthright discussion of women's leadership status and prospects must focus honestly on questions about the choices women are making.

NOTES

1. "Women in State Legislative Office 2001" (2001).

2. "Women in Statewide Elective Office 2000" (2000); "Women in Statewide Elective Office 2001" (2001).

3. Conducted by the Eagleton Institute of Politics at Rutgers University under a grant from The Pew Charitable Trusts, the Young Elected Leaders Project (YELP) is compiling a database of elected officials under age thirty-five and surveying them to learn about their personal histories, attitudes, opinions, and experiences in public life. The study will be completed in 2003.

4. Center for American Women and Politics (CAWP), *Women in State Legislatures: Past, Present, Future* (2001). This report is from a nationwide survey of state legislators conducted by CAWP in the spring and summer of 2001; findings about legislators' ages are reported in the section entitled "Demographics of Women in State Legislators." (The report is available from CAWP, Eagleton Institute of Politics, Rutgers University, 191 Ryders Lane, New Brunswick, NJ 08901).

5. Sumru Erkut, *Inside Women's Power: Learning from Leaders* 15 (2001).

6. Id., at 14.

7. Id., at 78.

8. Over the past thirty years of change in women's roles, professional aspirations, and status, the rate of progress has been incremental. In elective office, for example, women's numbers have grown steadily but glacially from under 5 percent representation nationwide in elective positions at local, state, and federal levels in the early 1970s to a little over 20 percent representation in local and state executive and legislative offices by 2001, with the federal legislative level lagging behind at 13 percent. As Deborah L. Rhode's chapter, "The Difference 'Difference' Makes," documents, these types of small incremental gains are typical in business and law, as well as in other sectors.

9. Of course, experiential knowledge is a valuable asset for elected representatives, no less so stereotypical "gender knowledge" than the professional knowledge gained from a physics degree, the knowledge of military life gained from serving in the armed services, or the knowledge of agricultural issues gained from a family farming background.

10. CAWP, *Women in State Legislatures: Past, Present, Future*; Janet A. Flammang, *Women's Political Voice: How Women Are Transforming the Practice and Study of Politics* (1997); Debra L. Dodson et al., *Voices, Views, Votes: The Impact of Women in the 103rd Congress* (1995); Susan J. Carroll, "The Politics of Difference: Women Public Officials as Agents of Change," 5 *Stanford Law and Policy Review* 11–20 (spring 1994); Sue Thomas, *How Women Legislate* (1994); Debra L. Dodson and Susan J. Carroll, *Reshaping the Agenda: Women in State Legislatures* (1991); Susan J. Carroll, Debra L. Dodson, and Ruth B. Mandel, *The Impact of Women in Public Office: An Overview* (1991).

11. Ruth B. Mandel, "Women's Leadership in American Politics: The Legacy and the Promise," in *The American Woman 2001–2002: Getting to the Top* (Cynthia B. Costello and Anne J. Stone, eds. 2001).

12. See *Women's Voices 2000*, a project of the Center for Policy Alternatives in collaboration with Lifetime Television (Washington, D.C. 2000). In a national study of women's values and priorities conducted in 2000, researchers found that, "Time emerged as a central theme . . . [and] is by far women's most precious resource. . . . " Id., at 13. The study reported that, "71 percent of all women surveyed said that they would chose a job with more flexibility and benefits over a job that offers more pay." Id., at 3.

13. Alex Witchel, "Trading Places: C.E.O. Does Mrs. Mom," *N. Y. Times*, Feb. 7, 2002, at F8.

14. The authors of *Inside Women's Power* argue the need for "a new leadership language," including "family metaphors," that will have the effect of making leadership more inclusive. See Erkut, *Inside Women's Power*, chapter 6.

5

JACOB H. HERRING

Can They Do It?

Can Law Firms, Corporate Counsel Departments, and Governmental Agencies Create a Level Playing Field for Women Attorneys?

In responding to Deborah L. Rhode's chapter, "The Difference 'Difference' Makes," I focus on three important challenges facing women in the contemporary professional organization.[1]

I start from the premise that there are indeed organizational, institutional, or systemic obstacles to women attorneys becoming leaders in today's corporations, law firms, and governmental agencies. The three that I discuss are (1) gender-based assumptions and practices, (2) a lack of mentoring, and (3) family-work conflicts.

THE PROBLEM OF GENDER

Is there a problem of women and leadership? Are there systemic obstacles to women achieving and wielding power in organizations and society at large? It's fascinating that this question is still being asked in 2001, when the evidence is so apparent to all but those who refuse to see it. The continual asking of this question, in the face of all kinds of evidence that answer affirmatively and identify multiple obstacles, leads me to believe that those who keep asking the question do so because it is in their self-interest to do so. That is, as long as we pretend not to be sure of the answer to the question, we need do nothing about solving "the problem."

The refusal on the part of some women and men to recognize the existence of gender-related obstacles is in itself a problem. This lack of recognition, accompanied by the reaction of incredulity on the part of some colleagues when the problems are pointed out, leave many women feeling as though they are out of touch with reality when they complain of not "getting their due." Lack of validation often leads to self-doubt, then confusion and anger, and sometimes rage.

The kinds of problems women experience are the *assumptions* that they can't be business developers; a discounting of their contributions to the organization's bottom line; a refusal to value (in monetary terms) their contributions to the smooth running of the organization (that is, administration, committee participation, and so forth)—all of these things lead to lower compensation, in general. This is by no means an exhaustive list of the obstacles that women face but just a few examples that appear to be among the most obvious.

Although I believe that white women lawyers, as a group, are doing better than attorneys of color, these women are still not playing on a level field when compared to white men in the legal profession. Part of the reason for this is that nearly all white men have had at least one authentic, interdependent relationship with a white woman, while few of them have had such a relationship with someone of color. However, white women have to put up with continual challenges to their authority; they have difficulty establishing a track record and are much more likely than white men to be assumed incompetent until they prove themselves otherwise. My experience as a management consultant to law firms over almost a decade and a half suggests that women lawyers are the angriest group in those organizations today. They are angry because they experience obstacles to their advancement on a regular basis, and they believe and in some cases know that these obstacles are based upon their gender and not upon their performance or other non-gender related factors.

This isn't to say that all women, regardless of color, are sterling performers or that some don't lose out fairly in any given instance of competition. However, it is to say that a growing number of women lawyers complain that they were not chosen for a given assignment when a man of no more or even less competence was chosen. Or women report not receiving a chance to inherit a major client when a man of no greater achievement got the opportunity. Some women experience better treatment and more respect outside their firms than among their colleagues within the firms. For example, male partners will introduce female colleagues to clients and other lawyers as though these women were associates, not partners. Such experiences rankle or embitter a growing number of women who either vote with their feet or stay and participate at levels far beneath their capabilities. In the latter case, the firm is an equal loser.

INADEQUATE MENTORING

As noted earlier, one of the most enduring and pervasive obstacles to women's success is the persistence of certain career-limiting "cultural assumptions" about women, such as "women can't be rainmakers." These cultural assumptions are destructive for women in a variety of ways; one involves their effect on women's access to mentors and mentoring. Mentoring is often essential to professional success. Yet if it is assumed, as it often is, that a woman can't be a rainmaker, then why bother supporting a "loser"? Since time is precious, why would anyone spend their time mentoring a woman who, it is assumed, probably can't do the job, when the alternative is mentoring a high-flying man, who probably can and, it is assumed, will do the job?

Even senior women who don't share that assumption often find it difficult to mentor younger women because of other gender inequities. Difficulties in balancing career and family needs leave many women without time to include mentoring in that mix. At least, they do not find time to mentor in the manner typically done by men—over drinks after work, on the golf course or squash court, and so forth. To some extent, this problem is exacerbated by the fact that women, more often than not, have to develop their own clients instead of inheriting them from more senior partners.

So too, senior men often fear mentoring more junior women because they believe they risk the appearance of impropriety as well as potential accusations of sexual harassment. Some men and women also complain that mentoring junior women is a waste of time because they have frequently done so only to have the junior woman leave the firm for other opportunities elsewhere or for family-related reasons, such as having a child or following their mate to another city.

A related problem is that women and people of color frequently find that the mentor they had on the way up—on the road to partnership or promotion—is no longer available to them once they arrive. Or they need a different kind of mentoring as partners than they had as associates, and this "higher-level" mentoring is often harder to come by. Once a woman becomes a partner, she may be perceived as a competitor and not a "subordinate" who still needs help, albeit of a different kind. In other cases, the problem is finding someone with the skills now currently needed—for example, business development or firm leadership.

FAMILY-CAREER CONFLICTS

For many women the most difficult issues are family-work or family-career conflicts. These issues have no easy resolution. Nearly everyone appears to lose from conventional solutions. Women who take time off or who work part-time in order to have children or to take care of elderly parents are still more often than not restricted from mainstream access to leadership positions. And they are frequently paid less than their contributions would suggest is fair. The unfairness is compounded by the expectation that they will be available for phone calls and faxes at home during their "off" time.

By the same token, single or childless women, as well as men, resent any special treatment for mothers because it imposes extra burdens on those who lack an acceptable "excuse" for turning down work. The non-child-rearing attorneys feel as though they are paying the price to "cover" for women who are primary caretakers. And frequently the client wants to relate only to one person on the team, not to a stand-in. Finally, firm managers feel as though they are caught between the proverbial rock and a hard place because their business model won't support paying part-time partners and associates commensurate with their contributions and because angry full-time attorneys complain to them about the part-timers.

The occasions that I've been asked to facilitate meetings that included these family-work issues have been the most trying of my career. No one feels like a winner and emotions are extremely high; everyone feels unfairly put upon—to say the least. Not only is this one of the most emotionally explosive issues facing law firms (and other organizations) today, it is also one for which there is no escape. People who should know believe that increasingly women have some of the best talent in today's law schools. Legal employers want the best talent. Also increasingly, young women coming into law today, unlike their predecessors of several decades ago, expect the institutions to adjust to them and their needs, not the other way around. In other words, the newer women entrants expect to be taken seriously as lawyers, be on the partnership track and have children, work part-time as associates and partners for a period of their careers, and not lose a "step" in the process.

APPROACHES TO RESOLUTIONS

There are a number of approaches to the problems I have discussed. I discuss here only a few the possibilities. First, it is necessary to recognize the existence of obstacles facing women in general, and professional women in particular. As James Baldwin said, "not everything that is faced can be changed, but nothing can be changed until it is faced." The sooner that leaders of the profession understand the obstacles preventing full participation, the sooner legal organizations will be able to utilize all the talent available for which they pay so handsomely.

A major challenge for women in these organizations is to enlist allies. Why? Allies increase a group's numerical weight beyond its membership. They allow women to make progress without doing everything themselves, and provide information and other resources. These allies will have to come from the ranks of white men, men of color, gays and lesbians, lawyers with disabilities—all individuals who share a self-interest in creating a fair system. This approach must be pursued at every level—personal, professional, and political.

At the personal level, I believe that all women who want to become successful leaders must learn to manage and channel their emotions—especially anger. My experience is that few organizations handle well people who are perceived as angry. Once lawyers acquire that label, they are avoided, isolated, and mistrusted. People almost never ask themselves or each other, What did we do to make her so angry? Instead, what they say is, How did she ever get hired here? Or they attribute the woman's behavior and mood to some aspect of her character or personal life, not to the obstacles she may be facing at work. Successful women, like successful men, have learned to focus beyond the obstacles in their path onto the goals they're striving to achieve.

It is important for women to bring new approaches to the acquisition of power in organizations. For example, some women report considerable success networking and acquiring clients through their children's day care center—a novel approach to rainmaking, if ever I've heard about one. Likewise, I've heard women discuss mentoring opportunities during a shopping excursion. Certainly I foresee an increased joining of forces between women in corporations and governmental agencies and women in law firms that have full diversity in their partnerships and leadership positions.

It may be that the problems of family-work conflict won't really be solved until many more men attorneys take on the challenges of raising children, either as primary caretakers or by playing a larger role together with their wives. Similarly, men as well as women attorneys, along with legal employers, must realize that mentoring is part of the professional role. Senior lawyers need to mentor their subordinates. If those junior attorneys leave the organization, it's in everyone's best interest to maintain good relationships. Departing lawyers are a source of referrals, information, and influence, but only if they and the resident lawyers share the same mindset.

Clearly, the issues raised in Professor Rhode's chapter and throughout this volume deserve far more time and space than I have here. I hope that I have done some justice to those issues that most concern me and that I think offer greatest opportunities for change.

NOTES

1. This discussion is specific to the issues of white women. Much of what is discussed also applies to women of color; however, their problems are compounded by issues of white supremacy and cross-cultural conflict in addition to those of male supremacy.

III

WHAT DIFFERENCE

DOES DIFFERENCE MAKE?

6

PATRICIA SCOTT SCHROEDER

Women's Leadership: Perspectives from a Recovering Politician

This historic collection makes me proud to be a lawyer and challenges me to find something important left to say. What I can perhaps offer is a perspective on leadership from a politician in the twelve-step recovery process.

The first thing to note is how far we have *not* come. When I attend an event like the one that prompted the chapters in this collection, I remind myself of when I was this thirty-two-year-old entering congresswoman from Colorado. This was 1973 and I recall thinking, "Wow! Women are on the move. This is going to be wonderful, we are going to have women everywhere; I am going to have colleagues coming soon. . . . " And with that freshman exuberance, I asked the Library of Congress research staff how long they thought it would be before half the House of Representatives would be female. And their answer was, "At this rate of change, four hundred years." I was totally outraged! I was ready to call out air strikes on the Library of Congress, but I am now beginning to think they were right.

Here we are, starting a new century, and we are so excited that women comprise 13 percent of the Senate and about 15 percent of the House. Woo hoo!! I mean, this is just too exciting. And when you look at governors, and you look at other elective offices, you see how much progress we haven't made. And that's just politics. I am not even going to *talk* about business.

Business is totally outrageous. Take the twenty-five mega-conglomerates, not one woman CEO in any of them. The Anneberg School for Communication just released a horrifying head count. There are almost no women CEOs at Fortune 1000 companies. And the new companies are worse than the old companies. You know, we kept hoping that they would evolve. But all these dot-coms are run by twenty-five-year-old males in T-shirts. There are no women anywhere. So I think we have to wonder why. The problems for women in all these settings are connected. It is difficult for women to break through in politics when they are not breaking through in the private sector and they are not breaking through in other leadership contexts. So what is wrong?

To begin with, here we are in a new century and "Barbie" is still the model of American women. If you take what the average American woman spends on outfits, hair, and shoes versus what she spends on political issues she cares about, the comparison is pretty scary. And if you look at women's magazines and you are not neurotic when you start them, you will be when you finish them. It is still the same old, same old story. Men age in our society, women rot. When I was a congresswoman I used to visit lots and lots of grade schools, and I would talk to the children. Some of the most depressing interchanges occurred when I asked young girls, "What is your favorite TV show?" I can't tell you how many of them would say, *Golden Girls*. And I'd say, "Why?" "Because it says you can be an old woman and have fun." Why are they worrying about that in grade school? What are the messages that the media sends?

We are in a period where we have moved past a great many of the overt barriers, but the covert obstacles are still very much there. And they are much more difficult to deal with. We are getting a great deal of lip service on gender equality. Nobody stands up and says, "Hey, I'm a sexist." But we really are trapped in a retro moment. Pray for me. Tuesday I have to go to the First Lady's lunch. I thought these ended in the 1950s! They are back! What is this? I went to law school to avoid it all and it is back, and we are in the twenty-first century! We have a cultural war going on that terrifies me, and it really is about women.

Why do I think there is a cultural war? Think of the response to a study that recently came out on child care. It claimed that children spending extended time in day care had more behavioral and other difficulties than other children. The entire time I was in Congress I used to get furious that taxpayers would fund studies like these. Europe, Canada, and other countries would take research on children and do something very productive with it. *We* would take the studies and just continue this cultural war that makes women who work feel guilty. At the same time, the message from welfare reforms is that poor mothers who don't work *should* feel guilty. It is a no-win situation for women.

If we do not deal more effectively with work and family issues, we are in deep trouble. I remember being so stunned after graduating from Harvard Law School and practicing law in Denver that raising children was so much more difficult than anything in my professional life. Being a mother required more skill, more patience, more self-discipline, and more judgement than being a lawyer. Part of the reason I was shocked by that discovery is that we live in a culture that says rearing children is not work. Everybody knows how to do it, it is easy, it is not a job, it is no problem. And then we say to women, "OK, so you think you are as smart as men? You think you are better than men, don't you. So you go out there and if you can keep your family straight, if you can look like a *Vogue* model, if you can keep your husband happy, if you can bake bread at home, and if your children can remain perfect, go ahead—work." Then when we all fall flat on our face they say, "See . . . ," and I say, "Wait a minute, this is about equality." If we want to ensure equal rights, we really need to work through these work and family issues, which are becoming issues for more and more men as well as women.

When I was in Congress trying to figure all this out, I was carrying 99.9 percent of all the work in family issues. It took me nine years to pass family leave; it has been law since 1993. But it is now eight years later and no one has done one thing to move the issue one inch further. We still don't have paid family leave. If you talk to anyone from Europe, Canada, South America, they will laugh at how backward we are. And we have not done much of anything about child care. We are still saying, "If you have a family, it is your problem." We still have a work environment where if someone brings up family issues we automatically assume that they are not fully committed to their career. You can bring up parking lot issues, you can bring up 401K issues, you can bring up food in the dining room, you can bring up anything else. It is only bringing up family issues that signals a problem. And men and women have to stand together and demand changes or it is unlikely to get any better.

About five years ago, some women lawyers did an amazing survey. They discovered that when you look at American society, only one family in ten resembles a Norman Rockwell painting—with a male bread-winner and full-time homemaker. When you look at elected officials, only one family in ten does *not* resemble a Norman Rockwell painting. So when you talk to political leaders about work and family, they just do not really get it. They are in another social strata where they have a full-time adult caregiver in the home. You mention "child care," and they hear "babysitting." There is just a huge disconnect between their perception and women's realities. But there is no money in "women's" issues so they don't get addressed. Other countries have done much better because they see "women's" issues as family issues. If we are going to move the American women's movement further, we need to do the same.

There is a great deal more we could learn from other countries. We just finished the five-year follow-up to the international conference on women held in Beijing in 1995. How many Americans know what our grades were as a country? They were terrible. Not only did we fail to make the Dean's List, we got mostly C's and D's. We got an F on raising women out of poverty during the last five-year period.

When I reflect on the twenty-four years that I spent in Congress, I admit to being discouraged that we did not move faster on women's issues. Patience is not one of my great virtues. So what would I do? One of my recent ideas is something that arose from a speech I recently gave about Wall Street to a group of men who thought they were being so progressive. After all, they were having *Pat Schroeder as a speaker*. Oooh! Halfway through the speech, one of the men in the audience stood up and said, "This woman must be stopped!"

But here is the idea. One way women can't be stopped is through their purchasing power. Part of the power that women have in this country is that they buy everything. They are the consumers. The only thing men buy is their own underwear and beer. That is about it. Even for corporations, it is women who are making the hotel reservations, the airline reservations, and pretty much everything else. We need a way to rank the major corporations in this country on whether they are good for women and let women purchasers know the numbers. Does the company have women on the board of directors? Does it have good work and family policies? Does it have women in their top line management? And so forth. And then we should tell every woman in America, "You can go to this Web site and check this out." So if you are deciding whether to book Hilton or Sheraton, you can pick out the one with the more progressive policies for women. You just think about how you could change this economy, because the entire game is about market share, market share, market share. Listen to the stock news every night. We want consumers to spend more, buy more. Fine, but they should be buying from businesses that do the right thing by women. So we need a Web site that is constantly brought up-to-date and marketed like mad.

Now the first response that people make is always, "There will be a lot of women who won't do that." And I respond, "I don't really care." Because I can tell you that if 10 percent of women change their buying habits, no one can stand to lose 10 percent of market share. Business would be in stark terror. Consider what has happened with the boards of directors. Those of you who get stock statements, do you see anyone on boards or among officers who looks like you? Rarely. I recall that back in 1960 when we first moved to Denver, I had a little stock, and I went to a couple of stockholders meetings. I remember going to the Continental Airlines shareholders' meeting with a friend. I didn't even have any stock but she did, and she didn't have the courage to stand up, so I did. I stood up and asked why they only had one woman on the board and it was the chairman's wife, who was Audrey Meadows. And they explained to me that you didn't get any prestige from having women on the board. I was a little shocked that they were so honest about it. Now today corporate leaders wouldn't say that, but they still don't have many women on boards.

So I just think maybe we ought to stop trying reasonable persuasion and figure out how we shop our way to freedom. I am tired of marching, I am tired of preaching, I am ready to start shopping. So give me the Web site; I want to move market shares.

7

SHEILA WELLINGTON

Making the Case:
Women in Law

For forty years, Catalyst has worked to advance women in business and the professions. The Women's Leadership Summit asked a question that is at the core of Catalyst's mission: How do we get more women in leadership positions? Our experience has taught us that the best way to achieve this goal is to ask a different question: Why care about women's advancement? We ask this question because change happens when women's retention and advancement is understood as a strategic goal rather than a personal goal for the individual. To make it a strategic goal, the economic benefits to the organization must be spelled out. What gets measured gets done, so to advance women, the link to profitability—always measured in private sector companies and firms—has to be drawn.

THE BUSINESS CASE FOR WOMEN'S RETENTION
AND ADVANCEMENT IN LAW

Nowhere is the need to make the link between the economic case and women's advancement more urgent than in the legal profession. The Catalyst study, *Women in Law: Making the Case*, identifies three prongs to the business case: (1) shrinking talent pool, (2) rising demand, and (3) hidden costs. With respect to the talent pool, the demographics are compelling: the

pool of people twenty-five to thirty-four years old from which law schools
and legal employers draw is declining.[1] At the same time, women are an increasing percentage of that shrinking pool. Women crossed the 40 percent
mark of law school graduates in 1985, the 50 percent mark in 2001, and
the trend line still climbs.[2]

With respect to rising demand, women are not only a greater percentage of law students, they are also an increasing percentage of the client
base for law firms.[3] In addition, many Fortune 1000 companies now consider diversity as a business imperative and are demanding that law firms
be diverse as well.[4] All of this leads to an increasing demand for senior
women within law firms. This demand is likely to increase still more in
years to come.

But the law firm pipeline continues to leak. *Women in Law: Making
the Case* reports that women leave law firms in greater numbers and earlier in their careers than men.[5] The third prong of the business case is the
hidden cost of this attrition. There is an old financial truism: It's not what
you earn but what you keep that matters. Turnover is a huge expense,
easily reaching millions of dollars a year for the large law firms. Further,
there is the additional, significant cost in client dissatisfaction that results
from turnover. During the course of Catalyst's research, clients told us
that they value stability in their service teams as much as, if not more
than, quick turnaround and twenty-four/seven access. Yet although it is
common knowledge that profit equals revenue minus costs, most law
firms give the revenue side all the glory but fail to keep track of turnover
and what is driving it. This is hardly a prudent business practice. Most
partners cannot tell you how much profit goes out the pipeline and down
the drain thanks to attrition. And they certainly can't tell you why their
high-potential people—male and female—leave. So to begin building the
business case, law firms must start to measure the rate of turnover by
level, the costs of turnover, and the reasons for it.

THE BARRIERS TO WOMEN'S ADVANCEMENT

Catalyst's study, *Women in Law: Making the Case*, based on responses
from more than 1,400 men and women graduates of the law schools at
Columbia, Harvard, Michigan, Berkeley, and Yale, shows that roughly
70 percent of these graduates, regardless of race, begin their careers in

law firms.[6] But today, only 35 percent of women of color and 41 percent of white women are still practicing in law firms, compared to 51 percent of men.[7] The higher rate of attrition for women is the result, in large part, of the fact that women are less satisfied with advancement opportunities than their male colleagues.[8] Not surprisingly, women intend to leave law firms three to four years earlier than do men.[9] These data indicate that one significant explanation for why women are not making it into law firm partnerships is that they leave before they can get there.

Although men and women in law firms generally agree on the strategies for success, listing communication skills and taking initiative among the top three, they don't see eye to eye on the barriers to women's advancement. Both rank commitment to family and personal life as the number one barrier to success. However, 74 percent of women in firms say this is a barrier, compared to 59 percent of men.[10] The fact that this barrier—conflict between work and personal life—ranked as the top barrier is unique among all the sectors that Catalyst has studied, including a major study of women in corporations, where this factor doesn't even make the top five barriers. Why is this factor so prominent in the law? A primary reason is that law firms are the sole organizations in the private sector that have a rigid, up-or-out career path.[11] According to the National Association of Law Placement, women law graduates were, on average in 2001, twenty-eight years old. Given that a typical partnership track is seven to eight years, it is clear that there is a serious structural issue: The partnership track is colliding with women's biological clocks. Should not the up-or-out system and the rigid time to partner schedule be reexamined? Are they so essential to the viability of law firms?

Commitment to family is not the only significant barrier to women's advancement, however. Over 50 percent of women in law firms also identified lack of client development experience, lack of mentors, and exclusion from internal informal networks as barriers.[12] When it comes to these obstacles that women experience, men simply don't get it. Whereas 52 percent of women cite lack of mentoring opportunities as a barrier, only 29 percent of men see this as a barrier.[13] Most striking is that whereas 52 percent of women rated exclusion from informal networks as a barrier, only 16 percent of men agreed.[14] In Catalyst's experience, this gendered perception gap about the barriers to women's advancement is *itself* a barrier—because it makes the case for change harder to make.

THE SEARCH FOR WORK-LIFE BALANCE

The prominence of work-life issues in the legal profession is underscored by the fact that over 70 percent of *both* men and women in the Catalyst study report work-life conflict.[15] Although lawyers with children report the highest conflict levels, 62 percent of women and 56 percent of men without children are also having difficulty balancing work and personal life.[16]

Why the conflict? Men and women agree that work-life conflict is related to the demands, expectations, and pace of work. The top three sources of work-life conflict they identified are (1) the pressure to provide fast turnaround, (2) excessive workload, and the (3) unpredictability of client demands.[17] Both men and women agree that control over when and where they work is the antidote for conflict. Over 50 percent of men and women in law firms want to be able to telecommute, which provides control over where work gets done.[18] In addition, 60 percent of men and an even higher percentage of women want more control over their work. Perhaps most significant is the fact that better work-life balance was the top factor for women in choosing their current jobs, but it was only the third-ranking factor for men.[19]

Although both men and women are seeking better work-life balance, men and women differ significantly in their interest in reduced hour schedules. Half of women in both law firms and in-house legal departments want reduced hour schedules, but fewer than 20 percent of men indicate that interest.[20] The long-term implications of these numbers is that women's career paths are affected by this issue in a way that men's are not. Although 80 percent of men in firms have worked continuously full-time throughout their careers, only 34 percent of women have.[21] Roughly a third of women had worked part-time at least at some point in their career, whereas fewer than 10 percent of the men had done so.

Why is there this disconnect between men and women's desire for better balance and their interest in part-time work arrangements? The answer lies in the link between part-time work arrangements and advancement. Only a third of the men and a quarter of the women believe they can use flexible work arrangements without affecting their career advancement. Women, whether by choice or necessity, make that tradeoff, whereas men by and large do not. Yet is it inevitable that part-time must be viewed as career suicide? Why can't law firms make this work?

LAW FIRMS AND CORPORATE LEGAL DEPARTMENTS COMPARED

Although more than 70 percent of the over 1,400 men and women respondents to the *Women in Law* study began their careers in law firms, currently 15 percent of both men and women work in corporate legal departments.[22] Women have traditionally left law firms and gone in-house in search of more regular hours. In fact, 61 percent of women in the Catalyst study who work in-house reported that they chose their job primarily for work-life balance.[23] However, the reality they find in corporate legal departments is different from what they expected.

Women in-house report work-life conflict at levels only slightly below their colleagues in law firms. Even more troubling is the fact that women in-house say they are more concerned about the career impacts of flexible schedules than the women in law firms. Only 9 percent of women in corporate legal departments, as opposed to 22 percent of women in law firms, believe they can use flexible work arrangements without affecting their career advancement.[24] In addition, women in-house are generally less satisfied with advancement opportunities than women in firms. The gender gap concerning advancement is most pronounced in corporate legal departments. These results from *Women in Law* tell us—to the surprise of many—that the corporate legal department is no haven for women.

PROMOTING WOMEN'S ADVANCEMENT IN LAW

In summary, measuring the costs of attrition, understanding the talent gap in the partnership and senior leadership pool, and exposing the perception gap on the barriers to women's advancement are the strategic foundation upon which a change initiative rests. Although attrition points to the case for women's retention, the case for women's advancement goes well beyond turnover—it rests on talent. Most law firms are still relying on the "myth of meritocracy" to determine their partnership pool. But the reality is that firms have lost much of their control over who leaves and who stays. Top talent is walking out. Prized colleagues are walking out. The revolving door is not just limited to associates—lateral movement at the partnership level is a serious issue as well.

Firms need to understand their talent gap by keeping track of the gender and race composition of their partnership pool and comparing that composition to who actually makes partner. Firms also need to understand why top talent leaves. Although many employers do exit interviews, Catalyst has found that the true story does not emerge unless these interviews are done by an outside person and in total anonymity. As a general proposition, women tell their bosses or the human resources department that they are quitting work to go home. But this is usually not the whole story. Of the *Women in Law* sample of law school graduates from 1970 to today, close to 90 percent of women lawyers were in the workforce. The notion that women lawyers leave to go home is, in fact, not borne out by the data.

Once lawyers have built the case for change, then they must specifically address each barrier. The most significant barrier to women's advancement is related to work-life issues. To address this barrier, written part-time policies are not enough. Those who use part-time policies must not be penalized. Part-time policies must be linked to the firm's strategic goals and must address compensation and advancement. In addition, the business case for flexibility must be communicated broadly. Reduced-hours schedules must be evaluated against the direct and indirect costs of losing a lawyer in whom the firm has invested heavily and who takes with her client-specific knowledge and relationships.

The other barriers identified by women in our study—lack of mentors and lack of access to informal networks—also need attention. A successful mentoring program includes clearly articulated objectives and performance standards for mentors, as well as incentives for meeting or exceeding standards. Besides mentoring, firms need to support affinity groups and networks by encouraging women's participation and by providing financial and other resources to accomplish their goals. Networks can provide personal support by reducing the isolation that many women and people of color feel in firms. And networks can provide professional support by creating business development opportunities and referral systems. That, in turn, can also help generate new business for the firm.

Whatever policies and programs law firms and corporate legal departments establish, Catalyst has learned that they won't be effective unless there is accountability and real commitment from the top. We find that formal structures establishing clear accountability for planning, monitoring, and evaluating action are key to a successful diversity initiative.

Getting women to the top starts by understanding why they leave and what would have kept them. Attracting and retaining talent—both male and female—is a major challenge facing the legal profession. Catalyst's study, *Women in Law: Making the Case*, indicates that women are like canaries in the coal mine—they are voicing the concerns of a growing number of men. Firms that make women's retention and advancement a strategic goal will not only improve their gender make-up at the top but will also have a competitive advantage in the war for talent that knows no gender.

NOTES

1. Catalyst, *Women in Law: Making the Case* 23 (2001).

2. Id., at 7.

3. See, e.g., Jane Pigott and Stephen Nowlan, "Success Stories from Women at the Top," *Diversity and the Bar*, Aug. 1999 (noting that the number of women general counsels of Fortune 500 companies grew exponentially throughout the 1990s).

4. See, e.g., *Diversity in the Workplace: A Statement of Principle*, signed by general counsel of Fortune 500 companies. For the list of signatories, go to the American Corporate Counsel Association Web site, [www.acca.com/gcadvocate/calltoaction/diversitystmt.html].

5. Id., at 13, 31.

6. Id., at 13.

7. Anne Weisberg and Meredith Moore, "The Concrete Ceiling: Women of Color in Law," *Diversity and the Bar*, Mar. 2002.

8. In law firms, 45 percent of women, compared to 59 percent of men, are satisfied with advancement opportunities. Catalyst, *Women in Law*, at 35.

9. Id., at 31.

10. Id., at 37.

11. Accounting firms were similarly structured, but over the last ten years have moved toward a more diversified career path model.

12. Catalyst, *Women in Law*, at 37.

13. Id.

14. Id.

15. Id., at 18. The numbers are higher for men and women in law firms. Id., at 40.

16. Id., at 18.

17. Id., at 18, 40.

18. Id., at 41.

19. Id., at 19. The top two factors for men were, first, the organization's reputation and, second, intellectual challenge. These same factors were identified by women, although women ranked the organization's reputation third, after intellectual challenge. Id.

20. Id., at 19, 41, 55.

21. Id., at 32–33.

22. Id., at 13.

23. Id., at 45.

24. Id., at 20.

8

Where Have All the Sisters Gone?

SO WHEN DOES DIFFERENCE
MAKE A DIFFERENCE?

In December 1996, a friend and I were talking, reflecting on the year that had just passed. In the life of a large firm partner, December is that special time of reckoning; you've either hit your targets in term of hours billed or revenue and you're totally exhausted, or you haven't hit the targets and you're totally exhausted in addition to being depressed or panicked. Whether it has been a good year or not, December is a time of introspection.

My friend was also at that time a partner in another large Chicago law firm. She told me that she was tired of big firm practice and tired of big firm politics. In fact, she said she was actually tired of practicing law altogether, and she was thinking about trying something different. I was just tired.

Somehow, our conversation turned to a "can you top this" context and, in focusing on the years we had spent at our respective firms, we reviewed the careers, tenure, and whereabouts of all the African American female partners at Chicago's large firms. The conversation did not take long.

There were nine of us. At that time, there were probably five thousand lawyers in Chicago's fifty largest firms, and there were nine African American female partners. Of the nine, my friend and I were the only equity partners. What was worse was that I realized that I had the longest tenure of the nine African American women partners. I was the only one who had joined as an associate and stayed at the same firm through to successful election to partnership. The crazier reality—the thing that really blew me away—was that I was only forty years old. It was 1996. Where were all the African American women who had come before us? Why did they leave?

At the risk of gross oversimplification, or even more dangerous, understatement, I suspect that they were gone because they were different, and the differences made a difference. Their differences were not celebrated, nurtured, or even valued or exploited. Their differences were misunderstood, punished, and ultimately used as a basis for their extinction. Where have all the sisters gone?

In the spring of 1996, I invited all nine of the African American female partners to a luncheon meeting, where we could get to know each other, and we decided we'd meet quarterly. By 1997, we had a victory; we hit double digits for the first time. There were ten of us. And we joked about our next milestone—the day when we couldn't be counted on two hands. By the spring of 1998, there were only six. And much to my surprise, I was one of the four escapees. I had been the first African American partner at Lord, Bissell and Brook, which was an eighty-five-year old firm at the time I was elected in 1991. The second, an income partner, was elected eight years later, and she has been the only one to follow me.

At the leadership summit that prompted this publication, we explored career paths, leadership styles, and use of influence. Having just described a career path, let me briefly address leadership style. It goes without saying that in my law firm environment, I was different from 95 percent of my colleagues. It took some doing, but the partners eventually learned to appreciate—and soon thereafter, being partners at large firms—to exploit that difference. In my formative years, I was assigned to a partner whose style ranged from street fighter to just plain mean. One year during my associate evaluation, that partner wrote in the evaluation that, "she tends to approach a case and an opponent as though she prefers to wound her enemies with a thousand paper cuts."

Now it doesn't take a genius to know that this type of assessment could have been my death knell if I had been labeled as weak, timid, tentative, indecisive—you fill in the blank. So during our evaluation, I read that remark back to him and I asked, "You thought those were paper cuts? You missed the point altogether. I use a razor." And then I told him something about using a razor. "When you attack your enemy with a razor, you can cut his throat without him even knowing it. And when you're done, he'll say, 'You missed me,' and you'll say, 'Uh-uh. Try to shake your head.'" From that day forward, I believe the partners in my firm learned to appreciate my difference.

At the leadership summit, we sat in a room full of phenomenal women. We were surrounded by trailblazers—or glasscutters, to use the ABA's terminology for those who have broken through the glass ceiling. We were in a room full of firsts. And I was one of those firsts. I was the first African American law clerk for the chief judge of the Eighth Circuit. I was the first African American partner in my firm's eighty-five-year history. I was the first large firm lawyer to be president of the Cook County Bar Association. I was the first African American woman to reach my leadership level at Ford Motor Credit Company. And the list goes on.

So why do I find this list just a little bit depressing, and why does this kind of piss me off? It's depressing because we're in the third millennium, and we are still counting "firsts" for 50 percent of the earth's population. And for women of color, we're going to be counting firsts a lot longer than everybody else. We're going to be counting firsts for a long, long time if we continue at the pace we are going.

It's depressing because as long as we are still counting firsts, we are still vulnerable to being isolated failures. Our accomplishments don't cause our numbers to approach anything resembling a critical mass, and we don't have any leaders or leadership opportunities to spare.

My grandmother used to measure our progress as African Americans using the step scale. Whenever an African American leader did something that was negative or received negative publicity, she would say, "You know, that person moved us two steps forward, but they set us three steps back." And for years, I wondered why the step scale didn't apply to white men. Why weren't they on the step scale? And as I was preparing this chapter, I figured it out. As Jacob Herring pointed out, it's because their successes are group successes and their failures are individual failures. They actually have leaders to spare.

All the contributors to this volume establish that in the workplace and in the professions, women have no leadership opportunities to spare. For every Eleanor Holmes Norton and Kim Campbell, there is a woman whose negative publicity will be used to question the next woman's fitness for office. And for every Sheila Wellington—well, there is only one Sheila Wellington. So her absence is too horrible to imagine. I just can't even go there.

So my vision is for a leadership summit to take place a few years from now. Get a hundred women leaders in the room, and have none of us be a first. When there are enough women in leadership positions at all levels so that one woman's failure can't set us three steps back, we will have made it. Then we'll have leadership opportunities to spare.

We are the beneficiaries of those who chose to lead. And not every woman who could make a difference is willing to make a difference. Leadership is a choice, and I believe that each woman must form her own definition of leadership and choose to use her influence in a way that best serves that definition. Accomplishment is not leadership. Achievement is not leadership. Notoriety is not leadership. For me, leadership is using that accomplishment, achievement, or notoriety to expand opportunities for others. Leadership is educating those who might otherwise overlook the value of our differences so that they learn to appreciate them. Leadership is mentoring, and not just mentoring other women. I believe it's just as important to mentor men as well so that they learn to be comfortable with women in leadership roles, whether or not the women choose to use a razor.

That's when difference makes a difference. When every "first" makes it her business to guarantee that there will be a second. When we use our success, leadership, and influence to support each other to affect change both inside and outside our organizations so that the definition of leadership is enlarged to embrace all of us—that's when difference makes a difference.

9

CHARISSE R. LILLIE[1]

Multicultural Women and Leadership Opportunities: Meeting the Challenges of Diversity in the American Legal Profession

In the twenty-five years that I have been at the bar, I have seen, on the one hand, enormous progress in terms of the steady entry of women of color into the profession. On the other hand, I still observe examples of unenlightened behavior and see substantial evidence that race and gender make a difference in leadership opportunities. This, of course, directly affects multicultural women's ability to be credible advocates in the courtroom and the board room.

There is ample evidence demonstrating that gender and ethnicity clearly have an impact on an attorney's dealings in courtrooms. Female and minority attorneys encounter problems such as nonrecognition as professionals, questions about their qualifications, inappropriate comments about their appearance, and outright antagonism. Although the number of female and minority judges on the bench has grown, their underrepresentation still has an adverse impact on the administration of justice. Increased diversity is necessary to ensure additional viewpoints and sensitivity to the problems faced by attorneys in their courtrooms.

The justice system, too, often seems like two different worlds from the perspectives of multicultural female attorneys. Unfortunately, when female and minority attorneys raise issues of concern to them and attempt to point out the differences in their treatment, many of their counterparts see them as whining or being oversensitive. For instance, in a survey of the perceptions and experiences of attorneys in the Second Circuit, one attorney commented, "I'm not trying to downplay the problem of racial prejudice or sexual prejudice *if it in fact exists*, but I'm in court almost every day and have been for fourteen years, and I just don't see these things as real factors in the daily operation of judicial business."[2] However, many organizations, including judicial commissions and task forces and the American Bar Association's Commission on Racial and Ethnic Diversity in the Profession, have recognized that these complaints have merit. Clear answers and solutions are urgently needed. Based on the comprehensive research of such organizations, it is clear that a difference does make a difference, often negatively, in the way female and minority attorneys are treated in courtrooms.

PROBLEMS FACING MULTICULTURAL WOMEN PROFESSIONALS IN THE JUSTICE SYSTEM

One of the primary problems that female and minority attorneys face in courtrooms is that others do not recognize them as attorneys, solely because of their gender or race. For example, an African American woman with over twenty years of litigation experience recalled "going to court in a small town and sitting in a row marked 'Attorneys Only,' just to have the bailiff ask loudly if I was seated in the wrong section."[3] In a similar situation, a Mexican American woman described instances in which her opposing counsel or co-counsel would mistake her for the receptionist or paralegal. In one instance, they asked her to label exhibits during a deposition even though the court reporter was sitting at a table with her equipment in front of her.[4]

The following comment further illustrates the extent to which some, even judges, are not recognized as professionals:

> There was the occasion where I was hearing a case in the courtroom of a federal agency at the World Trade Center in New York City, and at the conclusion of the day I discovered that I had locked myself out of the judicial chambers. It was 6:00 P.M., and the support staff had left for the day so I searched the hallway hoping to find someone who might assist me. I recognized a gentleman whom I had seen on the elevator that morning. I inquired of him where I might obtain a key. He asked me what business

I had on that floor that day. I was a little surprised by this inquiry in light of the fact that I was wearing my judicial robe and we were standing in front of the bank of elevators where there was a signboard that contained information pertaining to the case I was hearing.[5]

Instances such as these highlight the difficulties women and minority attorneys still encounter in being treated as equals and as professionals.

A related problem that female and minority attorneys often face in courtrooms is the questioning of their legal qualifications and skills. For instance, an African American supervising attorney in a city law department recounted an incident in which an elected official refused to accept her statement that she could make final decisions regarding a case. After being informed that she was the person with whom he had to deal, the official left court to avoid working out the situation with her.[6]

Unfortunately, some members of the bench also contribute to the devaluation of female and minorities appearing before them. As a minority attorney in private practice described the situation, "district court judges tend to ignore and under-value your comments and input, unless you are willing to stand up and confront the judge."[7] In a similar vein, women have often noted that the attention of judges noticeably diminishes when they speak, implying that what men have to say is more important. One Louisiana attorney recalled, "I was half way through my theory when the judge interrupted me and said, 'Oh, come on now, shut up. Let's hear what the men have to say.'"[8] A female Asian attorney noted the following similar incident:

> The judge asked that counselors state our name for the record. My opponent stated his name, and then I stated mine. The judge looked down at me from the bench, and in open court, and asked me, "Are you an attorney?" I said, "Yes, sir." He then asked, "Are you licensed to practice here?" I said, "Yes, sir." He continued to ask, "Will you provide me with your bar number after the trial?" I said, "Certainly sir."[9]

When viewed together, such seemingly isolated incidents reflect broader patterns that compromise commitments to equal justice under law.

Crude or subtle comments are often made about the physical appearance of female and minority attorneys that similarly impair their effectiveness. A classic illustration of such inappropriate comments are those made by former Texas Assistant Attorney General Jay Floyd in the *Roe v. Wade* litigation. After the female attorney for Jane Roe finished her oral argument and sat down next to another female attorney at the counsel table, Floyd began his address to the United States Supreme Court by stating "Mr. Chief Justice, May it please the Court. It's an old joke, but when a man argues against two beautiful ladies like this, they're going to have the last word."[10] More recent examples include the observation of a male attorney that, "women attorneys are effective in direct correlation to the length of their skirts and the size of their busts."[11] In another instance, a female minority attorney was told that she should not wear her hair braided to the courthouse because some people might think she was not professional.

Although they do not occur as frequently, dress and decorum issues can affect males as well. A case in point involved a District of Columbia appellate judge who removed an African American lawyer from a case after a dispute about the lawyer's appearance in a striped stole made of an African fabric known as kinte cloth.[12] Such negative comments about the dress and physical characteristics of female and minority attorneys can also interfere with their performance and devalue their competence and judgment.

Female and minority attorneys also have to confront overt hostility in courtrooms. In one instance, a male attorney reportedly demanded that his female opponent not interrupt him any further, and added that "women attorneys have a hard time keeping their mouths shut."[13] A Connecticut judge advised female attorneys arguing in court that "the trouble with you women is that you never learned to fight things out on a football field [and] . . . are too emotional."[14] In another instance, the same judge offered a gratuitously mean-spirited response to a female attorney's request to be heard at another calendar call due to difficulties with her case: "Women are the problem."[15] Even more disturbing is the fact that the audience in the courtroom greeted his remark with laughter and applause.[16] Similarly, an Illinois judge was reprimanded for telling pregnant attorneys that "[l]adies should be at home raising children" and "if your husband had kept his hands in his pocket, you would not be in the condition you are in."[17] In an incident just as appalling, a California judge asked a Jewish deputy district attorney, "Tell me something, with all the interbreeding that your people do, aren't you afraid that they will produce a race of idiots?"[18] Such comments obviously create hostile environments for female and minority attorneys in courtrooms.

One of the most effective strategies for combating such cases is to have more female and minority judges on the bench. As Philip S. Anderson, former president of the American Bar Association, recognized, "[t]he majority's perspective of the fairness of our system of justice is not generally shared by minorities in our society," and underrepresentation of minorities on the bench is at least part of the reason.[19] Both lawyers and judges have recognized that diversity brings crucial benefits to the quality of justice; a diverse judiciary adds varying ideas and views, which enhances the fact and appearance of fairness in the courtroom.[20] It is always judges' responsibility to intervene when they observe instances of bias in their courtrooms. Because gender and ethnicity inevitably influence judicial perspectives, a more diverse bench will increase sensitivity to problems confronting female and minority attorneys. The judiciary sets the tone and establishes the norms of proper professional conduct. Through example, authority, and influence, judges can work to ensure that their courtrooms are places in which a party's gender, race, or ethnicity does not hamper equal justice for all.

LEADERSHIP OPPORTUNITIES

Catalyst, the nonprofit research and advisory organization working to advance women in business and the legal profession, recently released a report entitled *Women in Law: Making the Case*. One of its key findings is that women law graduates, particularly women of color, are less satisfied with opportunities for advancement than men.[21] White men and white women are equally satisfied with networking and mentioning opportunities.[22] In the Catalyst study, 62 percent of white women law graduates are satisfied with their current employer compared with 46 percent of women of color.[23] The study also revealed that 41 percent of all white women law graduates are satisfied with respect to their advancement with their employer, compared with 30 percent of women of color.[24] Women of color also have lower levels of satisfaction with networking and mentoring as components of advancement.[25]

In summary, the Catalyst study notes:

> The low satisfaction rates registered by women of color law graduates can be explained in part by how they perceive the climate for diversity in their organizations. White men and women law graduates do not observe race

issues in the same way that people of color do. The greatest gap exists between white men and women of color, but even white women significantly underestimate the importance of race.[26]

The fact that more women lawyers of color perceive obstacles to advance as a hindrance to advancement than white men and women does not indicate oversensitivity or an eagerness to "play the race card." It does mean that persons of authority in law firms, governmental organizations, corporations, and other work environments need to be more responsive to the concerns of women of color. It means that managing partners, directors, and general counsels need to be trained and educated to be sensitive to the unconscious biases of race, ethnicity, and gender that persist in professional workplaces and that compromise commitment to equal opportunity.

THE AGENDA FOR CHANGE

"The Agenda for Change" proposed by the ABA Commission on Women in the Profession provides an important blueprint for the legal profession.[27] As the Commission report notes, diversity is a value that should guide leaders of the legal profession and should be among their highest priorities. The strategies proposed are excellent starting points for leaders who are concerned with making their organizations environments where women of color can thrive, survive, and at some point lead.

NOTES

1. The research and drafting of the first draft of this document was undertaken by Kyrus L. Freeman, a summer associate at Ballard Spahr Andrews & Ingersoll, LLP, in July 2001.

2. "A Report of the Perceptions and Experiences of Lawyers, Judges and Court Employees Concerning Gender, Racial and Ethnic Fairness in the Federal Courts of the Second Circuit of the United States," *Annual Survey of American Law* 419, 452 (1997).

3. Angela Langford Jacobs, in *Dear Sisters, Dear Daughters: Words of Wisdom from Multicultural Women Attorneys Who've Been There and Done That,* 179, 180 (Karen Clanton, ed. 2000).

4. Amalia S. Rioja, in *Dear Sisters,* at 288.

5. Covette Rooney, in *Dear Sisters,* at 120.

6. Rita Aliese Fry, in *Dear Sisters*, at 21.

7. "A Report of the Perceptions and Experiences," at 450.

8. Elizabeth A. Delfs, "Foul Play in the Courtroom: Persistence, Cause and Remedies," 17 *Women's Rights L. Rep.*, 309, 316 (1996).

9. Id., at 332.

10. Id., at 315.

11. Id.

12. Sabra Chartrand, "A Dispute Over Courtroom Attire and Principles," *N.Y. Times*, June 19, 1992, at B8.

13. Delfs, "Foul Play in the Courtroom," at 314.

14. Id., at 313.

15. Id., at 314.

16. Id.

17. Id., at 328.

18. Id.

19. Philip S. Anderson, "Striving for a Just Society," 85 *ABA J.*, Feb. 1999, at 66.

20. See e.g., "A More Diverse Group of PA Judges Is Changing the Way Law Is Practiced," *Pennsylvania Law Journal*, Nov. 6, 1995, at 61.

21. Catalyst, "Women in Law: Making the Case," *Executive Summary* 5 (2001).

22. Id.

23. Id., at 6.

24. Id.

25. Id.

26. Id.

27. ABA Commission on Women in the Profession, *The Unfinished Agenda: Women and The Legal Profession* 33–37 (2001).

10

ELEANOR HOLMES NORTON

Elected to Lead: A Challenge to Women in Public Office

A discussion of women and leadership is not merely another aspect of an important subject. Leadership by women is important to the hopes of the average woman for full equality. The first task of women and their movement for equality has been to infiltrate the rank and file of the workplace, education, elected office, the armed services, and almost all except a few places in society historically designated for women. This effort is still a work in progress, but there is no reason to proceed sequentially as though women are entitled to leadership only when sufficient numbers have served time in the ranks. I argue otherwise in this chapter: that it is important to press for women in leadership positions, not only for its own sake and for the virtuous reasons of fairness and elemental equality. In addition, women leaders serve two unique functions that can quicken the pace toward equality for the average woman. As leaders, these women are in a position to pave the way and clear the path for other women. As leaders, the success of their example also can help increase society's acceptance of women in new roles.

In this chapter, I explore how women in elected office, in particular, can multiply change for women. When women are elected to public office they are by definition leaders because they have been chosen to guide the public in important ways. Consequently, I first argue that elected women necessarily become important agents with the capacity to demonstrate that women can lead anything and anywhere. I then move to a second point, that women in elected office carry unique responsibilities for women here and around the world who depend disproportionately on the leadership of women who hold public office because such women are most likely to give priority to women's concerns. These two functional aspects of women's leadership in elected office provide an underpinning for the central point expressed here: that women in elected leadership can make a unique difference.

LEADERSHIP:
AN ISSUE WHOSE TIME HAS COME FOR WOMEN

The advances that have been achieved by women should make the issue of women's leadership unavoidable today. Women historically were excluded from so many employment, educational, athletic, business, and other opportunities that for almost forty years a major effort has been necessary even to secure entry. Today, the pressure from the women's movement and its allies, from changes in law and court decisions, and from the American public has produced countless victories. The principle that discrimination based on sex is wrong approaches consensus in the United States today.

This progress makes attention to women's leadership even more ripe and more compelling than four decades ago when the women's movement first gained national notice. More ripe because a critical mass of women has emerged in many fields; as a result many are or should be seeking and achieving leadership posts previously closed to them. More compelling because the achievements of women in many fields and at many levels make it difficult to argue that women cannot lead.

Ironically, women's progress in recent years has been so widespread that these improvements may obscure both the issue and the pace of leadership or, in some cases, may create the illusion that equality has been achieved. For example, rapidly increasing numbers of women in prestigious fields, such as law, improve the individual circumstance of these women but is not the equivalent of leadership. Increases in women lawyers do not necessarily translate into leadership positions in the field, such as partnerships and judicial appointments.[1]

Progress for women has required work, and leadership for women will be even less self-propelling. If women are thought less capable in many fields in which men predominate, it is unlikely that they will be regarded as natural or inevitable leaders in these fields. Even in traditional women's occupations, leadership and numerical dominance are not positively correlated. In elementary and secondary education, for example, men are vastly outnumbered by women, yet men are the professional leaders.[2] Moreover, as women leave women's occupations for nontraditional fields, men do not fill the women's ranks, but they continue to monopolize leadership in many traditional female fields.

Of course, there almost always are inherent structural barriers to leadership, quite apart from gender considerations. Leadership is competitive and rationed. Jobs may be won or ceded to women because of ability. However, leadership is not achieved through merit alone. Leadership depends on an exceptional set of personal characteristics and contextual factors. Among them are the nature and needs of particular institutions or groups; the often indefinable, personal qualities that particular leadership roles may require; and often, luck or chance.

Are there ways more rapidly to encourage the full integration of women not only into American life but also into leadership roles? How can the oldest and most rigid of stereotypes, that women are meant to follow, not lead, be changed? Women elected to public office have both a unique opportunity and a special burden to demonstrate that women can lead without reservation.

ELECTED WOMEN: AGENTS FOR WOMEN'S LEADERSHIP

The elected office I know best and that I draw on here is member of Congress, but much of that experience obviously applies to women elected to public office at every level. The opportunity to demonstrate that women can lead is inherent in obtaining public office and in performing official duties. In the first place, elected women attain office by convincing both men and women that they can lead. Large numbers of women and men in the particular electorate, divided between roughly equal numbers of men and women, choose political leaders in the privacy of the polling place. Because they are chosen by both men and women, elected women defeat the stereotype that women cannot win the confidence of others, especially men, necessary to be a leader.

Second, elected officials perform leadership tasks publicly and often. The visibility of their leadership is what distinguishes them from most other leaders.[3] When women are elected to executive or legislative office, people of many backgrounds see female leaders continuously in action.[4] These elected women are subject to immediate evaluation of their leadership in ongoing feedback that amounts to votes of confidence or no confidence from the public and media accounts. This public accountability ultimately translates into removal or reelection. The actions that women take in public office can go far toward encouraging the public to broaden its acceptance of women as leaders in all walks of life.

Women in legislative office are afforded many occasions to take command of a subject or situation. In the House and Senate, for example, women both lead and speak in committees and on the floor about the broadest range of complicated subjects and difficult policy choices, such as how economic surpluses and downturns in the economy should be accommodated, how conflict and corruption should be quelled, and whether human rights or trade interests should predominate.

Many of the same observations apply to women appointed to office, especially top executive office.[5] The presence of these women in public office can yield similar benefits even (but not always) when they are appointed by men who may control final policy decisions.[6] However, I focus on elected women for more than the public good that they, like appointed women, can accomplish. Election to public office via the same democratic processes as men gives elected women a unique role in breaking barriers to leadership for women.

The more the public has seen women in elected office, the more Americans have been willing to elect women. However, as in upper-level law and management positions, women have made only incremental changes in elective office. Elected women cannot help transform leadership opportunities for women across the society unless their numbers increase. Measured by objective standards, the House and Senate and most state legislatures are still male bastions. Cheering when a woman is added in the Senate or a few more in the House is natural but insufficient.[7] However, considering that the number of women in the House more than doubled from twenty-nine to sixty-two in a single decade, the pace of progress will be significant if the doubling continues. This pace can and should be quickened.

Where an elected woman stands on issues will make a critical difference on particular women's concerns and on the significance of her leadership to women. However, the style of her leadership is irrelevant to demonstrating that women can lead. What matters is for women to have the chance to lead. The absence of a predominant style of leadership among women in Congress should lay aside the notions that any particular set of leadership characteristics is necessary, that femininity is not conducive to leadership, and that men will not accept female leadership. Women already have shown that what makes a woman electable or effective as a senator or member of the House is her personal appeal and how she grapples with the concerns of her state or her district, not her gender. Should she be like the brilliantly witty Barbara Mikulski (Maryland), a single woman who is regularly elected by 70 percent of the vote, or like Patty Murray (Washington), a toned-down mother of two, who was the first woman to be selected as chair of the Democratic Senate Campaign Committee, the person who leads her party's fund-raising effort in the Senate? The women in Congress are as different as Senator Kay Bailey Hutchinson, every bit a Texas lady, who wants to be president, and Representative Maxine Waters, whose style is epitomized by the "no justice, no peace" slogan of the Los Angeles riots of 1992.

WOMEN'S LEADERSHIP FOR WOMEN'S SAKE

Art should be pursued for its own sake, but leadership for women today should have purposes beyond obtaining more leadership positions for more women. Of course, increasing the numbers is a particularly worthy goal and one that must be pursued. No society that strives to operate on the basis of merit, democracy, and equality has an alternative to finding ways to uncover and promote female talent and capability. Even societies that make no pretense of embracing these values may soon be pressed to uncover the sheer waste in suppressing or foregoing the contributions of women.

However, there is an important functional reason for encouraging greater leadership opportunities for women. It is reasonable to assume that when women lead, they will bring to the effort the experience of being a woman and often a special sensitivity to the needs of other women.[8]

Whether or not this assumption is true generally, it probably is true for elected women, regardless of party or place on the political spectrum. Although political candidates must cast a broad net of appeal, most women members of Congress regard it as an asset to match at least some women's concerns to their own experience as women.

This match also is a special obligation of elected women. More than other institutions, elected bodies if broadly representative, will have an easier time engaging the concerns of diverse constituencies. The theory of the framers in establishing the House of Representatives, for example, was that the electorate needed special and parochial pleading in at least one chamber. Similarly, most groups in the society, from business to poor people, need and seek elected officials attuned to their particular needs. Insurgent groups, especially women and people of color, are disproportionately dependent on elected officials from their groups, or on others who have a personal stake or an incentive to be especially attentive to the group's requirements.

If broadly democratic representation yields special attentiveness, many underrepresented groups, including women, have a considerable distance to go. Women have done better in opening male-dominated professions, such as medicine and law, previously all but closed to them, than they have in opening their own democratic legislatures. Especially considering that more than half the people and the electorate are women and that the votes of citizens are equal, the present participation of women in leadership roles is not the best a democratic society can or should do. Nor is this disparity beyond immediate change.

However, a more natural balance reflecting ability and appeal to the electorate should not be left to individual women, the electorate, or the women's movement alone. Women leaders, especially elected women, incur a special obligation. The access that elected leaders have to power at their particular levels and to the public gives reason to expect elected women to make use of their leadership for other women.

Assuming, as I do, that elected women are likely to give women's issues special attention, the unmet needs of women in this country and in the world are the best justification for doing more to increase the number of elected women leaders. Many of the problems of women that remain unsolved are more difficult than those where progress has been achieved in the most recent decades. This progress may distort what will be re-

quired to take on often equally urgent and more difficult issues. The progress is real, of course. As late as the 1960s, "help wanted" ads could be
segregated by sex. Women were virtually excluded from the armed forces
and from traditionally male professions and professional schools. Refusal
to hire and promote women was routine. Pregnancy was grounds for dis-
missal and received only token health insurance coverage. Abortion was
illegal. Women were excluded from many educational opportunities and
team sports in schools and college.

The problems that most affect women today are less about equal pro-
tection or intentional discrimination, as earlier issues often were, than they
are generally about equal access to resources or about new approaches to
long-standing social problems. Courts are rarely willing or effective in addressing such issues, and male-dominated legislatures often have been slow
to grapple with matters that require new resources or new strategies for
women. Two telling examples are child care, which requires additional resources, and pay equity, which requires a fresh approach.

As the average woman has become a working woman, child care has
become an increasingly urgent issue. However, as yet, there is nothing ap-
proaching a system of early childhood education for working families,
despite palpable harm to children and parents. Compelling scientific evidence suggests that the first years of life are when brain development is at
its height and learning is optimal.[9] Instead of taking advantage of this
unique and fleeting period in a child's life, parents, especially mothers,
scurry simply to find a safe place to leave children while the family is at
work. The educational component that might unlock learning potential
is a lesser priority, considering the basic need simply for facilities.

Why have not the obvious needs of parents and children made care-
taking an American priority? The considerable resources that would be
required are only part of the answer. Congress and the president have recently made the education of children a major priority, putting new fund-
ing and substantial energy into H.R. 1, the No Child Left Behind Act.
Yet this legislation offers almost nothing concerning the one aspect of a
child's education most in need of attention. Early childhood education
remains excluded from most public education appropriations. This omis-
sion is notable, inasmuch as early attention is uniquely able to advance
the statutory objective of H.R. 1—building a foundation for improved
education.

One reason that a major education bill focused on children excludes so desperate a need may be that child care and the task of finding child care surrogates have most often been left to women. Notwithstanding the importance of early education to the nation itself today, the issue is unlikely to receive the priority it needs unless women insist.

Educational child care is tailor-made for leadership by elected women. Women and families at most income levels encounter similar problems of lack of access to affordable child care. Organizing for reform at the grass-roots by such an unwieldy and uncohesive group is especially difficult. Elected women at the national or state level may be in an unique position to press early childhood education as a public education responsibility. Important efforts have been made, of course, and many are in place.[10] However, elected women have the power to help bring larger changes by pressing a bill with comprehensive objectives in keeping with the needs of children, women, and families. At the same time, women in elected office could help galvanize the electorate so that universal educational child care has the popular force it does in the rest of the Western world.

Another issue of great consequence to women and families that could be advanced by elected women is equal pay for the majority of women workers. Unlike educational child care, most pay issues involve the private sector and do not require public resources. To accomplish equal pay today, however, a new approach from government is necessary.

Equal pay has assumed new importance and appeal as the average woman has joined the workforce. The issue is a popular rhetorical issue for politicians of both parties. The Democrats, impressed by the appeal of an issue with which their party has been traditionally identified, pressed minor changes in the Equal Pay Act of 1963.[11, 12] The Equal Pay Act requires that employers pay the same wages to women and men who do the same or closely similar work. The Act has been successful in significantly reducing this form of discrimination. However, equal pay remains unrealized because most men and women are generally not doing the same or closely similar work.

The Fair Pay Act, which I have introduced, seeks to remedy the most common cause of male-female pay wage disparities.[13] Much of the gender gap is traceable to men and women who do work that is different in content but comparable in skill, effort, and responsibility.[14] Examples are social workers, a largely female occupation, and probation officers, a largely male occupation; or emergency services (911) operators, mostly females, and fire dispatchers, mostly males.

The Fair Pay Act addresses sex or occupational segregation, the primary cause of the pay gap between male and female full-time workers today. The bill differs from the Equal Pay Act in that it would allow a finding of discrimination if an employer pays a man and woman at different rates for jobs that are equal in skill, effort, and responsibility. The proposed Act is consistent with our market system. Under the bill, a woman who has filed such a claim, as in all discrimination cases, would have to prove that the reason for the wage gap in the same workplace is discrimination, and not other reasons, such as legitimate market forces. Gender, of course, is not a legitimate factor.

The bill is not unprecedented. Twenty states have done pay equity studies and adjusted wages for women in state government workforces, raising pay for teachers, nurses, clerical workers, librarians, and other female-dominated jobs that paid less than predominately male jobs with the same skill, effort, and responsibility. For example, New York State established a comprehensive pay equity plan for state workers, and Minnesota established a pay equity plan after finding that similarly skilled female jobs paid 20 percent less than male jobs.[15]

Part of the reason that too little progress has been made on salary issues for the average woman is the confusion today surrounding the term *equal pay*, an appealing and noncontroversial term but one that oversimplifies today's issues. Pay equity is a narrower concept used to refer to sex segregation that affects the average woman in traditionally female occupations.[16] An indication of the importance of pay equity is the broad coalition of women's groups consisting of eighty organizations that has formed a permanent organization, the National Committee on Pay Equity, to press the issue. However, without determined leadership from those with authority to both educate and move corrective action forward, pay equity is not likely to be achieved. Like child care, pay equity exemplifies an issue particularly suited for elected women because they are in a position to give it the necessary priority and are more likely to do so. Elected women have the additional motivation to stay the course.

Child care and pay equity have strong support from many elected women. However, despite this support and significant action, neither issue has galvanized elected women in Congress to provide the necessary, determined focus. Nevertheless, the work of the Congressional Caucus on Women's Issues suggests that these and other difficult policy reforms can be successfully pursued through the collective action of elected women.[17] Since 1977, when the women of the House of Representatives formed themselves into a women's caucus, these legislators have been the driving force behind major legislation benefiting women and their families. Many of these issues were complex and controversial, and progress could not have been achieved without a sustained effort, especially by women members of the House, who have been willing to give the problems continuing priority. Among the statutes championed by the Women's Caucus were the Family and Medical Leave Act,[18] the Pregnancy Discrimination Act,[19] the Child Support Enforcement Act,[20] the Breast and Cervical Cancer Mortality Prevention Act,[21] and the Mammography Quality Standard Act.[22]

SUMMARY

The values associated with democracy and representation should encourage a greater effort to elect more women to public office. A representative democracy that fairly reflects all segments of society would include a larger number of women. These values also are highly functional in the hands of elected women. These leaders are in a special position to challenge stereotypes about women's capabilities at all levels and to lead on issues of concern to women.

NOTES

1. Of the 489,530 lawyers in the United States, 30 percent are women. Only 10 percent of partners in law firms are women and only 12 percent of judges are women. ABA Commission on Women in the Profession, *The Unfinished Agenda: Women and the Legal Profession* 14 (2001).

2. Women are 66 percent of teachers but only 30 percent of principals and 5 percent of superintendents. Johnetta Hudson and Dorothy Rea, *Teachers' Perceptions of Women in the Principalship: A Current Perspective* (1998).

3. Many other leaders are equally important, especially in affecting large numbers of men and women and in their influence and ability to encourage change. The work they do, however, is less observable by the public than the work of elected officials and therefore may have less influence in changing attitudes about leadership. Examples are magazine editors and business executives.

4. Only seventeen women have been elected governors in the entire history of the United States, only thirteen in their own right. It is more difficult to be elected to executive than to legislative office, in part because there are fewer executive positions. However, the small numbers of women may also reflect the gender barriers that women still confront. National Women's Political Caucus, *Women & Political Progress Fact Sheet*, Mar. 7, 2002, [www.nwpc.org/about_women02.html].

5. Recent examples are Janet Reno, attorney general, and Madeline Albright, secretary of state in the Clinton administration, and Condoleezza Rice, national security advisor for President George W. Bush. Particularly when such offices are highly placed and visible, the effects may be even more powerful than those of elected office.

6. President Jimmy Carter gave me extraordinary policy latitude when I served as the chair of the Equal Employment Opportunity Commission during his administration. However, a public dispute developed when women in his administration were not able to get the president to change his position opposing abortion.

7. There were thirteen women in the Senate in 2001, up from two in 1990. National Women's Political Caucus, *Women & Political Progress Fact Sheet*, Mar. 7, 2002, [www.nwpc.org/about_women02.html]. There were sixty-two women in the House, up from twenty-nine in 1990. Id.

8. For evidence supporting this assumption see the studies reviewed in Deborah L. Rhode, "The Difference 'Difference' Makes."

9. *From Neurons to Neighborhoods: The Science of Early Childhood Development* (Jack P. Shonkoff and Deborah A. Phillips, eds. 2000).

10. The major federal example is the early childhood education bill known as Head Start enacted in 1965 (42 U.S.C. § 9801). However, this legislation is limited to low-income families. In 1999, I introduced H.R. 2865, the Universal Pre-Kindergarten and Early Childhood Education Act, to encourage school systems to use the experience achieved with designated early childhood grants to permanently add pre-kindergarten classes to their own school budgets.

11. See H.R. 781, the Paycheck Fairness Act, which would amend the Fair Labor Standards Act of 1938 to provide compensatory and punitive damages for victims of wage discrimination, among other changes.

12. 29 U.S.C. § 206(d).

13. H.R. 1362. Senator Tom Harkin was the Senate sponsor of the bill as S. 684.

14. These are the factors used to quantify the aspects of a job in job studies that are often used by private employers in this country to set wages.

15. For an overview of these efforts see Deborah L. Rhode, *Speaking of Sex* (1997).

16. Almost two-thirds, or 62 percent, of white women and almost three-quarters, or 72 percent, of African American women work in only one of three areas: clerical, service, and factory jobs. Bureau of Labor Statistics, *Employed*

Persons by Occupation, Race, and Sex (2000). The pay gap between men and women was reduced from $14,754 in 1980 to $10,087 in 1990. National Committee on Pay Equity, *The Wage Gap Over Time: In Real Dollars, Women See a Continuing Gap*, Mar. 8, 2002, [www.feminist.com/fairpay/f_change.htm]. Integration of women into male-dominated occupations, an important remedy, accounted for most of the change. However, women should not have to leave vital women's occupations to earn what a job is worth.

17. Early childhood education and pay equity may not become caucus issues because the Women's Caucus is bipartisan, and there are substantial differences in party approaches to these particular issues.

18. P.L. 103–3 permits employees to take up to twelve weeks of unpaid leave for the birth or adoption of a child, care for a family member, or serious health conditions.

19. P.L. 95–555 makes it illegal to discriminate against a woman because she is or may become pregnant.

20. P.L. 98–378 requires a parent who is delinquent in child support to include his unpaid obligation in gross income and to allow custodial parents a bad debt deduction for unpaid child support payments.

21. P.L. 101–354 established the National Breast and Cervical Cancer Early Detection Program and provides medical assistance for low and moderate income women diagnosed with breast or cervical cancer.

22. P.L. 102–539 requires that all mammography facilities be certified by the Food and Drug Administration or a designee.

Different Rulers—Different Rules

Shortly before participating in the summit that led to this publication, I was invited to appear on the television program *Politically Incorrect* with Bill Maher. Because the program prides itself on being provocative, I was selected partly because I was the only person the producer could find who supported the French Parity Law. It requires French political parties to present equal numbers of male and female candidates. The vehement opposition that this law inspires speaks volumes about the continuing obstacles to women's political leadership.

Let us put the French Parity Law in perspective. First of all, no one is advocating a similar law in the United States. It would be very difficult to apply in the American electoral system, whereas the French have party lists that can easily accommodate such a requirement. Second, the law was democratically enacted by the French National Assembly. Since only 8.9 percent of the members of the national government in France are women, there must have been a compelling reason for this male-dominated body to pass such a law. There was. The European Union was putting pressure on France to do something about the underrepresentation of women compared to other EU countries, including those that have not been at the forefront of equal opportunity for women leaders, such as Italy and Spain. If this law gives a "leg up" to some women candidates, it is nothing compared to the vise-like grip that white males, especially those who are graduates of the elite schools, have on French politics. It is interesting that such an extremely unrepresentative and, therefore, undemocratic political system is tolerable to Americans, but that they regard as unacceptably undemocratic the requirement that parties reach out into their communities and find credible female candidates.

The French Parity Law reflects the fact that "difference does make a difference," as Rhode's introductory chapter suggests. But we should not be sanguine about the numbers in our own countries. In the United States, only 14 percent of national legislators are women, and in Canada the number is 24 percent. The United States ranks fifty-third in the world. Sweden holds first place, with women representing 43 percent of its national politicians.[1] When we think about the sacrifices made a century ago by the suffragettes to get women the vote, we cannot, a century later, be complacent about those rankings and those numbers.

Although I am most often described as the former prime minister of Canada, I want to address this topic of "difference making a difference" as a former minister of justice and attorney general of Canada and a member of the legal profession. The law is an important mechanism of social change. Lawyers have an advantage in entering politics for two reasons. Not only are the skills in the two arenas complementary—familiarity with statutes, the skills of advocacy—but also the law is one of the few professional careers that can be interrupted during a political career and then resumed. In careers such as medicine, science, and others, interruptions can leave a person far more out of touch with the discipline. In addition, law is a mechanism of social change through litigation. So women in the law have an important opportunity to change the way society is governed and how the rules are made.

The American philosopher John Rawls had an interesting insight on this notion of making the rules. In A Theory of Justice, he uses the device of *social contract* to make his point. Philosophers have often described the relationship between people and the state as a social contract and, by describing the nature of that contract, have defined the relationship between government and the governed. According to Rawls, the only truly fair social contract is one negotiated behind a "veil of ignorance."[2] In effect, those who are deciding how to structure the government should have no knowledge about their own personal characteristics that may affect how they would fare under that structure. They should not know whether they are male, female, fat, thin, smart, stupid, strong, weak, disabled, and so forth. Under these circumstances, they would have to negotiate a social contract that they would be prepared to live by even if, when the veil of ignorance is lifted, they find themselves among the least advantaged. What Rawls' framework makes clear is that the rules of society are made by people who know very well what their personal circumstances are. People make rules that *they* can live by. When only a few people representing a small part of society make the rules, it is highly likely that many people will find the terms of the social contract onerous. So one of the ways that difference makes a difference is in terms of who makes the rules.

It is equally important how those rules are applied. A 1997 article in the *Wall Street Journal* reported that when symphony orchestras audition behind a screen, they hire 25 percent more women.[3] Since we can't live behind a screen or run for public office behind a screen, the question we have to try to answer is why that screen makes a difference. There is a growing literature on gender stereotypes and gender *schemas*, the unarticulated hypotheses that we bring to the understanding of gender roles. Books such as Virginia Valian's *Why So Slow? The Advancement of Women*, and Deborah L. Rhode's introduction to this volume describe the research findings that show how men are expected to be competent and women are not, how masculine qualities are seen as synonymous with leadership but feminine qualities are not.[4] Although the schemas are perceptions, not reality, they often keep women from being able to assume positions where they can participate in making the rules.

In February 1990, I was sworn into one of the great rule-making positions of the Canadian government—minister of justice and attorney general—the first woman ever to hold that position. It was a powerful position because the minister of justice is responsible for legislating the criminal law in Canada (our criminal law is a federal jurisdiction). When I described myself publicly as a "feminist," there was an audible intake of breath from coast to coast. But people got over it. I wasn't a single issue minister, but I wasn't prepared to pretend I was something I was not.

Now, why did I feel I could do that? Part of the reason is that I wasn't alone. I was one of six women in the cabinet. Although that isn't a crowd, it was enough so that my gender was not a novelty. I felt I could speak in my own voice. Often, when women in important positions disappoint us with their reticence, it is because they are in circumstances where they don't feel they can speak in their own voices, when they know that wherever they are, they are there on sufferance. The first generations of women in the legal profession often felt that way. Sandra Day O'Connor, third in her class at Stanford Law School, could not get a job at a major law firm. Often these pioneering women felt that if they could make it, others could too and should not look for special treatment. These women paved the way for the next generations with their sheer excellence. Some felt confident enough to mentor other women, but many understood the peril in such solidarity. If women today have the freedom to express their own values, it is because other women played by other rules and succeeded nonetheless. We should be grateful to them.

As justice minister, I defined three major priorities for my time in office, and one of those was inclusive justice. The two groups I focused on were women and aboriginal people. In 1991, I convened Canada's first-ever national symposium on women, law, and the administration of justice. Officials from the federal and provincial justice departments, members of the judiciary, and representatives from over sixty national organizations concerned with issues relating to women and the law attended. Some judges who took part told me after, "You know, I thought I was pretty liberal on these issues, but I realize that I didn't know anything!" For most of the participants, it was the first time they had been able to meet face-to-face with one another. It was—if I may use the term—a *seminal* event in mainstreaming women's issues in the Canadian legal system.

I also worked to increase the number of women in the judiciary. I was responsible for appointments to the superior and appellate courts of each province as well as the federal courts. One of the most important ways that women judges change the way rules are made is simply by broadening the judicial culture. I remember at a conference of Canadian judges, women judges said to me, "Because you are there, it gives us the courage to speak up." My goal was to make it natural and normal to address women's concerns. The willingness of a justice minister to do this encouraged and empowered others to do the same, and not just women but men, too.

What the presence of women also does, whether it is in Parliament or on the bench, is make it possible for men to be more of the things they want to be. Many men are not at their best in male-dominated organizations. As more women began to be elected to the House of Commons, the

House did away with night sittings. Most male members were delighted. They also had families that they wanted to see and marriages that they wanted to preserve. Many were happy to abandon the "fraternity brother" ethos that required you to stay up all night and drink and play cards in your office because the House was sitting and you might need to vote. Amazingly, it now appears possible to do the business of the country during normal business hours. We also have a day care center in the House of Commons. People who work on Parliament Hill—both inside and outside the Chamber—have children. It was the presence of women that began to push against the way the institution was created. Institutions are created by the people who inhabit them and have a voice in creating their structure.

But what of the women who feel ground down by their experience of "success"? In her latest book, *Sex and Power*, Susan Estrich, the first woman president of the *Harvard Law Review* and a tenured professor at the Law School at thirty-three, expresses her concern about women who are dropping out.[5] It is only by "being there" that women have made the next level of barriers visible and that scholars have been able to identify the cultural barriers to women. We are still struggling and we are still looking for the strategies that will enable women to overcome.

Leadership does matter and women can make great leaders. What can we do? We can create gender literacy—learn about the schemas that work against us and how they do so. We can also make women leaders more visible. I chair the Council of Women World Leaders. There are twenty-nine living women who have been president or prime minister of their countries. Because of the "masculine" connotations of leadership, women's accomplishments do not "stick" the same way men's do. When women trailblazers leave office, they often fall off the radar, too. Gender stereotypes insist that women don't lead well in a crisis or cannot make tough decisions. Tell that to Margaret Thatcher or Violetta Chamorro of Nicaragua or Hanna Suchocka of Poland. Tell that to the women who often get the job when the challenge is toughest. We have to keep making our women leaders visible and celebrating them—in government and in the professions. The talent is there. What is lacking is the access to power.

Power is essential. Women cannot afford to shy away from the leverage that will change society. But if we want power, we have to fight for it. No one gives power away without a struggle. We have to make a commitment. People ask me, "How do we get more women in government?"

I say, "Write a check." Women are very cheap—not because they are un-generous but because they are not clear on why they should be giving.

I throw out this challenge to American women. There must be, in this country, at least one million women who could afford to give $1,000 every presidential electoral cycle. That is $250 per year, just over $20 per month. If these women just put that contribution in a sock, in the next presidential electoral cycle they will have *$1 billion* to support feminist candidates in the primaries and the election. Now, consider what political parties would think about candidates for whom, say, $50 million or $100 million or $200 million are floating out there ready to support them. Mmmm! I can hear their lips smacking already! So leave us not be con-cerned that, "Oh, I couldn't spend the money. It's my family's money." Do you want your daughters and granddaughters to live in a world in which 15 percent of the national legislators in your country are women? It mat-ters who makes the rules. Karl Marx was not a great philosopher of his-tory, but he understood the notion of consciousness. He said, "The work-ing class has to move from being a class *in* itself to being a class *for* itself." And women—we have to move from being a gender *in* itself to being a gender *for* itself. Write those checks. Throw the bucks in the sock. I'm looking forward to seeing who you can produce for president in 2004.

NOTES

1. "Women in National Parliaments," as of May 15, 2002, compiled by the Inter-Parliamentary Union, [www.ipu.org/wmn-e/classif.htm].

2. J. Rawls, *A Theory of Justice* (1971).

3. Christina Duff, "Out of Sight Keeps Women in Mind for U.S. Orchestra Spots, Study Finds," *Wall Street Journal*, Mar. 7, 1997, at B68.

4. Virginia Valian, "Gender Schemas at Work," *Why So Slow? The Advance-ment of Women* (1998).

5. Susan Estrich, *Sex and Power* (2000).

IV

CHANGING THE CONTEXT AND

CHANGING THE CAST:

BREAKING THE BARRIERS

TO GENDER EQUALITY

12

DEBRA E. MEYERSON and ROBIN J. ELY[1]

Using Difference to Make a Difference

The title of Deborah L. Rhode's chapter, "The Difference 'Difference' Makes," suggests a host of fascinating questions about the role sex and gender might play in the practice of leadership. For example, are there sex differences in opportunity that make a difference in women's attainment of leadership roles? Rhode's review of the relevant literature points to a resounding yes. Gender stereotypes, limited access to mentors, and workplace practices that fail to accommodate family commitments have clearly made it more difficult for women to achieve and succeed in leadership roles. Do sex differences in leadership style make a difference in women's eligibility for these roles? According to Rhode's review, probably not. There is little empirical support for the notion that sex differences in leader attitudes and behaviors—of which there seem to be few—explain sex differences in who has managed to achieve leadership positions. Finally, Rhode's title begs the question, What difference would it make—in professions, corporations, politics, and the world—if there were more women leaders? Her review suggests that women leaders' impact is dubious at best, at least when it comes to advancing women's interests. Political leaders' party affiliation is a more important predictor of votes on issues of concern to women than is sex. Similarly, women lawyers and senior mangers are often not committed to or are reluctant to press gender issues openly. These findings are consistent with our own research and observations in organizations: The difference sex difference makes in how leaders, corporations, or politics function and in what they produce is probably negligible.

The question we address in this chapter is, Why? *Why has women's presence in leadership positions made so little difference? Will increasing their presence enhance prospects for change?* We say no, and propose that the reason lies in how various constituencies have framed the problem of women's underrepresentation. We have identified three such frames;[2] each rests on a different theory of gender and suggests a different approach to change, none of which by itself is adequate to produce the hoped for difference that women in leadership might make.

THREE TRADITIONAL APPROACHES TO UNDERSTANDING WOMEN AND LEADERSHIP

Frame 1: Fix the Women

According to the first frame, the problem is that too few women occupy leadership roles, and this is because they lack the requisite skills. Thus, the approach to change is to fix the women so that they can compete more effectively with men.

The theory of gender on which this approach rests casts gender as an individual characteristic marked by one's biological category as male or female. Sex-role socialization produces individual differences in attitudes and behaviors between men and women, which have rendered women less skilled than men to compete in the world of business. Accordingly, if women developed appropriate traits and skills, they would be better equipped to compete with men for leadership roles.

The change agenda of organizations that adopt this frame is therefore to minimize these differences, primarily through education and training. Executive training programs, leadership development courses, networking workshops, and assertiveness training programs that focus on helping women develop the skills and styles considered requisite for successful leadership are representative of this approach.[3]

Although better education has unquestionably increased the number of eligible women in "the pipeline," and training programs have helped women develop valuable skills and play the game as well as—or better than—many men, the glass ceiling persists.[4, 5] Moreover, with this approach there is no particular mandate for women other than simply to assimilate into organizations as they currently exist. The outcome of assimilation is that a sizeable proportion of women who occupy leadership positions behave just like their male counterparts, or even more so, to prove that they are "one of the boys."[6] Although the media may use the success of people like Carly Fiorina at Hewlett Packard as a harbinger of change and evidence of a new era of equality, they fail to take into account the socialization process that led to her selection. As Rhode suggests, these women are not necessarily feminists. In fact, they have typically succeeded by conforming to, rather than changing, the systems within which they operate.

In addition, these interventions are typically predicated solely on an understanding of the needs of white women in the managerial and professional ranks, as though those needs coincided with the needs of all women in the organization. This has left other women to fend for themselves as they aspire to leadership roles and places additional stresses on race and class relations in organizations, especially among women.[7]

In short, these interventions leave existing organizational policies and structures intact with minimal disruption to the status quo. Once assimilated, there is little to motivate those few, typically white, middle- and upper middle-class women who do make it to leadership positions to act any differently from their male counterparts.

Frame 2: Create Equal Opportunity

A second frame on the problem holds similarly that too few women occupy leadership roles, but here the cause is structural. Rather than fix the women, the approach to change is to fix the policies and practices that have blocked women's advancement.

This approach also rests on a theory of gender as differences between men and women; however, these differences result not from socialization processes but from differential structures of opportunity and power that block women's access and advancement. These include many of the problems Rhode identified in her review, including hiring, evaluation, and promotion processes that reflect sexist attitudes toward and expectations of women;[8] social and professional networks that give men greater access to information and support;[9] professional and managerial women's token status, which subjects them to increased performance pressures, isolation from informal social and professional networks, and stereotyped role encapsulation.[10]

Interventions designed within this frame are largely policy based. They include many familiar remedies and institutional changes of the sort Rhode proposes, such as instituting affirmative action programs that revise recruiting procedures with the aim of increasing the number of women in the pipeline to leadership positions; establishing more transparent promotion policies to ensure fairness;[11] instituting formal mentoring programs to compensate for men's greater access to informal networks;[12] constructing a range of possible career paths to provide alternatives to "up or out" internal labor market practices;[13] and introducing flexible work requirements and other work-family programs to accommodate women's disproportionate responsibility for dependent care.[14] All of these policy-based programs are designed to eliminate or compensate for structural barriers that make it more difficult for women to compete with men for leadership roles.

These interventions have undoubtedly helped improve the material conditions of women's lives. In particular, they have helped organizations recruit, retain, and promote more women in entry and middle levels and, to a lesser extent, senior levels as well. This, in turn, has increased the number of role models and same-sex mentors for women and decreased the constraints and stresses of tokenism, thereby creating an environment that is more hospitable to women.[15]

Nevertheless, they have provided no panacea. Some of these efforts have facilitated little progress and, in some cases, have even caused backlash and regress.[16] For example, formal mentoring programs have generally not proved successful in giving women useful connections to influential colleagues.[17] In addition, even though flexible work benefits might be on the books, many resist using them for fear that doing so will hurt their careers or create backlash.[18] These programs are typically implemented as accommodations to women, who rarely feel it is legitimate to use them, or they are used only as a device to placate and retain individual women who have proved their worthiness.[19] All of these accommodations attempt to change structures that produce inequality, but the stigma that is typically associated with using them diminishes their effectiveness as a tool for advancing women. Unless the stigma can be removed by, for example, widespread use or other clear evidence of these interventions' legitimacy, beliefs that legitimate inequality will persist, and gender inequality will play out in alternative structural forms.[20]

Finally, as with Frame 1, many of these efforts—especially those aimed at promotion and retention—have tended to assist only certain women: those who are white and relatively class-privileged. Race, class, and other aspects of identity, when considered, are rarely more than add-on concerns, despite many scholars' conclusions that these aspects of identity shape women's experiences differently from the way they shape men's.[21]

We conclude that although interventions recommended by this approach, unlike the previous one, target organizational policies and structures and thus have made an important difference for many women, their impact on who performs leadership roles, how, and for what purpose has been limited. Policies that accommodate existing systems do not fundamentally challenge the sources of power or the social interactions and belief systems that reinforce and maintain the status quo. As a result, even if women leaders are committed to women's issues, they may lack sufficient power or stamina to withstand the backlash that such commitment often brings. These interventions are necessary—but not sufficient—for transforming the workplace.

In the end, both Frames 1 and 2 posit increased representation of women in leadership roles *as an end in itself.* This goal, while laudable, is insufficient for advancing the more ambitious change agendas many feminists have in mind when addressing concerns about leadership.

Frame 3: Celebrate the Feminine

The third frame takes on some of these more ambitious change agendas at the outset, positing explicitly that increasing women's representation in leadership roles is not only an important end in its own right but is also a means to other ends as well. This frame rests on the belief that greater diversity—that is, more women—promotes more effective leadership and does so because women bring distinct perspectives and interests to bear on the role.

This frame, like Frame 1 above, rests on a theory of gender as socialized differences between men and women, but the argument here is that these differences should not be eliminated; they should be celebrated. According to this perspective, women's difference from men—in particular, their presumed relationship-orientation,[22] which has traditionally marked them as ill-suited for the hard-driving, task orientation of leadership—in fact, constitutes an effective and much-needed leadership style.[23] Women have been disadvantaged because organizations place a higher value on behaviors, styles, and forms of work traditionally associated with men, masculinity, and the public sphere of work while devaluing, suppressing, or otherwise ignoring those traditionally associated with women, femininity, and the private sphere of home and family.[24] The goal of interventions developed from within this frame, therefore, is to give voice to a women's perspective. It envisions a revised social order, one that would celebrate women in their feminized difference rather than devalue them as "imperfect copies of the Everyman."[25] According to this perspective, women leaders—if allowed to act like women—should lead differently, emphasize different ends, and, ultimately, make a difference in the world.

Interventions suggested by this approach include consciousness-raising and training to make people aware of the differences between women's and men's styles, skills, and perspectives; to point out the ways in which feminine activities, such as listening, collaborating, nurturing, and behind-the-scenes peacemaking, have been devalued in the public sphere of work; and to demonstrate the benefits of these activities. Rosener has been a strong and vocal proponent of this view, arguing further that capitalizing on "women's advantage" can strengthen a company's competitive advantage in its global markets.[26] This rationale holds broad appeal. Value-in-diversity advocates, for example, make the popularly touted business case for diversity, arguing that increasing the proportional representation of women and other traditionally underrepresented groups in leadership roles will bring particular perspectives that can directly benefit the organization. According to this logic, women would be particularly well suited for leadership roles that deal with the "people side" of work.

Although many corporations have undertaken the kinds of gender-awareness programs this approach recommends, usually under the rubric of "valuing diversity," there is no evidence that simply recognizing something as valuable will make it so.[27] Rather, in most cases, feminine attributes are valued only in the most marginal sense, since they stand in contrast to the organization's traditional norms, values, and practices, which remain intact.[28] Moreover, critics of this approach have suggested that calling attention to these differences reinforces sex stereotypes and the power imbalance between men and women.[29] Calas and Smircich, for example, have argued that the case for the "feminization" of leadership fails to alter the relative status and value of these traditionally female activities.[30] Rather, it does little more than reinforce women's appropriateness for performing what are essentially the "housekeeping" duties of management, tending the corporate fires on the home front, while men are out conquering the global frontiers and exercising the real power in today's multinational corporations. Thus, this approach may simply create and justify an ever more sophisticated form of sex segregation at work. Others have urged social scientists to abandon notions about women's unique qualities and contributions, based on the lack of quantitative empirical support for sex differences.[31]

In addition, feminist theorists of gender have pointed out that the attempt within this approach to preserve "women's difference" is also problematic because it does so at the expense of women's transformation and liberation from the oppressive conventions of femininity.[32] Proponents of this approach have mistakenly taken the meanings that have come to be associated with women under certain oppressive conditions of history to inhere in the real nature of women themselves. Ironically, if proponents of this view were to examine too critically the oppressive structures that give rise to this highly exalted, woman's point of view, they would invite a question that subverts their central premise: What would happen to woman's point of view if these oppressive structures were destroyed? Hence, the wish to celebrate woman's goodness would seem to require the perpetuation of her subordination.[33]

Finally, like the preceding frames, this one fails to incorporate other aspects of people's identity. Organizational interventions based on a Frame 3 understanding are predicated on particular, dominant images of feminine and masculine—those that are based on a heterosexual, white, middle-class model. They not only fail to challenge the hierarchical valuing of these categories, they are erroneously based on particular versions of masculine and feminine as if these were universal, enacted in the same way with the same meaning across all groups of men and women. As a result, this approach also targets a limited group of women.

USING DIFFERENCE TO MAKE A DIFFERENCE:
A NEW APPROACH

We propose that the goals people have focused on in each of these frames —whether increasing the proportion of women leaders as an end in itself or as a means to other ends—are the wrong goals. Feminists' change agendas have fallen short of their transformational potential because their goals are focused too narrowly on women—and a subset of women, at that— and on making change that is too limited in scope. We propose that to increase women's representation in leadership roles and thereby make a real difference in the practice of leadership requires a different perspective on the problem and a different set of goals. The problem is not only that there are too few women in leadership roles or that women's perspectives have been absent from the mix. The problem is much larger than this. First, what constitutes "women" and "women's perspectives" has been insufficiently inclusive or expansive to do justice to what is missing. There is a whole range of people and behaviors that have been excluded from leadership positions by virtue of the narrow definitions and constraining structures within which prospective leaders have had to fit. Moreover, those women and other "diverse" candidates who have made it have been, at best, a merely additive ingredient—and one that typically gets lost in the mix. Organizations have failed to tap these newcomers' potential as a resource for more fundamental individual and organizational learning, change, and renewal.

To address this problem, the approach we advocate is two-pronged. First, it requires an expansion of a Frame 2 strategy: the eradication of structural barriers that have excluded women—all kinds of women—and many men as well, who have been traditionally underrepresented in leadership and other organizational roles. These efforts must be driven, not only by concerns about equity and justice but also by concerns about the relatively limited knowledge and experience base on which organizations have traditionally operated. As Frame 3 suggests, women—some women —may well possess a kind of relationship orientation that has been either absent or devalued in organizations. Whether or not this orientation actually manifests in women leaders' behaviors is not at all certain, however, since most women who have achieved leadership positions have done so by assimilating into the traditionally prescribed role, just as their male counterparts have done. Moreover, many women—and men as well—have the potential to bring much more. For example, women, as a group, are situated differently in the world relative to those who have traditionally held organizational power. As a group, they are positioned to engage in different social relations and economic activities; structurally, they have a different relationship to power. Many women thus "know" a different set of interests, a different set of contingencies. This knowledge may be vital to the effective functioning of organizations, but not if it is isolated from the organization's core work and work processes, relegated to a behind-the-scenes, devalued organizational function. This knowledge is an organizational resource only if it is actually used as a basis for transforming at the core what already exists.[34] Finally, our research suggests that structural changes designed to expand the pool of leader candidates must be accompanied by legitimating explanations that explicitly link such changes to this rationale and become part of the social discourse of the organization.[35]

Hence, the second prong of our approach requires a shift in emphasis from simply *adding* different perspectives to the traditional mix to *using* different perspectives to transform the traditional mix itself. A diversity of perspectives—including, but not limited to those provided by women—becomes a potentially valuable resource that the organization can use to rethink and reconfigure its primary tasks, including, for example, leadership. These different perspectives might influence what *all* leaders do, not just those who are "different." Hence, the goal is not simply to increase the representation of women and "others" in leadership roles, but also to change what constitutes leadership, regardless of who is in the role. The entry of these newcomers provides the occasion for critical reflection on what is and creative thinking about what might be.

The theory that underlies this approach is not about gender alone, but about the ways in which differences of all kinds can become a resource for individual and organizational change. Research suggests that learning is one mechanism by which gender and other kinds of differences might foster such change.[36] This would require that people truly engage each other's differences and, themselves, become transformed in the process. To lead, for example, may involve an active state of learning—about self and other, about work and the organization. The leader in this context is constantly vigilant for opportunities to test old assumptions and new ideas. Work can be structured so that people are routinely called upon to speak their minds and encouraged to bring their whole selves to their work and to their interactions with others at work. In the course of these interactions, the organization's norms, values, and practices are open to scrutiny, providing the necessary impetus to question and change traditional beliefs, including those that legitimize inequalities.[37] These kinds of changes in turn drive and support structural changes in the organization that enable a more diverse group of people to achieve and succeed in leadership roles. Thus, by authorizing group members to use their culturally situated perspectives as a resource for rethinking and revising primary tasks, this approach, unlike those advocated in any of the previous three frames, challenges existing power relations and the social interactions and belief systems that reinforce and maintain them.

A small but growing body of research supports this approach. Ely and Thomas, for example, have demonstrated that for a work group to benefit from gender and other cultural differences requires a fundamental shift in power relations, whereby standard practice, traditionally derived from within the dominant (for example, white, male) culture, is no longer automatically and unquestionably assumed to be best practice.[38] Their research shows that simply bringing women and other traditionally underrepresented groups into the senior ranks of an organization, even in leadership roles, is not sufficient to produce this kind of shift. Instead, people must be able to use their cultural identity differences—which give rise to different life experiences, knowledge, and insights—to inform alternative views about their work and how best to accomplish it.

An example may help illustrate.[39] Dewey & Levin is a public interest law firm in the northeastern United States. The firm's primary practice is employment-related litigation aimed at protecting the rights of women. Although Dewey & Levin had a profitable practice by the mid-1980s, its all-white legal staff had become concerned that their clientele was limited largely to white women. The firm's attorneys viewed this as a problem in light of their mandate to advocate on behalf of all women. So they hired a Latina attorney to help them expand their reach and visibility in Latino communities. But their recruitment efforts did not stop there—people of color now form a majority of the firm's staff. More important, however, this change in staff composition precipitated a change in their work far beyond the "reach and visibility" they initially sought.

How did this happen? Initially, there was little awareness that bringing in more people of color would create an opportunity for organizational learning and development. The assumption was that attorneys of color would give the firm access to and credibility with their respective communities, thus helping expand the firm's client mix. But after much debate within the increasingly multicultural staff, Dewey & Levin came to the realization that if they viewed the employment issues of all women as an integral part of the firm's mission—and they did—then the work the firm defined as relevant to their mission needed to change. In time, changes in the composition of the staff increasingly fueled a reexamination process within the firm that, by virtually all accounts, has entirely reshaped the character and priorities of the firm's work in ways its founding attorneys say they never would have anticipated. The firm now pursues cases that its all-white legal staff would not previously have thought relevant or appropriate because the link between the firm's mission and these employment issues would not have been obvious to them. For example, the firm has pursued precedent-setting litigation that challenges "English-only" policies—an area that they would have previously ignored because it did not fall under the purview of traditional Title VII work. Yet they now see such policies as critically linked to employment issues for a large group of women—primarily recent immigrants—whom they had previously failed to serve adequately. As one of the white principals explained, the demographic composition of Dewey & Levin "has affected the work in terms of expanding notions of what are [relevant] issues and taking on issues and framing them in creative ways that would have never been done [with an all-white staff]. It's really changed the substance—and in that sense enhanced the quality—of our work."

Dewey & Levin's increased success has reinforced their commitment to diversity. In addition, attorneys of color at Dewey & Levin uniformly report feeling respected, not simply "brought along as window-dressing." As one woman of color put it, "The assumption about you is that you are competent." Not surprisingly, the firm has had little difficulty attracting and retaining a competent and diverse professional staff.

As this case illustrates, the goal of the approach we are advocating is to set in motion an ongoing process of incremental organizational change anchored on a vision of productive work and social interaction unconstrained by oppressive roles, images, and relations. The process relies heavily on learning as a primary motivation for people's interactions with each other. It is the mechanism by which people come to challenge old ideas and ways of doing things and generate new ones.

Although we are calling for fundamental organizational transformation, the approach to change we advocate is not a wholesale revolution. Our research in organizations suggests instead that the most effective strategy involves a series of localized, incremental changes in work practices, including leadership.[40] With this approach, people contribute to the goal of organizational transformation, even as they work within the constraints of their existing setting.[41] This is a far cry from the singular objective of promoting more women into leadership roles—itself, no small or insignificant feat. But for "difference" to really make a difference, we believe that that objective must be part of a larger transformation effort

NOTES

1. This was an entirely collaborative effort. Order of authorship was established by a coin toss.

2. Robin J. Ely and Debra E. Meyerson, "Theories of Gender in Organizations: A New Approach to Organizational Analysis and Change," in *Research in Organizational Behavior* 103–152 (B. Staw and R. Sutton, eds. 2000). We draw heavily from this article in the following section.

3. Margaret Hennig and Anne Jardim, *The Managerial Woman* (1977); Gary N. Powell, "The Effects of Sex and Gender on Recruitment," *Academy of Management Review* 731–743 (1987).

4. Pat Heim, *Hardball for Women* (1992).

5. Nijole V. Benokratis, *Subtle Sexism: Current Practices and Prospects for Change* (1997); Virginia Valian, *Why So Slow? The Advancement of Women* (1998).

6. Rosabeth Moss Kanter, *Men and Women of the Corporation* (1977).

7. S. Blake, "At the Crossroads of Race and Gender: Lessons From the Mentoring Experiences of Professional Black Women," in *Mentoring Dilemmas: Developmental Relationships Within Multicultural Organizations* 83–104 (Audrey J. Murrell, Faye J. Crosby, and Robin J. Ely, eds. 1999).

8. Kanter, *Men and Women of the Corporation*; Barbara F. Resskin, "Bringing the Men Back in: Sex Differentiation and the Devaluation of Women's Work," 2 *Gender and Society* 58–81 (1988); Cecilia L. Ridgeway, "Gender, Status, and the Social Psychology of Expectations," in *Theory on Gender/Feminism on Theory* 175–198 (P. England, ed. 1993); Myra H. Strober, "Toward a General

Theory of Occupational Sex Segregation: The Case of Public School Teaching," in *Sex Segregation in the Workplace* 144–156 (Barbara Reskin, ed. 1984); Myra H. Strober, "Gender and Occupational Segregation," in *The International Encyclopedia of Education* 248–252 (1994).

9. Joel Podolny and James N. Baron, "Resources and Relationships: Social Networks, Mobility and Satisfaction in the Workplace," *American Sociological Review* (1997); Ronald S. Burt, *Structural Holes* (1992); Herminia Ibarra, "Homophily and Differential Returns: Sex Differences in Network Structure and Access in an Advertising Firm," 37 *Administrative Science Quarterly* 422–447 (1992); Kathy E. Kram, *Mentoring at Work: Developmental Relationships in Organizational Life* (1986); Ann M. Morrison et al., *Breaking the Glass Ceiling: Can Women Reach the Top of America's Largest Corporations?* (1987).

10. For reviews, see Alison M. Konrad and Barbara A. Gutek, "Theory and Research on Group Composition: Applications to the Status of Women and Ethnic Minorities," in *Interpersonal Processes* 85–121 (S. Oskamp and S. Spacapan, eds. 1987); Alision M. Konrad, Susan Winter, and Barbara A. Gutek, "Diversity in Work Group Sex Composition: Implications for Majority and Minority Members," 10 *Research in the Sociology of Organizations* 115–140 (1992); Patricia Yancey Martin, "Group Sex Composition in Work Organizations: A Structural-Normative Model," 4 *Research in the Sociology of Organizations* 311–349 (1985).

11. Joan Acker and Donald R. Van Houten, "Differential Recruitment and Control: The Sex Structuring of Organizations," *Administrative Science Quarterly* 152–163 (1974).

12. E.g., Kram, *Mentoring at Work*; E. McCambley, "Testing Theory by Practice," in *Mentoring Dilemmas: Developmental Relationships within Multicultural Organizations* 173–188 (Audrey J. Murrell, Faye J. Crosby, and Robin J. Ely, eds. 1999).

13. Felice N. Schwartz, "Management Women and the New Facts of Life," *Harvard Business Review*, Jan.–Feb. 1989, at 65–76.

14. Arlie Hochschild, *The Second Shift* (1989); Ellen Kossek and Richard Block, *Management Human Resources in the 21st Century: From Core Concepts to Strategic Choice* (1999); *The Work-Family Challenge: Rethinking Employment* (Suzan Lewis and Jeremy Lewis, eds. 1996); Phyllis H. Raabe, "Constructing Pluralistic Work and Career Arrangements," in *The Work-Family Challenge: Rethinking Employment* (Suzan Lewis and Jeremy Lewis, eds. 1996).

15. Faye J. Crosby, "The Developing Literature on Developmental Relationships," in *Mentoring Dilemmas: Developmental Relationships Within Multicultural Organizations* 3–20 (Audrey J. Murrell, Faye J. Crosby, and Robin J. Ely, eds. 1999).

16. Lotte Bailyn, *Breaking the Mold: Women, Men and Time in the New Corporate World* (1993).

17. G. T. Chao, P. M. Walz, and P. D. Gardner, "Formal and Informal Mentorships: A Comparison on Network Functions and Contrast with Non-Mentored Counterparts," 45 *Personnel Psychology* 619–636 (1992).

18. Rhona Rapoport, Lotte Bailyn, Deborah Kolb, Joyce Fletcher, D. Friedman, S. Eaton, Maureen Harvey, and B. Miller, *Relinking Life and Work: Toward a Better Future, A Report to the Ford Foundation Based on a Collaborative Research Project with Three Corporations* (1996).

19. Hochschild, *The Second Shift.*

20. Cecilia L. Ridgeway, "Interaction and the Conservation of Gender Inequality: Considering Employment," 62 *American Sociological Review* 218–235 (1997).

21. Taylor Cox and Stella M. Nkomo, "Invisible Men and Women: A Status Report on Race as a Variable in Organizational Behavior and Research," 11 *Journal of Organizational Behavior* 419–431 (1990); Stella M. Nkomo, "The Emperor Has No Clothes: Rewriting Race in Organizations," 17 *Academy of Management Review* 487–513 (1992).

22. Mary F. Belenky, Blythe M. Clinchy, Nancy R. Goldberger, and Jill M. Tarule, *Women's Ways of Knowing: The Development of Self, Voice, and Mind* (1986); Carol Gilligan, *In a Different Voice* (1982).

23. Linda McGee Calvert and V. Jean Ramsey, "Bringing Women's Voice to Research on Women in Management: A Feminist Perspective," 1(1) *Journal of Management Inquiry* 79–88 (1992); Nanette Fondas, "Feminization Unveiled: Management Qualities in Contemporary Writings," 22 *Academy of Management Review* 257–282 (1997).

24. E.g., David Collinson and Jeff Hearn, "Naming Men as Men: Implications for Work, Organizations, and Management," 1 *Gender, Work and Organization* 2–22 (1994); Joyce K. Fletcher, *Disappearing Acts: Gender, Power, and Relational Practice at Work* (1999); Barbara Stanek Kilbourne et al., "Returns to Skill, Compensating Differentials, and Gender Bias: Effects of Occupational Characteristics on the Wages of White Women and Men," 100 *American Journal of Sociology* 689–719 (1994).

25. Christine Di Stefano, "Dilemmas of Difference: Feminism, Modernity, and Postmodernism," in *Feminism/Postmodernism* 63–82 (L. J. Nicholson, ed. 1990).

26. Judy B. Rosener, *America's Competitive Secret: Utilizing Women as Management Strategy* (1995).

27. Joyce Fletcher and Roy Jacques, "Relational Practice: An Emerging Stream of Theorizing and Its Significance," working paper #2, Center for Gender in Organizations, Simmons Graduate School of Management, Boston (1999).

28. Fletcher, *Disappearing Acts: Gender, Power, and Relational Practice at Work.*

29. E.g., Ridgeway, "Interaction and the Conservation of Gender Inequality," at 218–235.

30. Marta B. Calas and Linda Smircich, "Dangerous Liaisons: The 'Feminine-in-Management' Meets Globalization," *Business Horizons*, Mar.–Apr. 1993.

31. E.g., Cynthia Fuchs Epstein, *Deceptive Distinctions: Sex, Gender, and the Social Order* (1988); Martha T. Mednick, "On the Politics of Psychological Constructs: Stop the Bandwagon, I Want to Get Off," 44 *American Psychologist* 1118–1123 (1989).

32. Di Stefano, "Dilemmas of Difference," at 63–82.

33. Robin J. Ely, "Feminist Critiques of Research on Gender in Organizations," working paper #6, Center for Gender in Organizations, Simmons Graduate School of Management, Boston; R. T. Hare-Mustin and Jeanne Marecek, "The Meaning of Difference: Gender Theory, Postmodernism, and Psychology," 43 *American Psychologist* 455–464 (1988).

34. Robin J. Ely and David A. Thomas, "Cultural Diversity at Work: The Moderating Effects of Diversity Perspectives on Work Group Processes and Outcomes," *Administrative Science Quarterly* (2001); David A. Thomas and Robin J. Ely, "Making Differences Matter: A New Paradigm for Managing Diversity," *Harvard Business Review*, Sept.–Oct. 1996.

35. Robin J. Ely and Debra E. Meyerson, "Advancing Gender Equity in Organizations: The Challenge of Maintaining a Gender Focus in Participative Action Research," 7 *Organization* 589–608 (2000).

36. Ely and Thomas, "Cultural Diversity at Work."

37. Ely and Meyerson, "Theories of Gender in Organizations," at 103–152.

38. Thomas and Ely, "Making Differences Matter"; Ely and Thomas, "Cultural Diversity at Work."

39. This example appears in Thomas and Ely, "Making Differences Matter," and in greater detail in Ely and Thomas, "Cultural Diversity at Work."

40. See Debra E. Meyerson and Joyce K. Fletcher, "A Modest Manifesto for Shattering the Glass Ceiling," *Harvard Business Review*, Jan.–Feb. 2000, at 126–136.

41. Debra E. Meyerson, *Tempered Radicals: How People Use Difference to Inspire Change at Work* (2001).

13

LINDA A. HILL[1]

Are We Preparing
Ourselves to Lead?[2]

Through my research on leadership and globalization, I have come to understand that the best leaders are those individuals—women and men—who have an appetite for learning and are willing to work on themselves. Leadership is very hard, and even the most gifted individuals must commit themselves to lifelong learning and self-development. In the course of my work, I have had the privilege of developing teaching materials about many women leaders: from Meg Whitman, the CEO of eBay, a company revolutionizing the way we shop, to Irene Charnley, a black union leader under apartheid and now the executive director of Johnnic Communications, one of South Africa's foremost companies. In the following pages, I would like to offer advice to women on how to build a successful career. I can't say the advice would be very different if I were writing for men. However, women have fewer mentors and role models to guide them along the way, so addressing their experience can be particularly instructive.

This chapter builds on stories from some of the talented women I've encountered who are out there making a difference in their organizations. We can learn vicariously from their experiences. Consider, for example, Jeanne Lewis, who was about to step into a critical top management role as senior vice president of marketing at Staples, Inc., a nationwide office supplies superstore. Lewis recalled:

I'm not a good example of how to manage your career—I've just been willing to raise my hand several times for new opportunities. I've taken a lot of what others would perceive to be career risks, which fortunately have worked out. . . . I had proven myself in several different kinds of functional areas and I brought breadth, if not depth, of experience, coupled with the knowledge that I enjoyed operating in a high stress environment. From my perspective, this was the biggest job I'd had. It would require me to learn to deal with the top levels of the organization and across a broader span.[3]

Jeanne Lewis is much too modest. She is an excellent role model for how we, as women, need to manage our careers if we hope to move into senior executive positions. From Lewis' story, we see that leadership can be an exciting but arduous journey of self-development with few shortcuts for even the most talented. Over the course of her first six years at Staples, she made a series of upward and lateral moves that entailed a number of tough assignments across many functional areas.

Beginning as the director of New England operations, Lewis had profit and loss responsibility for fifty underperforming stores. Hiring a strong team of direct reports, Lewis set store standards, instituted training programs, and rejuvenated performance. Due to her success in operations, over the next two years, Lewis received two more challenging assignments. First, she became director of sales for 150 stores on the East Coast, and then, a year later, she was promoted to vice president and divisional merchandise manager for furniture and decorative supplies. There she had profit and loss responsibility for $350 million and twelve people in an area with poor assortment, flat sales, and low direct product profitability. She and her team turned over 75 percent of the assortment, tripled net direct product profitability, and increased sales. In 1996, Lewis advanced again, and moved back into the marketing department as senior vice president of small business and retail marketing. In 1999, based on her performance, she was appointed president of Staples.com, the company's e-commerce business, a key strategic initiative for the future success of the company.

Lewis, like the other women leaders whom I have studied, is a self-directed learner willing to reinvent herself time and again. In the pages that follow, I will set the stage with a brief discussion of what women need to learn if they hope to become leaders. Then I will present a power-and-influence framework for developing a successful career by addressing four challenges: (1) choosing the right position, (2) getting off to the right start, (3) landing stretch assignments, and (4) building a network of developmental relationships. In framing each of these four challenges from the point of view of the emerging leader, I hope to underscore my belief that leadership cannot be *taught*. Instead, potential leaders must ask themselves: Am I willing and able to prepare myself to lead? Gender inequality does exist in the workplace, and like the other writers in this volume, I am committed to creating an environment in which women leaders can emerge and flourish. But leadership development is fundamentally about self-development, and I hope to offer women a road map for taking charge of their own learning and development.

WHAT DO WE NEED TO LEARN?

If women want to get into the top echelons of organizations they must know how to lead. John Kotter, a renowned leadership expert, has identified three critical leadership functions and their attendant competencies.[4] *Establishing direction* involves developing a vision of the future and crafting strategies to produce the changes needed to achieve that vision. This requires developing skills such as inductive reasoning, strategic and multidimensional thinking, the ability to take risks, and the ability to make sense of complex and ambiguous data. *Aligning people* includes communicating the vision and strategies through words and deeds to all those whose cooperation may be needed. To accomplish alignment, a leader needs empathy, the ability to build credibility and communicate with diverse constituencies, and the willingness and ability to empower others. *Motivating and inspiring* involves energizing people to overcome major political, bureaucratic, and resource barriers to change by satisfying very basic, but often unfulfilled human needs. This requires the ability to acquire power and exercise influence to change the behavior, attitudes, and values of diverse constituencies and the ability to manage performance and to coach subordinates.

In short, leadership is an art requiring a mix of talents. Most of us understand that to be effective, leaders must do a great deal of task learning throughout their careers. In addition to acquiring expertise in technical, conceptual (for example, strategy formulation), and human arenas (for example, interpersonal skills), leaders also have personal learning to do.[5] They must adopt the psychological perspectives, attitudes, and values consistent with their roles and responsibilities. To be effective, managers must be prepared to learn about themselves (their identities, strengths, and limitations), be willing to make necessary changes, and cope with the associated stress and emotions of managing and leading others. It is no wonder that self-knowledge has consistently been found to be a key characteristic of effective leaders. Individuals are often surprised by just how demanding, and at times traumatic, such personal learning can be.[6]

To be effective in today's competitive environment, organizations are placing a premium on leadership capabilities. With more and more companies having access to the same technology, markets, methods of productivity, and channels of distribution, the competitive environment has changed fundamentally. The strategic management of talent has become the key to competitive advantage. The biggest obstacle to launching a successful company is no longer attracting financial capital, but rather attracting intellectual capital and finding leaders who can manage talent and build a sustainable enterprise.

HOW CAN WE LEARN TO LEAD?

Although some of the qualities of effective leadership are "innate" or acquired principally through prework socialization (for example, personal integrity, high energy level, and a drive to lead), much of leadership is learned.[7] There is growing evidence of a strong corelationship between leadership and learning, especially learning from social situations.[8] Leadership is primarily learned from on-the-job experiences—"by doing," observing, and interacting with others. In a groundbreaking study of executive development, Morgan McCall, an expert on leadership development, and his colleagues made this unsettling but all too accurate observation:

> The essence of development is that diversity and adversity beat repetition every time. The more dramatic the change in skill demands, the more severe the personnel problems, the more the bottom-line pressure, and the more sinuous and unexpected the turns in the road, the more opportunity there is for learning. Unappealing as that may seem, being shocked and pressured and having problems with other people teach the most. For future executives, comfortable circumstances are hardly the road to the top.[9]

The story of Dawn Riley is a prime example of the realities of leadership development.[10] Riley is the CEO and captain of America True, the first coed syndicate for the America's Cup.[11] Participating in the America's Cup had been Dawn Riley's dream from the time she began racing sailboats on the Great Lakes as a young child, a relatively unusual obsession for a girl from Detroit. Riley quickly grew accustomed to having to fight her way onto boats in the male-dominated world of sailing. She remembered, "As a girl, it was always a case of proving I was strong enough, a good enough sailor, and able to fit into the mostly male society onboard. It was always an uphill battle but I was willing to put up a fight." Her obvious talent, no-nonsense attitude, and competitive spirit compelled others to take her seriously once they gave her a chance, and by the time she entered college, she was captain of her sailing team. By then she had also developed a passion for entrepreneurship and hard work, which allowed her to pay her way through Michigan State University.

In 1993, Riley found herself in an unanticipated leadership role when, with one week's notice, she took over as skipper for the second all-women's boat in a Whitbred Round-the-World race. The crew had sailed the first leg of the race, then key members had mutinied. She flew down and joined the crew in South America. They successfully finished the race despite a damaged boat and difficult financial circumstances. In 1999, Riley decided it was time to take on the ultimate challenge of running a multimillion business as the CEO-captain of her own syndicate in the America's Cup. As Riley pointed out, building a syndicate from scratch in three years—bringing on investors and sponsors, designing and building a boat, and hiring and leading a sailing crew to race—was "one hell of an MBA."

As many have observed, however, people do not always learn from their experiences.[12] To make meaning from their experiences, leaders need to reflect on and consolidate the lessons of those experiences. In order to change and grow, they must be prepared to engage periodically in introspection—to collect feedback on and analyze their behavior, attitudes, and values. However, the difficulty in remaining objective about one's self, including the mechanisms that keep individuals from honestly evaluating themselves, is well documented.[13] The more candid feedback that managers can obtain from varied sources, the more accurate and precise their assessment will be.

Indeed, individuals find it nearly impossible to accomplish their development alone. To grow and develop, individuals must be prepared to seek assistance. They must devote time and energy to building and maintaining a network of developmental relationships (superior and lateral, internal and external to the organization). From these developmental relationships (for example, mentors or sponsors), potential leaders can better learn from their own experiences by receiving feedback, advice, and emotional support. These relationships can be helpful only if the managers are willing to take some risks, disclose some of their shortcomings, and open themselves to constructive criticism—admittedly a tall order.

Choosing the Right Position

Establishing a leadership career begins with choosing the right positions along the way. There are two factors managers should take into account when making decisions about which job opportunities to pursue: (1) How good is the *fit* between who they are and the position (and the organization)? (2) How good is the fit between who they are and who they want to be? That is, what types of *learning opportunities* does the position offer? To the extent that the fit is "perfect"—that the manager has the requisite talents and characteristics (for example, personal values that match the corporate culture) to do the job—the manager will be in a better position to make an immediate contribution to organizational performance.[14]

Admittedly, "fit" is subjective, and all too often women have been excluded because others have not found them to "fit." One way women have coped with this reality is to hide who they really are or how they really think until they get a foot in the door. This can be a dangerous tactic. If an individual's values are not consistent with those of the company, the compromises demanded may be considerable. Besides, it is hard to be a credible leader of others when acting out an inauthentic self.[15]

The best assignments from a developmental perspective are ones in which the fit is imperfect—it is a "stretch" (in terms of talent, not values). These assignments are riskier, since the manager is more likely to make mistakes that might set back her career progress or have a negative impact on organizational performance. But they are also the kinds of assignments from which managers can acquire new knowledge, skills, perspective, and judgment. Individuals should look for jobs in which they can leverage initial fit to establish a self-reinforcing cycle of success whereby, year after year, they acquire more of the sources of power necessary to be effective and successful. They should pursue situations in which their strengths are really needed, important weaknesses are not a *serious* drawback, and their core values are consistent with those of the organization; in other words, the stretch should not be too big or the risk too great.[16] Risk should be commensurate with the individual's ability to cope with and responsibly manage it (both for the sake of the organization and individual). As a general rule of thumb, the risk is probably too great if it will take more than six months to progress up the learning curve enough to be able to produce some meaningful results in a particular job.[17]

Women should seek out diverse experiences to facilitate and balance their development in multiple areas. This is precisely what Jeanne Lewis of Staples, Inc. did; she rotated through operations, sales, merchandising, and marketing. Individuals who are able to grow beyond their initial strengths and develop a *broad* repertoire of talents are more likely to progress in their careers because they have the requisite abilities to meet the ever-changing demands of their jobs. In this regard, studies that compare high-potential managers who have "derailed" (become plateaued or terminated) with high-potential managers who have made it to senior executive positions are enlightening.[18] One characteristic of those who derail is that initial strengths (for example, a "hands-on" style or technical virtuosity) later become "fatal flaws." When faced with new and different challenges, these managers continue to rely on their initial capabilities, even when they are no longer sufficient or appropriate. They are unable or unwilling to develop other supplementary or complementary capabilities.

In terms of developing leadership talents in particular, it can pay to look for stretch assignments involving change. Some examples include introducing a new product or information technology system, revitalizing a mature business, or starting up a subsidiary in an international market. These sorts of assignments, almost by definition, require individuals to establish direction, communicate that direction (vision and strategies) to diverse stakeholders, and figure out how to motivate and inspire the stakeholders to implement the strategies and fulfill the vision. The more revolutionary—as opposed to evolutionary—is the change, the more powerful are the leadership learning opportunities.

The case of Taran Swan illustrates this point.[19] Swan had spent three years in business development at Nickelodeon, a cable channel for kids. She was particularly wedded to the business plan she had developed for entry into Latin America. She believed Latin American children deserved better programming than they were currently getting. She explained, "Because it was largely a poorer, developing region, people thought they could put anything on the air, and they did. Nickelodeon was good for kids, gender-neutral, pro-social, and gave kids a voice." Rather than hand over the plan she had worked on for Nickelodeon Latin America, Swan asked to become the general manager of the effort. This was her chance to take what had begun as a "gleam in her eye" through the on-air launch and turn it into reality. Although she was nervous about the leap in responsibility, she was confident in her ability to learn.

As she reflected, "Before, in business development, I wasn't accountable. This time I was. We would meet the projections because I owned those numbers." On the one hand, Swan's superiors had some reservations about her lack of experience leading a larger organization and managing an on-going profit and loss. On the other hand, they knew her to be a clear thinker and had confidence she could handle the business and administrative responsibilities. She had a reputation for being exceptionally competent, warm, and personable, and people liked working with her. They knew her style involved a great deal of delegation, and although this had worked in the past, this position would offer new challenges. In addition, Swan did not speak Spanish fluently and had no previous experience working in Latin America, a difficult region from a macroeconomic point of view.

Swan and her team had to develop and implement a pan-regional strategy that would capitalize on the diversity of sixteen-plus countries and three languages across Latin America and the Caribbean. Swan's thoughts were never far from the bottom line. Despite the morass of detail to which she had to attend, she remained focused on the overall business strategy. She refined her leadership philosophy and style throughout her time at Nicklelodeon Latin America. Through inquiry, she created a culture in the organization in which people were both empowered and accountable:

> On the one hand, Taran was easygoing and fun. But she would ask and ask and ask and ask to get to the bottom of something. You would say to her, she would say it back to you, so that everyone would be 100 percent clear on what we were talking about. Once she got the information and knew what you were doing, you had to be consistent. She would say, "You told me x, why are you doing y? I'm confused." . . . You were held accountable. Taran's pet peeve was if you weren't thinking strategically. If you were just a worker-bee she would lose faith in you. She needed to know your brain was not just on the task at hand.

Swan was gratified to see her team put their "heart[s] and souls" into what had become their collective dream. She was learning a great deal about what it takes, given her talent and passions, to motivate and inspire people.

Getting Off to the Right Start

Women must be aware of their strengths, limitations, motives, and values in order to make the appropriate tradeoffs between fit and learning opportunity when selecting a position.[20] However, individuals only become aware of who they are and who they want to become through experience. As women accumulate work experience, they have an opportunity to make choices and test those choices and begin to clarify what they are good at and what is important to them.[21]

Hence, those early in their careers may have only a vague sense of their talents, motivations, and values. All too often, they get off to a bad start by selecting jobs and organizations that simply do not fit their capabilities, motives, and values very well. Because they are not clear about who they are and the kinds of jobs to which they are best suited, they are easily seduced by the money, glamour, or prestige associated with a given job. Some define the "good" opportunities as those that are popular in the social milieu in which they find themselves. These individuals end up taking jobs because the jobs are the "popular" choice and not because they are excited by the people with whom they will be spending time or the products or services with which they will be working. For women, given the special challenges of building developmental relationships (discussed below), it is best to pay particular attention to how comfortable they are with their potential colleagues.

In other instances, individuals choose jobs that are too demanding for them. Because they do not fully appreciate their strengths and weaknesses, they get themselves into situations where they are simply in over their heads. For example, newly minted MBAs or JDs who have never had subordinates reporting to them before may take jobs in which they will have considerable people management responsibilities, with little sense of the risk in doing so. Professional school graduates may take jobs in highly politicized environments where only those who are very skillful at handling difficult work relationships can prosper.

Those early in their careers can glean important self-insight through careful and systematic introspection. In particular, they should look for pervasive themes in their past and present experiences that say something about their key strengths, important limitations, and core values. For example, in trying to decide whether to move into a leadership role, individuals should ask themselves the following questions:

- What kind of work do I find most interesting and fulfilling?
- Do I like collaborative work?
- Do I tend to become the leader of groups in which I find myself?
- Have I ever volunteered to coach or tutor others?
- Do I find it intriguing to work on thorny, ambiguous problems?
- Do I cope well with stress (for example, extended hours, tough personal decisions)?

If they cannot answer most of these questions in the affirmative, it may suggest that they have neither the personal qualities, character, nor motivation required to be an effective leader.[22]

If women choose an appropriate position, they will be able to convert their general competencies into company- and job-specific expertise, develop relationships, and make a contribution to organizational performance in relatively short order. Once they begin to make a contribution to organizational performance (admittedly, perhaps in a limited way at first), their track record and credibility in the organization will begin to grow. People will then begin to seek them out and be more eager to work with them; in other words, their *network of relationships* will grow. Some will be willing to sponsor and perhaps even mentor them, taking risks on their behalf and promoting them into stretch assignments. From these assignments, they develop more expertise and more relationships and therefore are in an even better position to contribute to key organizational objectives. Soon this cycle of success becomes self-reinforcing; their track record and credibility continue to flourish. As they acquire more power and establish relationships with a broad range of people, they find themselves holding a more central position in their network of relationships, which enables them to gain still greater power and access to currencies.[23] Once these women begin to advance, they acquire more formal authority and can consolidate their power (see Figure 1 for a graphic depiction of this dynamic process).[24]

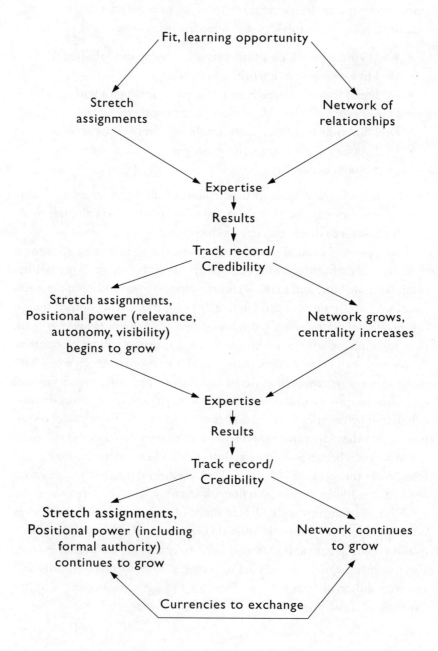

FIGURE I
*Building Power and Influence
Over the Course of a Career*

Landing Stretch Assignments

Stretch assignments are usually assignments with which considerable positional power is associated. Sources of positional power include *relevance*, *visibility*, and *autonomy*. By working on issues or projects that are highly *relevant* to organizational performance, individuals can acquire expertise critical to corporate objectives. Performing effectively and contributing to organizational success, however, is not enough. To reap the rewards associated with such success, others must be aware of an individual's performance. Assignments of strategic importance are generally *visible* to powerful people in an organization, and therefore persons working on highly relevant assignments are more likely to gain scarce organizational rewards (for example, other desirable assignments, salary increases, and promotions). And finally, with *autonomy*, comes the latitude to develop and demonstrate initiative and to innovate—in short, to lead and shape the direction in which the organization (or particular unit) will head. These particular talents are especially important in contemporary organizations, which are constantly confronted with the need to change and adapt to new environmental contingencies.

The most effective and successful individuals do not simply wait for such positions to be offered to them; they pursue or create them. They "invest" what power they have in the hope of getting it back with "interest." If a woman's ambition is to develop her leadership capabilities, especially the capacity to set direction, she should seek positions with ever increasing autonomy or superiors who are known for empowering their people. Of course, autonomy often comes with ambiguity, associated stress, and the opportunity to fail.

Leaders in the making focus on the right indices of career progress; they not only pay attention to the tangibles of titles, promotions, and salary increases, but also to the intangibles, such as the extent to which they are given progressively more challenging stretch assignments. For example, Ross Webber, professor of management at the Wharton School, found in his work that those who are most satisfied with their careers strive to move toward their firms' "power-axis functions." If offered a move toward the center, they never quibble about title, pay, or prerequisites.[25] They also resist corporate efforts to "fast-track" them before they are ready; if individuals move too quickly they never have a chance to consolidate or master the lessons of their experience. People often underestimate just how difficult it is and how long it can take to master a job assignment. As business management Professors Thomas Bonoma and J. Lawler observed, "Juniors are often their own worst enemies, mistaking the first five years of a career for the career itself. . . . A successful career in general management is analogous to climbing a ladder—skipped rungs almost always create a safety hazard for the whole crew."[26]

But to visualize one's career strictly as a ladder would be a mistake. Those individuals who are best at managing their careers approach them *strategically*—they know where they are and where they want to go. They set goals, periodically reevaluating and revising them; they are continually scanning the environment around them to anticipate what the organization will need and hence what knowledge and skills they should strive to develop. Instead of engaging in self-serving behavior focused primarily on achieving their personal ambitions, they are willing and able to take the risks necessary to seek out or create the kinds of assignments from which they can learn and contribute to corporate objectives. One woman described a critical lesson she learned from her mentor:

> He was my role model for not having a job title. He didn't have to have a job. He was very important in terms of my understanding of how to use the cracks in the company to achieve the things you felt needed to be done. Bill was a master at that. I remember asking him about career ladders. And he said, "Career ladder! Whatever gave you the thought that anything in life is as neat as a ladder?"

Managers thinking strategically about their careers may opt for a lateral as opposed to a vertical move if they believe that doing so will help broaden their skill set and put them in a better position to serve the organization. These individuals are willing to take calculated risks. For instance, they may move from a line position in which they had been in charge and their results had been measurable to a staff position so that they can develop their ability to exercise influence without formal authority and so that they can build a more varied network of relationships across the organization. Or they might volunteer to take positions in countries other than the ones in which their organizations are headquartered (for example, to help introduce a product to a new foreign market). Given the globalization of the economy, such positions can be quite relevant and visible; they frequently provide opportunities to acquire expertise and track records in areas of growing importance to the organization. In addition, these global placements provide particularly good opportunities for developing key leadership capabilities such as risk-taking, coping with ambiguous data, and developing empathy for diverse groups of people. Of course, risks are associated with such assignments; they often entail developing new functional or market expertise, acquiring a new language, or learning how to work with those from a different cultural background. In addition, there is always the risk of "being out of sight and out of mind."[27]

Building a Network of Developmental Relationships

Individuals who think strategically about their assignment choices also tend to do so about their relationships.[28] Devoting time and attention to growing and nurturing a network of relationships not only helps managers obtain stretch assignments but also helps them manage the risks associated with such assignments. For example, because they have connections with powerful people, they are less likely to be forgotten and neglected when they return home from expatriate assignments.

Instead of searching for that one "perfect" mentor (something far too many people do), those who are most effective at managing their careers cultivate multiple and diverse developmental relationships in an effort to build a "personal board of directors" (for example, coaches, sponsors, protectors, role models, counselors). Prospective leaders spend time on critical relationships based on the needs of their work and their development rather than on habit or comfort level. They recognize and seize opportunities to form such partnerships. For instance, they may elect to join a task force even though it means extra work because it also provides a unique opportunity to encounter superiors and peers in different functional areas. Over time, these contacts may yield developmental relationships. Such work also provides an opportunity to refine communication skills with diverse constituencies—a critical leadership talent.

In addition, instead of fretting about who will make a "good mentor," leaders focus on being a "perfect protégé" so that others will be attracted to working with them. They recognize that mentoring relationships demand considerable investment and risk on the part of both partners. They share responsibility with their mentors for ensuring that the relationship is productive and mutually beneficial; they make an effort to give back as much as they receive.

To help students understand what it means to be a perfect protégé, I wrote a case about Joline Godfrey that described her unlikely evolution from interning in Polaroid's employee assistance program to heading a new initiative, which Polaroid later spun off as an independent company. Godfrey was continuously learning and preparing herself to make a difference. She was always aware that she could learn from others, as evidenced in her description of her interactions with a senior executive she first met while working on a new hiring policy:

> He was an extraordinary man. If I needed to talk something over with him, he would suggest I drop by his office at the end of the day. We might meet for 15 to 20 minutes and then, informally, others would slowly gather in his office to discuss company politics, policy issues under discussion, or projects under way. He never asked me to leave and it was in this way that I came to feel comfortable in this milieu. So, I, this young thing right out of graduate school, would be sitting in the office with the CEO, etc. For the first time in my life, I was smart enough to be quiet so they wouldn't notice I was there. Later, when projects came down that were important to the company, I was often involved. No doubt, not everyone supported his ways of giving some of us opportunity. But he brought us into contact with company officers and helped us gain a more intimate understanding of the company culture.[29]

Godfrey was open to feedback, so her mentors could tell her honestly how they felt both about what she had accomplished (or not accomplished) and the means by which she had done so (for example, how others in the organization felt about her leadership style). Godfrey was able to use the latter information to develop a more effective leadership style by hearing others answer the following questions: How did they feel about working with her? How did others feel about themselves with her? Did they feel energized and inspired? If not, what about her behavior was not working? Such insights can help individuals modify their behavior and improve their ability to motivate and inspire. Godfrey is now the CEO of Independent Means, a company founded in 1992 initially to meet what Godfrey defined as the "unserved needs of teen women who were ready and hungry to learn about money and business."[30]

Effective leaders also know that they can learn from peers and subordinates as well as superiors. Meg Whitman knew she had much to learn about technology when she arrived at eBay.[31] In fact, some predicted she would fail in her new assignment because she could not get up the learning curve fast enough. Two weeks after Whitman started at eBay, the company's site went down for over eight hours, angering hundreds of thousands of eBay users who had auctions in process. Whitman recalled, "it was a wake-up call" for her. She turned her attention to mastering the key strategic choices eBay faced with regard to technology. Whitman was willing to admit her need to learn, and the eBay culture was conducive to her doing so. Whitman explained:

> I've worked in a few companies where senior managers are so afraid of appearing "weak" that they stand by a point of view even in the face of better, more informed data. At eBay, we have a "no penalty" culture, meaning that there is no penalty for being on the wrong side of an issue or changing your mind in the face of better information. If you come to a meeting with one point of view and a colleague says something that convinces you that you're wrong, the culture is to say, "O.K.—that's smart. You're right. Let's move on."

After rigorous discussions, Whitman and the eBay team were able to move decisively and make the necessary investments in system capacity. That has helped enable eBay to be one of the few dot-coms to survive.

For emerging leaders, relationships become the linchpin that ensures continuous development and career success. Mentors and sponsors provide progressively more challenging assignments from which women can learn, cultivate an even wider network of relationships, and contribute to the organization. If individuals do not get stretch assignments, they have no opportunity to continually upgrade and update their expertise.[32] Given the pace of change in organizations today, individuals' expertise can rapidly become obsolete. This insidious process of *deskilling* appears to happen disproportionately to women and those in the minority in organizations (for instance, African American managers in the United States). This process may account in large measure for why such individuals can find it difficult to break corporate "glass ceilings," that is, apparent barriers to advancement to the highest level of the organization.[33] For example, there is evidence that many women actually may be less prepared than men for handling upper-level management jobs because they have been denied access to developmental jobs, accorded less responsibility in jobs comparable to men, and given fewer resources with which to do their jobs effectively.[34]

As research summarized throughout this book makes clear, mentors and sponsor relationships are especially critical for women. Without strong relationships with people who will take risks on their behalf, women have difficulty gaining access to the experiences necessary for growth and development.[35] Unfortunately, there is considerable evidence that women and minorities encounter unique dilemmas in establishing such developmental relationships. Because most of these relationships require some degree of identification, affinity, and trust, it is not surprising that mentoring relationships occur more naturally between "like" individuals."[36] Establishing mentoring relationships is not an easy task for women, but it is not an insurmountable task. However, women can ill afford to be naïve or cynical about their circumstances.

As mentioned earlier, when considering a position women should pay attention to their comfort level with potential coworkers. Instead of getting caught up in "fit" with form, they should pay attention to fit with substance: Do they have similar approaches to business issues? Do they have similar values? Because mentors often believe that it is riskier to support a woman than a man (and frankly, it can be), women will have to be prepared to give back more than they receive. As one woman explained, "If you are sent out to get a flounder, you had better bring back a whale." This is not fair but true. Women must take the initiative and work to establish a network of developmental relationships, one that ideally includes women as well as men. Women must be prepared to discuss and explore issues that arise because of their gender with those whom they wish to build developmental relationships. Although superficial conformity on some issues can be effective, overconformity on key ones is detrimental in the long run. Harvard Professor David Thomas has found that relationships in which difference was "embraced" and sensitive issues discussed were more successful than those in which tough topics were ignored.

CONCLUSION

There are many structural and cultural barriers to be addressed if women are to get ahead in organizations. We all need to work hard at removing them. But the fact remains, if we want to lead, we need to take charge of our own development. No one can teach us to lead; we have to teach ourselves. We must be ready to work on ourselves. We must be ready to proactively pursue or create developmental opportunities—experiences and relationships from which we can learn to lead. In addition, there is yet another responsibility to be addressed. Today, to be effective leaders, women must ask themselves not only, "Am I willing and able to lead?" but also, "Am I creating a context in which others are willing and able to lead?"

Currently, I am writing a book on leadership in the global economy in which I consider what world-class companies will be like and what it will take to lead them. In the twenty-first century, world-class companies will act, look, and feel like the most successful entrepreneurial ventures. Corporations, no matter how large and established, will need to behave with the agility and creativity that characterize small, aggressive start-ups. They will be ever-evolving collectives of talented, passionate, and diverse individuals. What will the leaders of these world-class companies look like? Leaders will be architects of these collectives. They will lead, figuratively, from the back, shaping what is, in essence, *collective genius*.[37] Perhaps Nelson Mandela said it best:

> A leader . . . is like a shepherd. He stays behind the flock, letting the most nimble go on ahead, whereupon the others follow, not realizing that all along they are being directed from behind.

Fundamentally, outstanding leaders today are comfortable sharing power and creating leadership opportunities for others. Despite all the talk about empowerment, many people are afraid to give up the control it implies. But the outstanding leaders are secure in themselves; they know their strengths and weaknesses. They know they don't have to have all of the answers. When eBay was looking for a CEO for the company, the founder, Pierre Omidyar and his colleagues quickly settled on Meg Whitman as their top choice. As one explained:

> I remember the most important question she asked during the recruiting process—a question that demonstrated to me that she was exactly the right person—was "Pierre's not going anywhere, is he?" I can tell you from my perspective that it's relatively rare that you find a new CEO mature enough to be more concerned about keeping the good people than making their mark and taking control. Her comment displayed an unusual perceptiveness into that fact that what was going on at eBay was pretty special and that Pierre had been the architect of it.

Effective leaders surround themselves with great people who can cover for them when necessary. These leaders are an inspiration to be around because they truly and deeply believe in people. For them, leadership is about getting the very best out of people.

Taran Swan, who I discussed earlier, made a number of "big bets" in developing her team. Virtually all of its members recognized that they were in stretch assignments—with opportunities other managers would not have given them. They felt quite indebted to Swan for believing in their potential and providing them with the autonomy to lead. As one member of her team noted, "[Taran's] always seen things that a lot of other people don't see." A member of a coleadership marketing team elaborated on this idea: "Taran was the one who proposed and championed our sharing the marketing position. She was willing to take the risk because she wanted to create a structure that tapped into both Donna's and my respective talents. Donna and I were individual leaders in certain projects, but always consulted with each other and gave approval." Swan helped her team members learn how to work collaboratively and be leaders of collective genius —a critical talent in twenty-first century organizations.

When I joined the faculty of Harvard Business School in 1984, I am ashamed to report that there were very few materials about women leaders in our curriculum. The first two cases I developed were about women: Suzanne de Passe, the CEO of Motown Productions and an African American woman, and Karen Leary, one of the first women branch managers at Merrill Lynch.[38] Admittedly, I probably developed these cases to affirm my own place at Harvard Business School and to create a space where I "fit." When I became the head of our required leadership course, my priority was to develop cases that represented the diverse student body we have from around the globe. Women have been generous and allowed me to develop materials about them that showed both their successes and missteps and, perhaps most importantly, how they learned to lead. MBAs can see that these charismatic leaders were not simply born so, but rather that they worked hard at their own development.

Does difference make a difference? I can't say, but what I do know is that there are women out there changing their organizations and their societies. What do these women have in common? They have ambition, the courage to have a dream, and the commitment to work to see it realized.[39] Their careers represent years of hard work and dedication to prepare themselves to meet the challenges and opportunities of our new century. From the early days of their careers, they were willing to take responsibil-

ity and be held accountable. They have taken risks and made mistakes—
and they have learned from them. They have been helped by others—and
they have helped others in return. They exemplify leadership for both
women *and* men in the twenty-first century.

NOTES

1. In this chapter, I draw heavily from a previously published paper, Linda
Hill, "Managing Your Career." Copyright © 1994 by the President and Fellows
of Harvard College. Harvard Business School No. 494-082.

2. I would like to acknowledge the insights and able editorial assistance of
Maria Farkas and Jennifer Suesse.

3. Linda Hill and Kristin Doughty, "Jeanne Lewis at Staples, Inc. (A)," Harvard Business School No. 499–041.

4. John. P. Kotter, "What Leaders Really Do," *Harvard Business Review*,
May–June 1990, at 103, 111.

5. For a discussion of the varying mix of expertise required at different levels
of management and in different functional areas, see for example N. Fondas, "A
Behavioral Job Description for Managers," 47 *Organizational Dynamics*, summer 1992; R. L. Katz, "Skills of an Effective Administrator," *Harvard Business
Review*, Sept.–Oct. 1974, at 90–103; H. Mintzberg, "The Manager's Job: Folklore and Fact," *Harvard Business Review*, July–Aug. 1974, at 49–71; R. Stewart,
Choices for the Manager (1982).

6. For additional information about task and personal learning see, for example, D. T. Hall, "Dilemmas in Linking Succession Planning to Individual Executive
Learning," 25 *Human Resource Management* 235–265 (1986); L. A. Hill, *Becoming a Manager: Mastery of a New Identity* (1992). For a discussion of some of the
psychological traps managers can fall into if they do not engage in self-assessment
and self-development, see for example M. F. R. Kets de Vries, *Leaders, Fools, and
Impostors: Essays on the Psychology of Leadership* (1993). For a discussion of the
importance of characteristics such as self-awareness, empathy, and personal motivation in success see Daniel Goleman, *Emotional Intelligence* (1995).

7. See for example M. W. McCall, *High Flyers* (1998).

8. Warren Bennis, *On Becoming a Leader* (1989).

9. See for example M. W. McCall, M. M. Lombardo, A. M. Morrison, *The
Lessons of Experience* 58 (1988); Jay A. Conger and Beth Benjamin, *Building
Leaders: How Successful Companies Develop the Next Generation* (1999).

10. Linda Hill and Kristin Doughty, "Dawn Riley at America True (A)," Harvard Business School No. 401–006.

11. *Coed syndicate* refers to a syndicate that includes sailors of both genders.

12. McCall et al., *The Lessons of Experience*, at 9; Donald A. Schön, *The Reflective Practitioner: How Professionals Think in Action* (1983).

13. See for example C. Argyris, "Teaching Smart People How to Learn," *Harvard Business Review*, May–June 1991, at 99–109; H. Levinson, *Career Mastery: Keys to Taking Charge of Your Career Throughout Your Work Life* (1992).

14. For a discussion of how to assess person/job fit, see, for example, T. A. Judge and G. R. Ferris, "The Elusive Criterion of Fit in Human Resource Staffing Decisions," 15 *Human Resource Planning* 47–68 (1992). The authors discuss the variety of criteria that individuals and organizations use when assessing fit. Moreover, they identify how to avoid an all-too-common pitfall of confusing form (those who match the *images* of competence and qualifications) with substance (those who are truly qualified).

15. Herminia Ibarra, "Making Partner: The Mentor's Guide to the Psychological Journey," *Harvard Business Review*, Mar.–Apr. 2000, at 146–155.

16. Because it is more difficult to change values than attitudes and behaviors, it is usually recommended that people select positions in organizations whose cultures basically match their values.

17. If the individual chooses to accept a job in which the risk is indeed great, it pays to discuss the risks explicitly with superiors and agree on an action plan in which expectations are clarified as much as possible about what the individual's goals should be and how he or she can achieve those goals.

18. See for example M. M. Lombardo and C. D. McCauley, *The Dynamics of Management Derailment* (1988).

19. Linda Hill and Kristin Doughty, "Taran Swan at Nickelodeon Latin America (A)," Harvard Business School No. 400–036.

20. In choosing a position, people should think broadly about how they define success, taking into consideration both their work and nonwork values and goals. Managers today are attending more to the integration of their work, personal, and family priorities; they are finding it pays to confront early on their desire for balance between their work and nonwork lives and organizational expectations about effort and commitment. For insight about how to think through and manage these issues effectively, see for example L. Bailyn, *Breaking the Mold: Women, Men, and Time in the New Corporate World* (1993); F. Bartolome and P. A. Lee Evans, "Must Success Cost So Much?," *Harvard Business Review*, Mar.–Apr. 1980, at 137–148; D. T. Hall and V. A. Parker, "The Role of Workplace Flexibility in Managing Diversity," *Organizational Dynamics*, summer 1993, at 5–18.

21. Edgar H. Schein has done much of the seminal research on how individuals go about discovering and accepting their "career anchor." He has identified eight types of career anchors: security/stability, autonomy/independence, technical/functional, managerial competence, entrepreneurial creativity, sense of service/ded-

ication to a cause, pure challenge, and lifestyle. See for example E. H. Schein, *Career Dynamics: Matching Individual and Organizational Needs* (1978); E. H. Schein, "Individuals and Careers," in *Handbook of Organizational Behavior* 155–172 (J. W. Lorsch, ed. 1987).

22. Many have written about the managerial character or temperament and motivation required to be a manager. See for example Hill, *Becoming a Manager*; McCall et al., *The Lessons of Experience*; M. W. McCall, *High Flyers*; D. C. McClelland, *Power: The Inner Experience* (1975); E. H. Schein, "Individuals and Careers"; A. Zaleznik and M. F. R. Kets de Vries, *Power and the Corporate Mind* (1975); H. Levinson, *The Exceptional Executive: A Psychological Conception* (1968).

23. Networks are mutually beneficial alliances or exchange relationships based on the law of reciprocity; that is, that "one good (or bad) deed deserves another." The primary way managers exercise influence and get things done is by providing resources and services to others in exchange for resources and services they require. Cohen and Bradford use the metaphor of "currencies" to describe this process of exchange. As they point out, just as many types of currencies are traded in the world financial market, many types are "traded" in organizational life. See, for example, A. R. Cohen and D. L. Bradford, *Influence Without Authority* (1990). Managers with a broad repertoire of sources of power are more likely to have access to a variety of currencies. And managers with more currencies are more likely to have "just the right one" for building a network with a given person or group on whom they are dependent. See for example Linda Hill, "Exercising Influence," Harvard Business School No. 494–080; Linda Hill, "Building Effective One-on-One Work Relationships," Harvard Business School No. 497–028.

24. There are five positional sources of power (formal authority, relevance, centrality, autonomy, visibility) and four personal sources of power (expertise, track record, attractiveness, and effort). See Linda Hill, "Power Dynamics in Organizations," Harvard Business School No. 494–083. For more on building a success syndrome, see John Kotter, *Power and Influence: Beyond Formal Authority* (1985).

25. R. A. Webber, *Becoming a Courageous Manager: Overcoming Career Problems of New Managers* (1991).

26. T. Bonoma and J. Lawler, "Chutes and Ladders: Growing a General Manager," *Sloan Management Review*, spring 1989, at 30.

27. For more in-depth discussion of expatriate assignments, see for example R. L. Tung, "Expatriate Assignments: Enhancing Success and Minimizing Failure," 2 *Academy of Management Executive* 117–126 (1987); Ely and J. McCormick, *The New International Executive: Business Leadership for the 21st Century* (a global research report published by Amrop International, 1993); Morgan W. McCall and George P. Hollenbeck, *Developing Global Executives* (2002).

28. Relationships play a pivotal role in individual development at every career

stage. For an in-depth discussion of sponsor and mentor relationships, see Linda Hill, "Beyond the Myth of the Perfect Mentor," Harvard Business School No. 491–096. Prospective leaders need to pay attention to building both instrumental and developmental relationships. Instrumental relationships are relationships from which an individual acquires job-specific resources (such as information, advice, material resources). Developmental relationships, by contrast, are ones in which individuals obtain needed support for the enhancement of their career developmental and organizational experience (e.g., career advice, coaching, emotional support). The distinction between instrumental and developmental relationships is not hard and fast. Temporary instrumental relationships can evolve into developmental relationships.

29. Linda Hill, Melinda Conrad, and Nancy Kamprath, "Joline Godfrey and the Polaroid Corp. (A)," Harvard Business School No. 492–037.

30. Godfrey was exposed to the need for independent means while researching her book on women entrepreneurs, *Our Wildest Dreams: Women Entrepreneurs Making Money, Having Fun, Doing Good* (1992).

31. Linda Hill and Maria Farkas, "Meg Whitman at eBay Inc. (A)," Harvard Business School No. 401–024. For further information about Meg Whitman's career at eBay, see Linda Hill and Maria Farkas, "Meg Whitman and eBay Germany," Harvard Business School No. 402–006.

32. For a more in-depth discussion of "powerless" positions, see R. M. Kanter, "Power Failure in Management Circuits," *Harvard Business Review*, July–Aug. 1979, at 65–75.

33. For discussions of the special dilemmas minorities face, see for example E. L. Bell, ed., "Special Issue on the Career and Life Experiences of Black Professionals," *Journal of Organizational Behavior*, Nov. 1990; David A. Thomas and Robin Ely, "Making Differences Matter: A New Paradigm for Managing Diversity," *Harvard Business Review*, Sept.–Oct. 1996. For insight into the challenges women face in building their careers, see for example Lisa A. Mainiero, "Getting Anointed for Advancement: The Case of Executive Women, 8(2) *"Academy of Management Executive* 53–63 (1994); A. M. Morrison, R. P. White, E. Van Velsor, and the Center for Creative Leadership, *Breaking the Glass Ceiling: Can Women Reach the Top of America's Largest Corporations?* (1987). To examine how women are faring in management, the *Wall Street Journal* studied employment records of companies filing reports with the U.S. Equal Employment Opportunity Commission from 1982 to 1994. The findings are reported in two articles: R. Sharpe, "The Waiting Game: Women Make Strides, but Men Stay Firmly in Top Company Jobs," *Wall Street Journal*, Mar. 29, 1994, at A1, A10; R. Sharpe, "Family Friendly Firms Don't Always Promote Females," *Wall Street Journal*, Mar. 29, 1994, at B1, B5.

34. Deborah L. Rhode, "The Difference 'Difference' Makes"; P. J. Ohlott,

M. N. Ruderman, and C. D. McCauley, "Gender Differences in Managers' Developmental Job Experiences," *Academy of Management Journal*, Feb. 1994, at 61–62.

35. See for example K. E. Kram, *Mentoring at Work: Developmental Relationships in Organizational Life* (1988); H. Ibarra, "Personal Networks of Women and Minorities in Management: A Conceptual Framework," 18 *Academy of Management Review* 56–87 (1993).

36. For a broader discussion of race and mentoring relationships, see for example D. A. Thomas, "The Impact of Race on Managers' Experiences of Developmental Relationships (Mentoring and Sponsorship): An Intra-Organizational Study," 11 *Journal of Organizational Behavior* 479–492 (1990); "Mentoring and Irrationality: The Role of Racial Taboos," 28 *Human Resource Management* 279–290 (1989); "Racial Dynamics in Cross-race Developmental Relationship," 38 *Administrative Science Quarterly* 169–194 (1993); David Thomas and Jack Gabarro, *Breaking Through: The Making of Minority Executives in Corporate America* (1999).

37. Linda Hill, "Leadership as Collective Genius," in *Management 21C* (Subir Chowdhury, ed. 2000).

38. See Linda Hill, Melinda Conrad, and Katherine Weber, "De Passe Entertainment and Creative Partners," Harvard Business School No. 494–013; Linda Hill and Jaan Elias, "Suzanne de Passe at Motown Productions (A)," Harvard Business School No. 487–042.

39. James Champy and Nitin Nohria, *The Arc of Ambition: Defining the Leadership Journey* (2000).

14

ELAINE R. JONES

Breaking the Barriers
to Equality

In thinking about opportunities for leadership, particularly for women of color, I want to offer some brief thoughts about how we achieve such positions and what we should do when we get there. I start from the premise that one crucial requirement is a measure of mental toughness. Women especially need that quality because when we run into barriers and obstacles, if we do not have something from within that allows us to overcome the small and large indignities and problems, we will cave in. I do not have the answers as to where that strength comes from and how we get it, but I suspect for most of us that it is developed during the formative years. In her comments on this issue, Charisse Lillie talked about the importance of having grandparents and parents who believed that she could do whatever she wanted to do. I was fortunate as well in that respect.

I, too, grew up in an all-black environment in the segregated South. My first experience with whites in America was in law school at the University of Virginia. I was the only black woman, and there were six white women. I encountered no shortage of discrimination but I generally did not know whether it was because I was African American or because I was female. I could not figure it out. But when the seven of us got together in the ladies room at the end of the day, which was the only place we had to congregate, and when I heard the experiences of the other women, then I could start to tell whether what was happening to me was due to race or gender or some combination. We had some great laughs and the shared experiences helped me gain perspective and start thinking in a very serious way about gender, as well as racial discrimination.

The chapters in this collection make it clear that—in Rhode's phrase—"what works best depends heavily on context, most research underscores one generalizable strategy. In order to retain both an insider's influence and an outsider's critical perspective, women need allies." Teveia Barnes makes a similar point. As she notes, women need white male allies because they need support from people with power.

As I look back at my experience starting with the NAACP Legal Defense Fund (LDF) as a young lawyer, I did have allies. My professor of contracts who left to go to the Wall Street firm Mudge, Rose, Guthrie & Alexander saw that I was interviewed for a job there. I had no interest in a Wall Street practice but it was helpful to have an interview and an offer. Having a white male ally who wanted to support me made the difference.

Tevia Barnes notes that it is unusual for women of color to have white male allies. Part of the reason is because these men do not see themselves reflected in our contributions and our leadership style. I was fortunate to encounter an exception. Jack Greenberg was head of the NAACP Legal Defense Fund. And Jack is a man of great vision and good judgment. As a young lawyer, I had his support. And I had a mentor in Chairman of the Board William T. Coleman, one of this nation's leading lawyers, who happens to be African American.

But as we discuss strategies to help women in advancing to leadership positions, the question we need to keep in view is, What are they going to do when they get there? Is the point of a Women's Leadership Summit to talk about women advancing for the sake of advancing? Well, you climb a mountain because it is there; however, if you simply want to advance for the sake of advancing, then how does that distinguish you from anybody else?

If our claim is that women want to advance for the sake of changing the institution that claim may be viewed as threatening. The response from insiders often is, "What's wrong with it? It was here before you came along. Why do you think that you will make it better?"

One answer is that we want to advance for the special skills set that we bring. Then a frequent response is, "Well, that is arrogance. There are others who have special skills. Why should you be singled out?"

Another answer is that we are carrying the flag for all the women who came before and are coming behind us who have not yet had leadership opportunities. Then the question becomes, "Well, who anointed you? Why you?"

What can often end the discussion is when we say women should be able to advance not only for all the reasons we just offered, but also because we can make an important difference in achieving the goals of an organization. Because of our knowledge base, we can make a better widget, gain a larger market share, bring in more paying clients, and improve the way we do business. My point is that women need to think about why their leadership matters and make sure they have reasons that resonate in their particular institutions.

Now as I look at the history of my own organization, I see that the first woman on the staff of the Legal Defense Fund was Constance Baker Motley. She came to LDF as a law student in 1947. Jack Greenberg followed in 1948. Thurgood Marshall was the director. In total, Connie and Jack argued almost fifty cases before the United States Supreme Court. Connie's first argument was in 1961. That is the year that Thurgood left to go on the Second Circuit Court of Appeals. It was only during the period from 1961 to 1965, after which she became Manhattan Borough president, that she argued ten cases. It may not be coincidental that she gained opportunities when Jack became director in 1961. It is important to know the history of how women advance or fail to advance in their own institutions.

Now I am head of the Legal Defense Fund. And it is my obligation and the obligation of other women leaders when we are the first to hold a leadership position to make sure we are not the last and to open the door for others. That is the importance of being first. Otherwise, why be there? What is the point of being a leader if you cannot give access and use your power and influence to help others?

So I am very conscious of women's issues at LDF. To remain that way, I need to listen and continue to give access to everyone, ranging from the folks in the mailroom all the way up to my associate director counsel. Fortunately, our organization is small enough, about seventy employees, so people feel free to stop me in the hall. No matter how busy I am, I have to find time to respond to their concerns. I think that is a very important way to keep informed as to what is going on within the institution that I am privileged to serve.

But although I accept the obligation to help women, I am not interested in spending my time and capital on those who do not do the same—those who do not look beyond themselves. I have a problem putting my shoulder to the wheel to support women for positions of power if they do not provide their support on broader issues of social justice. I do not want to spend my time helping those who turn a deaf ear to problems of ethnic and racial prejudice or religious freedom. Just as my issue cannot only be race discrimination, other women's issues cannot only be gender. We have to care about all of the sources of injustice.

And we have battles still to fight on all these issues. We have got to do it with humor. We have got to smile. We have got to get along. We have got to be nonthreatening. We know how to do that. But we have to be very clear. Issues such as judicial independence and individual rights cannot be taken for granted. We have some important protections and we have fought hard to keep them. It is our obligation as women leaders to pass them on. And we can only do that by not just talking but by rolling up our sleeves and getting involved with causes that matter.

15

MICHELE COLEMAN MAYES

Did I Forget to Tell You I'm in Control?

It took more than a while to decide what I wanted to impart to those who read what follows. Since I have spent most of my career working in corporate legal departments, I finally decided to write about what I know best. Let me begin with a premise that I have long ago stopped debating: A rich sustenance can come from being inclusive. Although I mean this in the broadest sense, for purposes of this discussion I shall talk about the inclusion of women in corporate leadership positions and, more specifically, what they can do to facilitate attaining such leadership positions.

What is readily apparent when you look at the ranks of the company for which I work is that women comprise a significant number of the total staff. Having said that, it is also true that to create the rich sustenance I mentioned, numbers alone will not do it, although it is a good start. The environment also has to be welcoming. To create such an environment requires commitment, openness, and focus on the part of the organization. Each individual woman also has a major role, not the least of which is determining whether and how she wants to "fit" into the organization. Inclusiveness simply does not just happen. The balance of this discussion will be about seven important questions one should ask in tackling the "fit" question. Though the responses will undoubtedly vary based on workplace context and organizational culture, the questions themselves should not.

This focus is not meant to relieve the employer of responsibility or accountability. Nor do I want to stir up images of clones by using the term *fit*. But if you are part of an organization, then it is to your advantage to examine and understand how you fit into the whole. Although these issues are not limited to gender or race, they have special relevance to those who have historically been underrepresented in leadership positions.

A common threshold question is: How much of my identity can I retain? My first reaction is to ask another question. Do most women consciously know who they are in a professional sense? That takes a bit of effort to sort out (and is beyond the focus of this paper), but once it is done I generally tell women that there are aspects of their identity that are inextricably part of who they are or are nonnegotiable, and then there are those that are up for examination. Understanding what falls in which column is absolutely critical, and that is certainly dependent on the person. For example, one's personal style or appearance could be, on the one hand, either so inherently part of the individual as to be nonnegotiable or, on the other hand, simply not a big deal. Some folks change their hairstyle based on the weather or latest trends. For others, it is a more complex and critical issue.

Do I know how the organization perceives me? We've all heard the statement that perception is reality. Therefore, it is imperative to gain access to this information. Of course, this should be done in a way that is constructive. There are a number of tools available to assist with the collection of data. Indeed, I think that an organization that is committed to inclusiveness must employ such tools to ferret out harmful stereotypes and false assumptions. Once in possession of these critical data, you can more concretely assess the entity and your standing within it.

Have I established priorities? Over the years, I have come to appreciate that what was important yesterday may well not be critical today or tomorrow for any number of reasons. Some individuals are unwilling to make hard choices, and that does not work. Setting priorities forces a very conscious decision about what sacrifices you are willing to make, which I think is far better than awakening one day and realizing that the process has happened by default. The point is to identify what you think matters and why and be willing to voice those priorities. Ask for what you want. If there is an untenable tension between your needs and organizational priorities, it is far better to know that immediately.

Am I willing to take risks? The safe path is one that is well traveled. Frankly, it is also less exciting. You need to assess your appetite for risk. Numerous factors will affect that appetite. You should also be receptive to exploring nonlinear opportunities. If you have the confidence to step off the path, the rewards can be huge, but they are in no way guaranteed. Once again, knowing yourself well enough, without letting that automatically stop you, is the key.

Do I have the right mentors? It goes without saying that mentors are a must no matter by what label you choose to call them (teacher, friend, adviser, confidante, and so forth). The essential question truly is whether you have been strategic when answering this question. You should be able to articulate what it is you expect to gain from such relationships. If you cannot do that then you are missing the point. Notice that I wrote "mentors." Is it plural because there is no reason to restrict yourself to just one. We are not talking about dessert. One mentor might well be unable to address all of your needs. Needless to say, mentors will come in all shapes, sizes, and colors. Don't make the mistake of only looking for those who look like you. Finally, your age has absolutely, positively nothing to do with whether you should have mentors. If you find yourself in a new role or situation, start looking in a big hurry both within and outside the organization. It is amazing how many people welcome the chance to impart their wisdom if asked. It's no excuse that your mentors have not found you.[1]

Do I know what my strengths and weaknesses are? Quite simply, you want to build on your strengths and fix or compensate for your weaknesses. You cannot do that if you don't have a clue as to what they are. Certainly you can engage in self-evaluation, but as is clear from the discussion above, you should approach this in a more systematic fashion to get a sound grasp. Having this understanding will affect so much of what you do, such as deciding whether a new position is an unacceptable risk. Further, I would urge you not to become cavalier about this assessment process, since, when the stakes go up, you might not be as good as you assumed you were at the outset. Continuous improvement and vigilance are the watchwords.

What management styles do I want to use? Now I could turn to a discussion about how women are team builders, consensus-oriented, and so forth. That is too simple for my taste, for reasons that other chapters in this volume make clear. In general, I think women's management styles differ. They cannot be so neatly classified, nor should they be. A savvy leader comes to understand that you need different approaches depending on the people and the context. You should become adept at using the right style at the right time.

There you have my seven questions. Obviously, there is no such thing as a sure formula for success. As I stated at the beginning, you can, however, increase your chances of attaining it by focusing on important issues that *you* control. And you should also ask yourself one threshold question: Do I truly enjoy what I do—at least most days? If you respond to that question in the affirmative, then by all means do answer the remaining seven—and see you at the top.

NOTE

1. A useful resource is Ida O. Abbott, *The Lawyer's Guide to Mentoring* (2000).

16

MARY B. CRANSTON

Some Thoughts on Dealing with Cultural Bias Against Women

As a twenty-five-year veteran of a large and venerable law firm, I can think of no more persistent irritant than the subtle (and not so subtle) biases that make it much more challenging for women to be effective and successful. All professional women know exactly what I mean: the exclusion from "old boy's club" events; the attribution of your idea to the guy next to you; the assumption that you cannot do something until you indisputably prove that you can. In our culture the playing field is simply not level.

The irritant persists in the context of a world that has improved every year for women. When I started in the law firm all those years ago, the environment was a wall of tall white men in gray suits. There were a few women, but you had to go hunting to find them. There were no women in firm leadership roles and few women who were succeeding at top performance levels. When I became pregnant with my first child (she is now twenty-three) there were no maternity policies at any firm in San Francisco. Part-time was unheard of. Firm events were held at discriminatory clubs. Women were expected to just deal with day-to-day harassment and mean-spirited denigration. So I am very grateful for the tremendous advances in the opportunities and choices for women lawyers. Still, the irritant persists.

I have dealt with subtle bias differently at different times in my career. At first, and I still cringe to admit this, I didn't notice it. Bias was such an ingrained part of the world I saw growing up that I just took it as the way things were meant to be. I felt lucky that law schools had started to admit more women and that law firms had decided to hire women a year or two before I appeared on the scene. I attached myself to compassionate male mentors and began to develop my skill sets.

About the time I became a partner, the firm had hired sufficient women that we began to have critical mass. I also linked up with women partners in other San Francisco firms. Talking with women both within and without my firm began to awaken a new consciousness in me. I saw clearly the higher bar that women were asked to jump over, and I became enraged. I discovered a passion to protect the younger women coming into the profession. So for many years, I became an activist, joining with other similarly minded women to push for reforms. My favorite campaign was taking on the discriminatory clubs, including the one where my firm had had its annual partner dinner for years. All of the women partners were sick of sneaking in through the kitchen door, and we simply boycotted the event. I am happy to say that was the last dinner at the club. In general in those years, I felt I had right on my side and did not feel the need to be tactful. Although we accomplished a lot, we also sometimes alienated friends as well as foes.

Over time, I changed course. I never lost my passion to open the profession for women, but I became more interested in building alliances with men and women to create change. I found that consensus led to more lasting and wiser solutions with broader institutional acceptance. I also came to believe that my anger-based confrontational approach masked a deeper and more complex issue.

I came to see that my anger was because I thought that someone with power was stopping me and other women from achieving our goals. Although at one level that is exactly what was going on, I began to realize that I was contributing to the problem by unconsciously conceding men that power. I was pouring all my energy into wresting that power back from men, when instead I could have been looking within and nurturing my own power to control my destiny. Ironically, the cultural bias was in my own head as well as in the culture.

With that insight, I began a long process of study and self-evaluation.

I studied the lives of great leaders and visionaries who had made a significant contribution. I saw that great leaders know in their hearts and guts that they could do what they need to do. I worked to get a clear sense of my own inner drives and goals. I tried to get very conscious of fears and culturally conditioned beliefs about limitations on women, so that those fears and beliefs would not stop me before I even began. I saw that the biggest block to my success was not male cultural bias but my own fears about that bias. I worked on building optimism and excitement about change into my worldview. With these tools, I began to create and shape a very different life. I set stretch goals for myself and stayed focused on those goals, every day taking little steps that I intuitively knew would move me toward my goals. I patted my fears on the head, and made forward progress anyway. Over time, I was able to accomplish things that had seemed literally impossible a few years earlier.

I offer these thoughts because I no longer believe that taking the cultural bias head-on "out there" is enough, or even the most effective approach. I think that if each of us worked instead on building our own inner source of power and stayed focused on our goals, the very real bias would simply slip by us without hampering us. I am not saying that we should stop identifying the bias when we see it, or that we should stop doing all we can to help each other deal with bias. I am simply saying, don't get stuck fighting that fight.

I do think the persistent irritants will continue for some time to come. It will probably take critical mass in all sectors of our business world before blessed relief will finally arrive. In the meantime, it really need not matter to your success.

WHAT ABOUT MEN?

17

TEVEIA R. BARNES

Strategies for Developing White Men as Change Agents for Women Leaders

For the legal profession, government, and business, the numbers in Deborah L. Rhode's, "The Difference 'Difference' Makes" reflect the distance women must overcome before they may even dream of leadership in significant numbers in this country. Women will need powerful allies to overcome this distance to leadership.

> Women now account for about half of managerial and professional positions but only 12 percent of corporate officers, 4 percent of top corporate earners, and two of the Fortune 500 CEOs.[1] Almost 30 percent of lawyers are women, but they represent only about 15 percent of federal judges and law firm partners, and about 10 percent of law school deans and general counsel positions at Fortune 500 companies.[2] Women constitute over half of American voters, but only 22 percent of their state legislators, 15 percent of their Congressional representatives, and 10 percent of their state governors.[3]

To be effective, the agenda for change has to identify and develop white men as the initial focus.[4] White men must be brought to the table to participate actively in the dialogue for change and to become champions for women's leadership. Although there certainly are women and men of color in leadership positions who promote the advancement of women (and we should not lose sight of these very rare individuals), the real untapped champions of women are white men.

When seeking their successors, white men often select reflections of themselves—younger white men who will carry on their vision. White men generally do not see women (certainly not women of color) as their reflection, as people capable of carrying on their vision to success. If a white man does not perceive a person to be someone who can succeed and lead, he will not support that person. Consequently, many white men do not seek out women as their successors because they do not expect women to succeed. However, white men who understand and appreciate that women can be successful and enormously effective leaders generally surround themselves with very able and talented women. Men who expect women to succeed have women in line to be their successors. An effective agenda for change must include a strategy for raising the awareness of white men to the very real possibility that women can be their successors. The agenda for change also must bring white men to the process of advancing women to the highest positions of true leadership.

Women should not need to alter their fundamental being by adapting a "style that men are comfortable with."[5] Women should not be imposters. Too often women fail because it is extremely difficult, if not impossible, to maintain the charade. Moreover, a style that is most likely to make a white man comfortable may not be the most effective style for success for any person, regardless of gender. In many instances, women are put in untenable positions just to lower a white man's stress level. White men often perceive "decisive and forceful" women as "arrogant and confrontational," not because the women necessarily have interpersonal problems, but because white men simply are not ready to accept and work with women on those terms.[6]

Yes, women need allies. The best allies for women's advancement are white men. Of course, women also need women mentors and networks. Those resources are extremely important. But if a woman is up for partner, executive, or potential party representative, in that room of male decision makers, she needs a male ally. If there is no man, and particularly no man of influence, to advocate on her behalf, she will not advance. She needs a champion who will fight for her success. If there is a woman of influence in that decision-making room, a woman leader can certainly be another woman's champion. But given the low numbers of women in leadership positions, the likelihood of finding a woman with sufficient influence in that room is slim. So let's get real, the focus must be on developing white, male champions.

First, a white, male champion must be identified within an organization. A potential champion is someone who has influence, power, and authority —a leader who can be persuaded to take on women's issues as his personal mission. The best advocate may be the CEO or chairman of the firm, but only if the person in that position has real influence. Position alone will not be effective in bringing women to positions of leadership if the person in that position is not committed to changing the status quo and sharing the power chair with women. He might say the words, but his failure to act is more likely to be destructive to all women in that organization.

Second, after the potential champion has been identified, the questions become who will approach him and how best to approach him. One possibility is to find an emissary who has the ear of the potential champion. The emissary also may be someone outside of the organization who is regarded by the potential champion as a respected peer, colleague, or mentor. The emissary must be committed to sharing the power chair with women within his or her own organization, to presenting the business case for the advancement of women, and to furthering the recruitment, retention, and advancement of women.

Once the champion is identified and committed to breaking the glass ceiling, women in the organization must seize the opportunity to help him succeed in meeting his newfound goal by

- Emphasizing the need to have a diversity program that includes women
- Supporting diversity training for all members of the organization, from top management on down
- Changing behavior and practices that are prejudicial to women in order to effectuate institutional changes
- Ensuring that the organization's strategic plans include substantial provisions relating to the hiring, retention, and advancement of women, with concrete programs focused on achieving specific goals
- Insisting on public goals and timetables for the hiring and advancement of women, as well as written policies on nondiscrimination

- Monitoring and measuring progress on realistic goals and time-tables for the advancement of women
- Ensuring that organizational leaders hold all managers account-able by rewarding and publicly recognizing those who meet or exceed the goals within the timetables
- Ensuring that the rewards and recognition are seen as an added bonus, not a penalty
- Ensuring that women are included on influential committees within the organization
- Publicly supporting leaders in their efforts to share the power chair

Many women have succeeded to positions of leadership in this country. Most have had at least one white, male ally—at least one white, male champion willing to support, mentor, and share influence with a woman successor. In this new century, women confronting a glass ceiling must enlist more white, male leaders to help shatter the glass.

NOTES

1. Catalyst, *Catalyst Facts: Women in Business* (2000); and *2000 Census of Women Corporate Officers and Top Earners* (2000).

2. ABA Commission on Women in the Profession, *A Snapshot of Women in the Law in the Year 2000*.

3. Deborah L. Rhode, "The Difference 'Difference' Makes"; "Pro Choice Forces Pick Up Senate House Seats," *WomenNews*, Nov. 9, 2000.

4. I use the term *white men* specifically to make it clear that this is not solely a gender issue. White women and men and women of color generally are not in positions of leadership in this country.

5. Catalyst, *Women in Corporate Leadership: Progress and Prospects* 15, 21 (1996); Deborah Graham, "Second to None: Best Practices for Women Lawyers and Their Employers" (ABA Commission on Women in the Profession, unpublished discussion draft, 2001); Eleanor Clift and Tome Brazaitis, *Madame President: Shattering the Last Glass Ceiling* 321, 324 (2000).

6. Rhode, "The Difference 'Difference' Makes."

18

J E R O M E   J .   S H E S T A C K[1]

What Men Can Give to Women's Quest for Leadership

Leadership is a goal sought by many in the legal profession.[2] The path for would-be leaders in our profession is not a primrose path but an obstacle course beset by daunting questions: Who anointed you? How are you qualified? What do you offer? What are your motives? How does your leadership affect my own ambitions? Why should I support your quest, rather than my own? These are only a few of the challenging questions a would-be leader faces—some expressed openly, some indirectly or by innuendo, some revealed by attitude. A woman's quest for leadership is complicated further by an uneven playing field.

My focus here, however, is not how women lawyers traverse the obstacle course to leadership but what men can do to help them. There is a certain presumption in even undertaking such an assignment, but here it goes.[3]

At the outset, in their quest for leadership in the legal profession, women must demand, and male colleagues must accept, the need for an equal playing field. In the past, women were required to demonstrate qualities far superior to their male contenders to gain leadership positions; when female contenders were merely equal they lost out. In trial phraseology, women had to prove their case not just by a preponderance of the evidence but also by a clear and convincing standard.[4]

Not so very long ago this kind of double standard applied to minorities and still exists for many. For example, for a Jew to be chosen for a high judicial post he had to be a Brandeis or Cardoza, not just a Vinson or Burton. For a black lawyer to be so chosen for the appellate bench he had to be a Hastie or a Marshall, that is, superior to others chosen for the same post. Over the years, the same extraordinary standard applied to women. Women chosen for the judiciary, a law firm's executive committee, or a corporate general counsel had to be far superior to men chosen for similar posts. Adopting the concept of an equal playing field in judging the qualities of leadership requires a mindset that many men simply do not have. Those men must cultivate a mindset that levels the field.

More men must also develop an understanding of and an empathy for the pain women have suffered over the centuries in being subordinate to men. Sensitivity to another's pain is surely critical to human understanding.

There is an old Hasidic tale of two peasants conversing:

The first: My friend, do you love me?
The second: Of course, I love you.
The first: Do you know what gives me pain?
The second: How can I know what gives you pain?
The first: If you don't know what gives me pain, how can you say you love me?

For most of our nation's history, women have suffered from being treated as second-class citizens, a status that carries with it humiliation, devaluation, and unfairness. Understanding that history and its pain helps us appreciate the natural desire for inclusive leadership and the obstacles that have stood in the way.

Justice requires no less. Put plainly, discrimination engenders injustice, while advancing women's leadership is intertwined with rectifying such injustices. A lawyer worthy of the calling should understand the obligation to redress an historic pattern of devaluation and exclusion.[5]

Beyond providing understanding, empathy, and leadership opportunities, men can offer a variety of proactive and practical forms of support. Such support involves more than a removal of resistance to women's ambitions. It requires feeling comfortable with women's issues and goals. And it requires actively mentoring junior women. Cross-gender mentoring is necessary in most legal workplaces, since the number of junior women colleagues substantially exceeds the number of women senior colleagues. Most current mentoring programs fail because they are poorly implemented.

For the upper levels of leadership, encouragement from male colleagues, and particularly male leaders, is vital. We all value the esteem of colleagues, and encouragement is a stimulus to leadership aspirations, particularly within a law firm or corporate counsel department. Leadership is rarely a solo enterprise. To be effective it needs the support of followers and other leaders as well. On all levels, men should be willing, not reluctant, advocates for gender equality in advancement opportunities. Indeed, for both men and women, sharing leadership is in itself a sign of leadership.

A negative attitude is frequently revealed in the differing ways that men describe leadership qualities in males and females. Consider the following characteristics of leadership as men delineate them: A man is described as being (1) aggressive, (2) creative, (3) determined, (4) engaging, and (5) tough. But those same exemplary characteristics in a woman are described as (1) abrasive, (2) tricky, (3) strident, (4) fawning, and (5) bitchy. Such stereotypical characterizations foster a mindset that consciously or subconsciously denigrates women's leadership ability and thwarts their leadership aspirations.[6]

Men must not only reconsider their perceptions of women's capabilities but also reconstruct their own responses and priorities. Unhelpful attitudes include

1. Abdication: I am too busy or too far removed from the problem.
2. Apathy: It's not my concern.
3. Skepticism: It's rare for a woman to be both good at work and good at home. Men are a safer investment.
4. Ego: It is humiliating to lose out to a woman or threatening to be led by a woman.
5. Complacency: Progress has been made in my workplace; the problems are anywhere and everywhere else.

Finally, there is an aspect, which for want of a better term I call *the value-added quality of diversity*.[7] Diverse leadership may provide sensitivities to issues that the white male majority tends to gloss over. For example, in the context of a law firm, women leaders are often perceived as being more nurturing, more supportive, and more empathetic on such issues as putting human considerations above the bottom line; providing adaptable work hours; securing child-care assistance; and recognizing different modes of client development (for example, theater rather than golf invitations). In short, women leaders are especially likely to see the need to improve the quality of life for both sexes.[8] Such aspects of law practice are often given short shrift by male law firm leaders whose focus is largely on service, hours, marketing, and the bottom line.

Whether women in leadership positions follow the same priorities as men is not entirely clear. The evidence is mixed, but there is at least some indication that many women who obtain leadership positions feel an obligation to address issues of social responsibility, particularly those of special concern to women.[9] But regardless of whether women leaders lead differently than men, diversity in leadership is a desirable value. It reflects the face of our nation and it provides a democratic dimension to organizational decision making.

Will women leadership make a beneficial difference in our profession and society? The answer to this question can only be yes.

NOTES

1. Past president of the American Bar Association (1997–98). As chair of the Section of Individual Rights, he initiated the ABA's first Women's Rights Committee in 1969. He chairs the Litigation Department at Wolf, Block, Schorr & Solis-Cohen, LLP.

2. Women's Leadership Summit, Presented by the ABA Office of the President, the ABA Commission on Women in the Profession and the Center for Public Leadership at the John F. Kennedy School of Government, Harvard University, Cambridge, Mass., April 27–28, 2001.

3. My focus is on leadership in the legal profession. Leadership in the larger community, including business and public arenas, involves a myriad of other considerations that these remarks do not attempt to address.

4. There is a fairly widespread assumption among men lawyers, and even among women lawyers, that an equal playing field exists in the profession. But the statistics thus far available demonstrate the error of this assumption. See Deborah L. Rhode, "The Difference 'Difference' Makes."

5. This aspect of understanding also encompasses a moral plane. In Kantian terms, each individual is autonomous so long as the exercise of that autonomy does not interfere with the legitimate rights of another. This element transcends

gender and recognizes the dignity and worth of the individual. Understanding and acceptance of this concept counters parochial and selfish obstacles to women's quest for equality.

6. See Rhode, "The Difference 'Difference' Makes," at notes 27–28, and notes 146–147, for a discussion of traditional stereotypes and other biases.

7. Beyond reasons of history and redress, it is easier for both men and women to support a quest for leadership if the leadership is sought not only for power, or self-gratification, but for transformative purposes—i.e., to achieve good objectives. In short, leadership sharing is more compelling if good ends are seen as the goals of the leadership quests. Professor Deborah L. Rhode's impressive chapter, "The Difference 'Difference' Makes," suggests an underlying premise that women leaders are more likely to focus on issues of social responsibility than are men and thus make a positive or beneficial difference. The premise has considerable anecdotal support.

8. Although quality-of-life issues affect both men and women, women bear the brunt of the hardship from a sweatshop atmosphere.

9. See Rhode, "The Difference 'Difference' Makes," at notes 135–136.

VI

MEETING THE CHALLENGES

19

PATRICIA IRELAND

Progress Versus Equality:
Are We There Yet?

The story of my first job after college is just one of many stories—and we all have them—that reflect how far women have come in the past thirty-some years.

I flew for Pan American Airlines in an era when we were not flight attendants; we were stewardesses. The airline ad campaigns included such classics as Continental's, "We really move our tails for you!" and, one of my favorites, National Airlines', "I'm Cheryl; fly me!" to which some of my colleagues responded by wearing buttons that said, "Fly yourself!"

And yet we didn't even have the words "sexual harassment" to describe the behavior such ads engendered, much less a legal remedy for it. So, believe me, I've seen a lot of progress just in my adult life, and I want us to celebrate that progress. How can we encourage activism without acknowledging and celebrating the reality that when we fight back, we move forward?

However, in this chapter I want to make three important points about progress: progress is not inevitable, progress is not equality, and progress is not irreversible. Along the way, I'd like to highlight some of the tactics used to slow our progress. I'll argue that to continue making progress, we need to examine the nature of power and privilege; and at the risk of be-

ing tagged with some ugly label such as "man-hater" or the formerly popular "Commie pinko," we need to ask, "Who benefits from inequality?"

The most important point is that every one of us has a role to play and
a price to pay in continuing to move forward. I hasten to add that I have
always found the costs to be very low indeed compared to the benefits of
being part of an historic movement that is quite literally changing the
course of history in this country and around the world!

My first point is that progress is not inevitable; it only happens when
individuals and movements give society a big push. Let's start at the beginning of our country and make four stops through history to illustrate
what I mean.

When John Adams was off with the other founding fathers writing the
basic documents for the new nation, as many of us know, Abigail Adams
wrote to her husband that they should, "Remember the ladies." Probably
fewer of us are familiar with John's reply to his beloved wife. He wrote,
"Depend on it. We know better than to dismantle our masculine system"!

Now John may have been teasing Abigail. But humor is often used as
a means to convey hard truths. And the truth is that, right from the beginning, a hierarchy of inequality was built into our system. As women
discovered when we began talking openly about our lives, many of the
problems we thought were personal turned out to be problems that all
(or most) women in our culture faced, all (or most) African Americans
and other people of color faced, and all (or most) people with disabilities
faced. The problems are structural; they are systemic.

Now flash forward to 1848 in Seneca Falls and the first women's rights
conference ever held. When Elizabeth Cady Stanton, one of the six women
who called that meeting, and the other women presented their demands in
the Declaration of Sentiments, most of them were adopted unanimously.
The demand for economic equality ("a purse of her own"), an equal role
in all of the institutions of society, including the family and religion—none
of the demands caused the uproar that resulted from the wholly unrea-
sonable and radical notion that women should have the right to vote.

The very idea was so outrageous that Elizabeth's husband, Henry Stanton, good liberal and abolitionist though he was, nevertheless left town the
day the conference started rather than stay to be embarrassed when his
wife made such a ridiculous demand. The plank calling for women's suf-

frage might not have passed at all had it not been for the impassioned advocacy of former slave, abolitionist, and suffragist Frederick Douglass.

The newspapers had a field day. They called the women "unnatural," "mannish," "spinsters." (I guess that was as close as they could come to calling them "sapphists," the then-current term for lesbians.) The attacks were so ferocious that some who had signed the Declaration of Sentiments withdrew their names.

Now let's move to the campaign for ratification of the Equal Rights Amendment from 1972 through 1982. When the time ran out, thirty-five states had ratified the amendment, three less than required for it to become part of the United States Constitution. Still, the National Organization for Women's ERA Countdown Campaign and other efforts to ratify the ERA gave a huge boost to women's leadership.

For ten years, we had a public dialogue in this country about what equal rights for women would mean and how far we were from equality. By the end of the campaign, the majority of people in the United States supported a constitutional guarantee of equality of rights under the law regardless of sex. Supporters of the ERA included a majority of women across a broad spectrum of race, religion, age, and economic, marital and parental status. Even among homemakers, the women that anti-ERA spokesperson Phyllis Schlafly purported to champion, a majority agreed with the Equal Rights Amendment.

Many women cut their political teeth campaigning for the ERA. They had learned how to organize politically; they became skilled in community organizing, public speaking, fund raising, door-to-door and telephone canvassing, voter registration, media outreach, and more. By the end of the ERA campaign, women had, for the first time since suffrage, a nationwide network of experienced, effective activists. And they were angry.

Despite winning the majority of public opinion, they had not been able to win the final three of the necessary thirty-eight state legislatures. Neither the legislatures nor the Congress had been redistricted in nearly ten years to reflect shifts in population, legislatures in unratified states were disproportionately dominated by conservative, rural members, and Congress had set the deadline for ratification as June 30, 1982, which preceded the first post-reapportionment-redistricting elections in a decade. Many supporters had gone to their state capitols to advocate for the ERA and, often for the first time, had met their legislators. They had looked at those guys and realized, "I could do that job. In fact, I could do that job a whole lot better!"

The next steps became clear when NOW analyzed the fifteen state legislatures that had refused to ratify the ERA: more than half of the white men opposed the ERA, while nearly two-thirds of the women and practically all of the African American legislators favored it.[1] There simply were not enough women in elective office. NOW and other women's rights groups vowed to change that. And change it we did, recruiting unprecedented numbers of women to run for state and local office, getting them elected and laying the groundwork for the breakthrough at the federal level in 1992, the so-called Year of the Woman, after the next post-census redistricting helped open the field once again for nonincumbents.

The news media coined the phrase "Year of the Woman" as though we would be satisfied with one year and one woman! But if I did have to pick just one woman from the 1992 elections, my choice would be Carrie Meek from Miami. We had worked together when she was a pro-ERA state legislator, and I was proud to support her campaign for Congress. Carrie Meek is the granddaughter of slaves. Her parents were sharecroppers, working someone else's land in order to feed their family. Carrie and her sister both had jobs as so-called "domestics," cleaning other people's houses so their family could have a home. Now Carrie Meek sits in the United States House of Representatives. And you can be sure that she has a different reaction from someone born with a silver spoon in his mouth when a proposal comes up to cut public health or public education.

The life experiences of Representative Carrie Meek and other women we get elected in 1992 mean that as a rule, they have priorities different from those of the men who have traditionally held office. That is, of course, a gross generalization, subject to the same exceptions as any generalization. In a given race, the male candidate may be better than the female on feminist issues, and in such cases NOW's Political Action Committee has endorsed and will continue to support the better feminist. But if I had to choose in the dark, knowing nothing else about the candidates, I would play the odds and fill the Congress fifty-fifty with women and men.

With this history and experience in mind, it is not a surprise to read in Professor Deborah L. Rhode's excellent chapter that in contrast to women in leadership in other institutions, women in government have made a difference through the substance and style of their leadership. For some twenty years, the feminist movement has been recruiting women to run for election and appointment to office based on those very differences, seeking out and supporting women who support public health and education; abortion and other reproductive rights; antidiscrimination, antipoverty and antiviolence programs; and equality for women.

I mention appointed office, because the 1992 elections were followed by a concerted campaign by NOW and others to move more women into positions of policymaking and power in the new president's administration. The ultimately successful efforts by President Clinton to keep his campaign pledge to appoint the first woman ever to serve as United States attorney general are illustrative of some of the barriers that still work against women's progress.

The president initially named Zoë Baird as his choice for attorney general. During her confirmation hearing, as senators asked questions about how many hours she worked and who took care of her young son, I fumed, "If her name were *Joey* instead of *Zoë*, they'd never even think of such questions." And it was true. After Baird's nomination was withdrawn, we learned that at least two men had been confirmed to cabinet-level positions who, like Baird, had employed undocumented household help and failed to pay Social Security taxes for these workers. They laid the blame on their wives who, of course, had responsibility for running the household.

The president next named Kimba Wood, but she never had a hearing and was gone before most people had learned that she did not have an "s" at the end of her last name. Wood also had hired undocumented workers, although it was not illegal to do so at the time. Apparently she was supposed to use her woman's intuition to anticipate that the law would be changed and comply in advance.

After Wood's nomination was withdrawn, I started saying in interviews and speeches that if Clinton were going to keep his campaign promise, the new attorney general would have to be a childless woman with a dirty house. And sure enough, along came Janet Reno, a woman with no children and a self-confessed bad housekeeper. But no sooner had Washington wags breathed a sigh of relief that she would not have what the media had dubbed a "nanny-gate problem," than tongues started wagging again.

"Oh, a woman in her fifties, never been married, no kids? Must be queer!" Just that quickly the discussion veered away from her qualifications to whom she loved.

Reno, an experienced campaigner, came up with the perfect political answer: "I'm an awkward old maid with a great affection for men." Delivering her nondefensive non-answer with just the hint of a self-effacing smile, she effectively turned the focus back to whether she was tough enough, smart enough, and had the integrity to handle the job for which she had been nominated. And from my point of view, she turned out to be.

It certainly is progress to have the first woman attorney general; however, as this sequence of events illustrates, progress is not the same thing as equality. For women's efforts to move into leadership are still hindered by women continuing to bear primary responsibility for our families' well-being and by very personal attacks, often implicating our sexuality. And although we cheered the 1992 election that tripled the number of women in the Senate, that was simply a more encouraging way of saying we had moved from two to six out of a hundred! Today, women senators number thirteen.

Clinton's election not only brought us a record number of women in the Cabinet, but also the spectacle of an impeachment and Senate trial of the President. I remember seeing Cheryl Mills, from the White House counsel's office, on television and thinking as this strong African American woman lawyer argued passionately and persuasively to the United States Senate not to overturn the presidential election, "Now there's a measure of how far we have come!" But then I looked at the senators to whom she made her argument and thought, "And there's a measure of how far we have to go!" The United States Senate is 87 percent male, 98 percent white, and, I would venture a guess, about 100 percent rich. Daniel Inouye and Daniel Akaka of Hawaii, and Ben Nighthorse Campbell of Colorado keep the Senate from being totally white. We have no African American senators. It is hardly a representative body.

Also, progress is not irreversible. In 2002 we have fewer women in state legislatures than before. The wage gap between women and men has widened. During the Equal Rights Amendment campaign, we wore 59 cent buttons, representing the median annual wage of women for every dollar paid to men. That number came up to nearly 75 cents in 1997, and although I still wanted for my last quarter, the progress was gratifying.

But by 1999 the direction had reversed and women were down to less than 73 cents on the dollar.[2]

A more dramatic example can be seen in Afghanistan, where women had participated in the life and work of their country in important ways. Women accounted for 40 percent of the physicians in Kabul, 50 percent of the students and 60 percent of the teachers at Kabul University, 70 percent of the teachers overall, and 50 percent of the civilian government workers.[3] With the ascendancy of the Taliban militia into government power, women were pushed back in terrible ways. Under the Taliban, women were thrown out of the workforce and schools. Access to health care for women was essentially nonexistent, as male doctors were not allowed to fully examine female patients and female doctors were not allowed to practice. Women could not leave their homes except while wearing a burqua that had to cover them from head to toe, with only a thick mesh through which to breathe and see, and even then they had to be accompanied by a close male relative. With so many men having been killed in the decades of war in Afghanistan, women often had no way to support their families and were virtual prisoners in their homes.

To continue making progress for women and women's leadership, it is helpful to examine the nature of privilege and power and ask who benefits when women are excluded or face discrimination. Individuals and institutions often think, consciously or unconsciously, that discrimination is to their advantage. Surely it must have been easier for a man who wanted to be a lawyer, neurosurgeon, welder, or factory worker when he could wipe out more than half the population because he would never have to compete with women for those jobs. I think the cadets at the Virginia Military Institute and the Citadel opposed admission of women to those state-sponsored schools because they knew at some level what would happen: with women allowed into the competition, students would have to have higher grade point averages and Scholastic Aptitude Test scores to get in, and if admitted, would have to work harder to excel.

Similarly, sexual harassment is used as a weapon to keep women from competing on an equal basis for higher-paying jobs previously reserved for men. For example, in a town ironically named Normal, Illinois, jobs in the Mitsubishi manufacturing plant were prized union jobs with good benefits and pay and some measure of job security. Some of the men in the plant were extremely uncomfortable with even a small percentage of women workers. Their sexual harassment of the women served two purposes. It put the relationship back into a context in which the men were more comfortable, a sexualized context in which, since the Garden of Eden, men have been dominant and women have taken the blame. The harassment also put such strains on the women that they could not do their best work. They suffered stress-related illnesses and related absenteeism, and could not concentrate on the job, because they were always worrying about when the next verbal or physical assault would come.

Having said that, I may surprise some of you when I state that feminism's success does not require most men to give up power. Most men have not had power. For some two hundred years in our country, power was held in a very narrow range of hands. They were hands that looked very much like those of John Adams, the hands of rich, white, able-bodied, and apparently straight men. And the further you are from those parameters, the less likely you are to have power, even today.

But if most men do not have power, they do have privilege that comes from being male, just as I am privileged by my white skin. Although I do not want that privilege and I work against racism, I will never, for example, be arrested for the crime of driving-while-black, even in New Jersey. Similarly, men benefit from an assumption that they possess certain desirable leadership qualities, such as decisiveness. Although the trend continues in a positive direction, polls asking voters about supporting a woman for president of the United States still reflect this and other assumptions that favor men.

Institutions may also see a benefit to themselves from discrimination. Employers may think it is advantageous to maintain a level of insecurity and mistrust among their employees, viewing this as a way to keep employees from taking collective action and making demands for better pay or working conditions. The insurance lobby was prominent in the fight against the Equal Rights Amendment, despite its efforts to hide behind Phyllis Schlafly's skirts. With its pricing and benefit structure subject to government regulation, the insurance industry did not want to face a requirement of equal treatment of women and men. Current pricing reflects widespread discrimination against women. For example, the oft-cited break the industry gives on young women's auto insurance rates ignores the reality that women have better driving records our whole lives and are unfairly charged after our early years.

Part of the strategy for moving forward for women must be to reframe the discussion and the information. For individual men, the emphasis can be moved productively to a focus on the economic welfare of their families as a whole. In most families these days, every adult, and often the children as well, must be in the waged workforce in order to pay for health care, housing, and higher education. In California a number of years ago, I ran into one of my favorite groups, Angry White Guys *for* Affirmative Action. These were men who clearly had figured out that if their wives, mothers, daughters, and sisters had equal opportunity and access to better positions, their families would have greater economic stability.

With employers, an appeal to the bottom line can be effective. Discrimination and harassment are, in fact, bad business. Absenteeism and turnover are expensive, as is the low morale and lost productivity of a workforce in conflict and workers who feel unfairly treated. And with the prospect of trials by jury and both compensatory and punitive damages in discrimination cases, failure to comply with equal opportunity laws also has the potential to eat into profits. Although the reasons are somewhat speculative, the data indicate that companies with more women on their boards of directors have also been more profitable.

Another shift in our culture that will benefit women's leadership is to increase recognition of the value of women's traditional work in the family. As the White House and the Congress examine the Social Security system, NOW and dozens of other women's advocates are arguing that workers who take time out from the waged workforce to care for their families should be given a credit, rather than have zeros averaged into their wage records, for purposes of determining their Social Security retirement benefits. To the extent that we move beyond lip service to give concrete financial compensation for this work, we are more likely to credit those who perform it with talents and traits of character that are also important for leadership outside the family.

All of us have a role to play in continuing to advance women's leadership and contributions to our society. Some will work from the inside of the institutions that shape our culture; others will push from the outside. Some will figuratively—or in some cases literally—kick open the doors of opportunity, knowing that more moderate women will then walk through and, we can hope, will serve as role models and mentors and create change from within.

I want us to respect the various roles necessary to make change and the women and men who play those roles. None of us should be so arrogant as to imagine that she has the ultimate or only strategy in order to bring to bear on society's problems the full talents and commitment of women as leaders. Each of us must find her own style and place, but each of us must be willing to step outside her circle of comfort to continue making progress. Creating change, even positive change, makes people uncomfortable. But stretching ourselves is how we grow, individually and as a society.

And so, I urge each of us to take the next step to move forward, whatever it is for us, in whatever way suits us best at this point in our lives. I know that if we do, just as we began the twentieth century by winning the right to vote, women can begin the twenty-first century by taking full and equal leadership.

NOTES

1. *National NOW Times* (1982).

2. U.S. Census Bureau, Table P-38, Full-Time, Year-Round Workers (All Races) by Median Earnings and Sex: 1960 to 2000.

3. Feminist Majority Foundation, "The Taliban and Afghan Women: Background" [www.feminist.org/afghan/facts.html].

20

JUDITH RESNIK

Women, Meeting (Again), in and Beyond the United States

The basic message of this book is that the project of women's equality is far from complete. Despite having been to many meetings and conferences and despite having written or read many books on women and leadership, those dedicated to equality need to go to yet other meetings, lobby yet again, organize more, and to do so more collectively, and write yet more pamphlets, position papers, and books. Such activities must simultaneously acknowledge the real gains over the past few decades and detail the work required to achieve deeper and more substantive forms of change.

By way of introduction to this volume, Deborah L. Rhode probed the question of what difference "difference" does—and does not—make to the project of substantive equality of women and men of all colors. By way of conclusion, I consider the difference that meetings have in fact made, and I suggest some of the topics that the current and the coming sets of meetings, conferences, and books need to address.[1]

Over hundreds of years and with particular intensity in the nineteenth and twentieth centuries, women came together to create or continue organizations aimed at making new rights for women and all persons.[2] A powerful example comes from the year 1840, during which women from North America traveled to a first-ever conference, the World Anti-Slavery

Conference, held in London and organized by the British Foreign Anti-Slavery Association.[3] Although antislavery organizations in Britain were sex segregated, not all of those in the United States were. Thus, women were among the delegates sent from the states.[4] But they were not seated. Rather, the all-male World Anti-Slavery Conference debated the question of admitting the women delegates from the United States and then voted them out.[5]

Although women were prevented from serving as delegates, their work could not be excluded. Indeed, that 1840 conference was built on efforts of women and men, working on both sides of the Atlantic, and in Calcutta, Sierra Leone, and the Cape of Good Hope. During the 1820s and 1830s, around the world, women had actively campaigned against slavery. Some of those women's groups were independent organizations standing on their own, such as The Female Society of Birmingham, England. Others were "auxiliary" institutions, women's wings of men's associations.

These women accomplished an astonishing amount. They launched a campaign against using sugar that had been grown by slaves. "Abstain!" was their banner, as they urged other women not to buy or use sugar in their households. In addition to waging abstention campaigns (today termed boycotts), women wrote pamphlets and held fairs to disseminate information about the injuries caused by slavery.[6] And they petitioned Parliament. In fact more than 187,000 women signed their names to a petition, filed in 1833, calling for the abolition of slavery.[7] Some historians point to this protest as the first public presence in English history of women as a group speaking out as a group.[8] (Commentary by queens does not count, for this purpose.) Parliament responded in 1833 by banning slavery in the British Empire.[9]

From the perspective of those in the United States, something else important happened in London in 1840 when the men rejected women as delegates to the World Anti-Slavery Conference. Lucretia Mott, a delegate from Pennsylvania, and Elizabeth Cady Stanton, a delegate from Massachusetts, met for the first time in London. In their exclusion from that meeting, they understood that they had something in common as women. As Mott explained in her diary, there "[we] resolved to hold a convention as soon as we returned home, and form a society to advocate the rights of women."[10] That conference took place eight years later, in 1848. It is called Seneca Falls, and as is familiar, it stands as a marker of the beginning of the United States women's rights movement, with Mott and Stanton among its leaders.[11]

Consider the themes running through the antislavery and women's equality work as it developed during the nineteenth century:

- Women held meetings because they were concerned about subjugation and inequality.
- At those meetings, contacts and connections were made, as women found common ground both within localities and across the nation-states.
- At some meetings, women were excluded, so they decided to hold meetings of their own.
- Through such meetings, women made serious efforts to alter power relationships.
- And they did so by seeking to change laws and practices, both within their own townships and around the world.

This pattern of interactions has been reiterated in hundreds of other settings and about a diverse set of problems over many decades and on many continents. Time and again, women created institutions, societies, clubs, caucuses, and associations. Some were auxiliaries of men's organizations, and some were independent. Many were race segregated, and a few were interracial.[12] Some were service organizations, some fellowships or religiously based, some expressly devoted to advocacy. Sometimes their focus was friendship, sometimes the goal was specifically to make spaces for women's rights, and in other instances the shared work stemmed from efforts to alter the shape and understanding of human rights more generally. Today, we rely on many of the same methods. We, too, form connections and groups around exclusion and use a host of methods, law included, to try to change power relationships and lessen inequality.

The list of the many international and transnational organizations of women is long.[13] We share some shorthand by which to refer to these events. At times, we use the name of the organization, such as the Women's International League for Peace and Freedom. Sometimes, we talk about the places at which the meetings occurred—Mexico City, Nairobi, Copenhagen, Vienna, Beijing—locales now famous for marking the United Nations' efforts related to women's and human rights. And sometimes, the names of the meetings and even of the associations get lost, but their products do not.

I think we should understand such women's groups as constituting the original "NGOs"—nongovernmental organizations, existing outside of governments but aimed at changing policies and practices of governance.[14] NGOs are much in focus in American literature on transnational human rights work, which tends to put their beginnings in the early 1960s by citing some of the great international human rights organizations.[15] With respect, women were doing and being NGOs long before that name became popular in the development literature and long before questions emerged about their status, relationship to governance, and effects. Women's NGOs have an ironic history. We were nongovernmental in the deepest sense, in that governments would not have us. Until all too recently, women could not vote, could not run for office, could not become lawyers, could not be in the military, could not serve as jurors, could not contract, could not hold property. We had no juridical voice. But we nevertheless *voiced* our views through the means then available to us—by getting together in religious groups, sewing groups, or other voluntary associations. And when those associations would not have us, we made up our own.

From my own discipline of law come several examples. In 1886, a handful of women formed the Equity Club, the first national organization of women lawyers in the United States.[16] Although that organization lasted only a short time, another, the National Association of Women Lawyers, was formed in 1899 and continues today as a part of the National Conference of Women's Bar Associations.[17] Almost a century later, in 1979, a group of women judges created the National Association of Women Judges,[18] which in turn has also helped support the International Association of Women Judges. And such organizations have also helped spawn dozens of other organizations, such that women's bar associations, women's law student associations, women's caucuses, and their journals are now common features of the landscape. Solidarity has always been one goal; sisterhood and companionship are others. We enjoy each others' friendships. And we need to learn from each other how to cope, given male domination of so many institutions in which we work. But as soon as the numbers are enough, the focus enlarges beyond the problem of how to manage within a world run by men to the question of how to change the ways in which the world is run.

This book and the conference that generated it depend on that insight. The authors hope that their commentary will prompt and support others, continuing to shape political change. To do so, we need to appreciate the women of the nineteenth and twentieth century, many of whom encountered substantial hostility, barred from participation in a host of endeavors not only by men, but also sometimes by women of different colors, classes, or ethnicities. Thus, I invoke their efforts in this volume as one of many means of acknowledging their contributions.

But just as we need to remember their struggles, we must also neither blindly emulate nor romanticize them. The quick rendition just provided does not detail the internal debates and disputes between and among early feminists. For example, some from North America thought that their English counterparts had not pressed hard enough for women's entry into the World Anti-Slavery Conference,[19] and, as is familiar, efforts to abolish slavery were undertaken by groups and individuals who had profound differences about how to proceed.[20] Moreover, the names of leaders readily accessible to many contemporary readers are often those of white women, whereas fuller narratives would include a wider range of individuals. Our attention should not only be turned to Lucretia Mott and Elizabeth Cady Stanton but also to many others, such as Sojourner Truth,[21] Sarah and Caroline Remond,[22] Mary Ann Shadd Cary,[23] and Harriet Jacobs,[24] as we acknowledge how certain meetings excluded women of diverse classes and colors and selected certain issues for attention and ignored others.[25] Further, having skimmed a rich literature, I have invoked images of many women's organizations without elaborating how they differed in terms of their focus, function, form, and scale. Also, a good deal of this literature has, thus far, been framed through knowledge of activism in the United States and Great Britain rather than by exploring a wider set of interactions across more continents.[26]

While I have thus far emphasized the continuity of the project over time, in some respects the contemporary work about women's leadership is discontinuous from that which preceded and enabled it. The very exclusions of Mott, Stanton, the Remond sisters, Cary, Truth, and Jacobs from specific circles of power prompted them to shape others. Leaders of those generations thereby gained a peculiar form of advantage: focus. Unable to be a part of government, banned from attending certain meetings, prohibited from access to a range of organizations, those women had both fewer meetings to attend and clarity about which barriers needed breaking. In contrast, women leaders today have achieved access to some circles of power. As a consequence, they have many more meetings in which they have to participate. Moreover, they are at risk of being confused by their own enjoyment of certain forms of power. Further, they may themselves be used to engender misperceptions about the kind of work yet to be done. The women who have "made it" are often held up as exemplary of the fact that the "problem of women" no longer exists.[27] And finally, with the very wealth of organizations invoking "women" comes the risk of diffusion and competition for self-importance.

The challenge for leaders today who are concerned about equality is how to be in (and to enjoy the access to) places of power, while understanding that their privilege is not as widely shared as it ought to be. To do so, such leaders need, in essence, to be in many places at once: inside circles of obvious authority and yet also in the many circles (also authoritative in other senses of the word) that have been formed by those still excluded from certain places of leadership.[28] Further, when inhabiting the plainly powerful institutions, women need to develop means to prevent their presence from being (mis)used as evidence that all the problems of women have been redressed. As vivid barriers fall, the willingness of many to attend to remaining forms of inequality has waned. The pull toward assuming the quality of the status quo, particularly in the United States, has proven strong.

If the access gained during the intervening decades distinguishes some of today's women leaders from their many grandmothers, the problems faced are, however, familiar. Perhaps most painfully, even the most horrific symbols of the nineteenth century remain in the twenty-first. Return to the 1840 World Anti-Slavery Conference and recall that its goal was to abolish the hideous practices of slavery. Yet more than 160 years later, our goals must also include the very same aspiration—the abolition of practices, many of them routed in colonialism, some, sadly enough, still accurately described as *slavery*.

It may seem odd—in a volume dedicated to women as leaders—to end by insisting on the centrality of the contemporary problem of slavery. Indeed, it *ought* to seem odd that such a focus is demanded in the beginning of the twenty-first century. Yet as newspaper headlines periodically remind us, slavery has not been abolished. Sometimes the reference is to children, transported in slavery from one country to another.[29] But at other times, the word is connected to women. For example, in the winter of 2001, the problem of slavery was linked specifically to women, as press headlines announced the conviction of individuals at the United Nation's International Criminal Court for the Former Territories of Yugoslavia.[30] As the *New York Times* put it, in February 2001, a decision from that Court was the "first international judgment to condemn sexual slavery" as a crime against humanity.[31] Its relevance to the topic of women's leadership is revealed by considering who held the power of judgment and by the terrible facts of the case. The decision for the three-judge court was given by the presiding judge—Judge Florence Mumba, of Zambia, joined by Judges David Hunt and Fausto Pocar. The lengthy opinion detailed how rape was used "as an instrument of terror." As the prosecutor, Peggy Kuo, from the United Nation's team at the Hague explained, "the judgment makes clear that slavery means not only slave labor but that it can also be sexual slavery."[32]

Thus, a woman prosecutor, on behalf of the United Nations, presented evidence to a three-judge tribunal about war crimes against women. Another woman served as the presiding judge, and three perpetrators have now been called to account.[33] That historic trial developed out of meetings, and specifically, a several-decades-long effort to bring attention to female sexual enslavement.[34] Women leaders invoked the word "slavery" to underscore the gravity of the harms—physical, economic, social, and legal—that contributed both to mistreatment and toleration of mistreatment of women. Through meetings, women helped to shape a series of initiatives at the United Nations that have changed the formal rules of war, if not yet the actual practices.[35] Through examples such as the judgment that holds that sexual slavery can be a crime against humanity, it becomes clear that women have not only gained recognition as rights holders. Women have changed the meaning of what counts as rights, of what wrongs law must address.

And war is but one of many templates in which, through women's leadership, efforts are under way to alter both formal legal regimes and daily practices. Across a vast spectrum of human activity, experimentation is going on to unleash a wide and creative range of remedial strategies.[36] For an audience of readers in the United States, it is important to underscore how much innovation is occurring beyond this country's shores. For example, more than a dozen countries are experimenting with "democratic parity," mandating that women hold certain percentages of elected or appointed offices.[37] Other innovations come from the intersection of household work, wage labor, and unpaid labor. A few countries have developed rules termed "daddy quotas," laws that provide benefits on the birth or adoption of a child but withhold some of the payments if both parents do not take time with the new child.[38] Such efforts have begun to unravel positions of privilege and to shift understandings of what equality entails.

The judgment on sexual slavery trials offers special instruction for those concerned about women and leadership. The existence of that judgment results from women leaders, who for the first time hold the power to make laws. Women prosecutors, legislators, judges, activists, and investigators created the space in which women besieged by violence could articulate claims of wrongdoing and call perpetrators to account. That is a stunning achievement, and it is a rapid achievement. One hundred sixty years ago, women were shut out of the World Anti-Slavery Conference and forbidden to speak as public delegates. Today, women *preside* in courtrooms, as well as in law offices and law classrooms, around the world.

But that judgment also points to another task facing contemporary women leaders. Today, as it was 160 years ago, women remain the recipients of brutal and demeaning attacks such as those that gave rise to the Hague verdict. It is hard to read the horrid details that form the basis of that judgment; described there are acts that ought to be unimaginable but that in fact haunted the lives of young women for many months. Moreover, those events are unique in neither time nor place. With variations, they are repeated not only in venues of war but also in homes and on streets, in countries throughout the world—this one included.

Thus, a volume on women and leadership in the twenty-first century must encompass multiple aspects of contemporary women's roles. Some now have the luxury of speaking from places of obvious power. Yet women of all classes and colors continue to be subjected to persistent harms visited upon them because they are women. The challenge is to understand and to enjoy the changes that enable women to speak from positions of authority while simultaneously retaining an acute awareness that not all women and not all peoples enjoy such opportunities. Far worse, many women remain excluded, sometimes silenced, beaten, raped, and harmed, sometimes unpaid for their work in their households, or underpaid for their participation in the wage labor force, or undervalued for their contributions in a host of places. Women with privilege and with some power must seek to sustain both a celebratory posture (complete with moments of genuine exhilaration) and a deep sense of distress (founded on a painful consciousness of so much more work to be done). Further, women with certain forms of power must also be respectful of women who lack those trappings and careful not to presume to know more than they do and to speak "for" others.

How are women in roles of leadership, who occupy positions of authority, who hold titles and enjoy access, to keep their awareness of the narrowness of those places of power and of their own perspectives? Return then to the central questions of this volume, about the difference that difference can (but need not necessarily) make, and to my inquiry about the role of meetings and associations. Why, given the many places one can now be, do women nevertheless continue to need to attend women-centered meetings? These meetings are to remind us to be different and to make a difference in other persons' lives.

Here the 1840 World Anti-Slavery Conference offers yet one further lesson. Although women who are not slaves and not specifically subjugated because of race have sometimes used the term *slavery* to understand their own conditions, many of the women who fought against slavery did not understand themselves to be enslaved. But they knew that others were and that they were obliged to try to intervene. Today, as then, in deciding about which meetings to attend and which projects to embrace, one has to consider not only one's own problems but also those of others. Further, such meetings need to be populated by individuals wary of assuming their own ability to know all facets of subordination and aware that the nomenclature women and the deployment of the proposition "we" can often be simplistic. While appropriate in some moments to share rhetoric space through use of the category "women," it has proven insufficient to the task of crafting complex social policies aimed at remediating deeply rooted inequality. Through watching women leaders, it is plain that not all align themselves with women in either the most general sense or, more important, attend to the diversity of problems with which a range of women struggle. Further, as histories of the antislavery efforts illuminate, the mechanisms for inequality rely on a complex interaction among gender, race, class, sexual orientation, and age. To seek "women-centered" policies then and now requires an elaboration of how which women can enjoy what forms of opportunity.

What are leaders committed to movements toward equality to do today? If, for every meeting with those acknowledged holders of formal power, leaders also attend meetings with others not in those inner circles, such leaders might indeed bring different content to the power of meetings and the purposes to which such power should be put.

NOTES

1. This is also the occasion on which to proffer a collective note of appreciation for the leadership that produced the meeting and subsequently this volume. Thanks are due specifically to Martha Barnett, Barbara Kellerman, Deborah L. Rhode, and Kim Youngblood, and to the staffs of the ABA, its Commission on Women, and the Kennedy School, for creating a two-day gathering of women and men focused on understanding the import of women's recent emergence (in still small numbers) as leaders in the United States, and for bringing this book to fruition. And for help in shaping this chapter, thanks are owed to Kate Andrias, Elizabeth Brundige, Joshua Civin, Reema El-Amamy, Deborah Martinez, Cori Van Noy, and Laura Viscomi, who also make plain that new and generative leaders abound.

2. Several histories are instructive, some focused on collective efforts, others on individuals, and still others on particular aspects of social policy. See, e.g., Christine Bold, *The Women's Movement in the United States and Britain from the 1970s to the 1920s* (1993); Nancy Cott, *The Grounding of Modern Feminism* (1987); Nell Painter, *Sojourner Truth: A Life, A Symbol* (1996); Theda Skocpol, *Protecting Soldiers and Mothers: The Political Origins of Social Policy in the United States* (1992).

3. My discussion of that conference is drawn primarily from the following sources: Clare Midgley, *Women Against Slavery: The British Champions, 1780–1870* (1992); and from Kathryn Kish Sklar, "Women Who Speak for the Entire Nation: American and British Women at the World Anti-Slavery Convention, London, 1840," in *The Abolitionist Sisterhood* (Jean Fagan Yellin and John C. Van Horne, eds. 1994). See also Clare Taylor, *British and American Abolitionists: An Episode in Transatlantic Understanding* (1974); Betty Fladeland, *Men and Brothers, Anglo-American Anti Slavery Cooperation* (1972); Margaret H. McFadden, *Golden Cables of Sympathy: Transatlantic Sources of Nineteenth Century Feminism* (1999).

4. Sklar, "Women Who Speak for the Entire Nation," at 308. Women also had their own conventions in the United States; for example, Lucretia Mott

presided at the 1837 Anti-Slavery Convention of American Women. Id., at 307. The admission of women to some antislavery societies was a source of controversy. Taylor, *British and American Abolitionists*, at 13 (describing the breaking apart of the American Anti-Slavery Society, in part over this issue).

5. Sklar, "Women Who Speak for the Entire Nation," at 308–12; Midgley, *Women Against Slavery*, at 158–161.

6. See *An Appeal to the Hearts and Consciences of British Women*, published in 1828 by Elizabeth Heyrick, considered one of the foremost antislavery pamphleteers. See Midgley, *Women Against Slavery*, at 58, 750. Heyrick is credited with writing the pamphlet *Immediate, Not Gradual Abolition; or, An Inquiry into the Shortest, Safest, and Most Effective Means of Getting Rid of West Indian Slavery*, which, published in 1824, was the first to call for immediate abolition and served as an inspiration for William Lloyd Garrison's subsequent abolition campaign as well as for campaigns by women abolitionists in the United States and Great Britain. See McFadden, *Golden Cables of Sympathy*, at 109–110; Sklar, "Women Who Speak for the Entire Nation," at 322–23; Fladeland, *Men and Brothers*, at 178, 181.

7. The practice of petitioning remained important in both Great Britain and the United States. Women participated in many petition drives, including the 1838 effort seeking to end the apprenticeship system. For discussion of more recent petitions filed in the 1990s at the UN Conference on Human Rights, see Wendy Schoener, "Non-Governmental Organizations and Global Activism: Legal and Informal Approaches," 4 *Indiana J. Global L. Studies* 537, 560 (1997).

8. An earlier example may have been efforts against sati. See Joshua Civin, "Slaves, Sati, and Sugar: Constructing Imperial Identity through Liverpool Petition Struggles," in *Parliaments, Nations and Identities in Britain 660–1850* (Julian Hoppit, ed. 2002).

9. The Act provided that all slaves under the age of six were to be freed immediately; those older were to be partially freed over a period of four years and paid wages for a quarter of their work undertaken as "free." The government gave compensation to slave owners for such a loss of their property. See Fladeland, *Men and Brothers*, at 206. See, generally, David Brion Davis, *The Problem of Slavery in Western Culture* (1966).

10. See Sklar, "Women Who Speak for the Entire Nation," at 302 (quoting Mott).

11. Of course, histories of feminism are more complex and the roots of the efforts in the United States more variegated than only this strand. See, generally, Suzanne M. Marilley, *Women Suffrage and the Origins of Liberal Feminism in the United States, 1820–1920* (1996); Nancy A. Hewitt, *Women's Activism and Social Change: Rochester, New York, 1822–1872* (1984); Barbara Berg, *The Remembered Gate: Origins of American Feminism* (1978).

12. See Carolyn Williams, "The Female Anti-Slavery Movement: Fighting Against Racial Prejudice and Promoting Women's Rights in Antebellum America," in *The Abolitionist Sisterhood*, at 159, 164–167.

13. See Leila J. Ruff, *Worlds of Women: The Making of an International Women's Movement* (1997) (providing an analysis of the development of the International Council of Women, the International Alliance of Women, and the Women's International League for Peace and Freedom).

14. See Nitza Berkovitch, "The Emergence and Transformation of the International Women's Movement," in *Constructing World Culture: International Nongovernmental Organizations Since 1875* (John Boli and George M. Thomas, eds. 1999); Jane Connors, "NGOs and the Human Rights of Women at the United Nations," in *The Conscience of the World: The Influence of Non-Governmental Organizations in the UN System* 147 (Peter Willets, ed. 1996).

15. See, e.g., Michael H. Posner and Candy Whittome, "The Status of Human Rights NGOs," 25 *Colum. Hum. Rts. L. Rev.* 269, 270 (1994).

16. See Virginia G. Drachman, *Women Lawyers and the Origins of Professional Identity in America: The Letters of the Equity Club, 1887–1890* 1 (1993). According to Drachman, several women began the club, which lasted four years and included thirty-two members, several of whom were European. See also Karen Berger Morello, *The Invisible Bar* 54–55 (1986).

17. See National Conference of Women's Bar Associations, [www.ncwba.org/History.html].

18. See Gladys Kessler, "Foreword to the Symposium Issue: The National Association of Women Judges," 14 *Golden Gate L. Rev.* 473 (1984) (describing the meeting, with about a hundred women from around the country).

19. Sklar, "Women Who Speak for the Entire Nation," at 314–315; Midgley, *Women Against Slavery*, at 161.

20. See Taylor, *British and American Abolitionists*, at 2 (describing bitter disputes, in which the factions "agreed upon only one thing—that slavery was a sin and should be abolished.")

21. See Painter, *Sojourner Truth*, at 114–115 (detailing Truth's work at a number of antislavery meetings, including those held in Massachusetts, New York, and Rhode Island, and her work, along with Mott, at the women's rights meeting held in Worcester, Massachusetts, in 1850).

22. McFadden, *Golden Cables of Sympathy*, at 112–113 (describing Sarah Remond's work, as a "free person of color" in Massachusetts, her travels to Britain for an antislavery lecture tour, and the controversy—played out in the press and in Parliament—prompted by a passenger ship's refusal to serve Caroline Remond Putnam).

23. Id., at 113 (discussing her publication in 1852 of *A Plea for Emigration; or, Notes of Canada West, in its Moral, Social and Political Aspect.*)

24. See Harriet A. Jacobs, *Incidents in the Life of a Slave Girl: Written by Herself* (Jean Fagan Yellin, ed. 1987); Anne Goodwyn Jones, "Engendered in the South: Blood and Irony in Douglass and Jacobs," in *Liberating Sojourn: Frederick Douglas & Transatlantic Reform* 93–111 (Alan J. Rice and Martin Crawfords, eds. 1999).

25. For example, as Jean Fagan Yellin explains in her introduction to the Jacobs volume, *Incidents in the Life of a Slave Girl*, at xiv–xxi, Jacobs broke ground by presenting sexual oppression (id., at 53–57) as an aspect of slavery.

26. See *Gender, Sexuality, and Colonial Modernities* (Antoinette Burton, ed. 1999).

27. See Deborah L. Rhode, "The 'No-Problem' Problem: Feminist Challenges and Cultural Change," 100 *Yale L.J.* 1731 (1991).

28. See, generally, *Democracy and Difference: Contesting the Boundaries of the Political* (Seyla Benhabib, ed. 1996).

29. See, e.g., Barbara Crossett, "What It Takes to Stop Slavery," *N.Y. Times*, Apr. 22, 2001, Sect. 4, at 5; "Benin Unsure if Ship Carried Child Slaves," *N.Y. Times*, Apr. 18, 2001, at A10.

30. See *Prosecutor v. Kunarac, Kovac, and Vukovic*, Cas Nos. IT-96-23-T, IT-96-23/1-T) (Int'l Crim. Trib. for Former Yugoslavia, Feb. 22, 2001), [www.un.org/icty/inde-e.htm]. The case is pending on appeal.

31. See Marlise Simons, "Three Serbs Convicted in Wartime Rapes," *N.Y. Times*, Feb. 23, 2001, at A1 (also discussing that the tribunal had before tried cases of rape through definitions of torture).

32. Id. Distressingly, the report from a syndicated Associated Press story described the judgment not in terms of rejecting particular behaviors of men so much as underscoring women's "special vulnerability during war." See "U.N. Tribunal Convicts 3 of 'Sexual Enslavement' over Bosnian Atrocities" (reprinted by the *New Haven Register*, Feb. 23, 2001).

33. As of this writing, that decision is pending on appeal.

34. See *International Feminism: Networking Against Female Sexual Slavery: Report of the Global Feminist Workshop to Organize Against Traffic in Women* (Kathleen Barry, Charlotte Bunch, and Shirley Castley, eds., Apr. 6–15, 1983).

35. See Kathleen Barry, "The Opening Paper: International Politics of Female Sexual Slavery," in *International Feminism*, at 21–25 (discussing the decision to form an international network). The focus of that work was on forced prostitution; one essay in the collection addressed the use of sexual slavery as a political weapon. See Ximena Bunster, "The Torture of Women Political Prisoners: A Case Study in Female Sexual Slavery," in *International Feminism*, at 94–102. Other work has developed the relationship between sexual slavery and war crimes. See, generally, Judith Gardam and Michelle Jarvis, "Women and Armed Conflict: The International Response to the Beijing Platform for Action," 32 *Colum Hum. Rts.*

L. Rev. 1 (2000): Patricia Wald, "Judging War Crimes," 1 *Chi. J. Int'l L.* 189 (2000); Cate Steains, "Gender Issues," in *The International Criminal Court: The Making of the Rome Statute* 357 (Roy S. Lee, ed. 1999).

36. See, generally, Judith Resnik, "Categorical Federalism," 111 *Yale L. J.* 619 (2001); Joyce Gelb, "Globalization and Feminism: The Impact of the New Transnationalisms," *Center for German and European Studies, Working Paper* 2.74 (2000).

37. See, e.g., Noelle Lenoir, "The Representation of Women in Politics: From Quotas to Parity in Elections," 50 *Int'l & Comp. L. Q.* 217 (2001); Eliane Vogel-Polsky, "Parity Democracy—Law and Europe," in *Gender Policies in the European Union* 61 (Mariagrazi Rossilli, ed. 2000).

38. See, e.g., Arnlaug Leira, "Caring as Social Right: Cash for Child Care and Daddy Leave," 5 *Soc. Pol.* 362 (1998); *Parental Leave* (Peter Moss and Fred Deven, eds. 1999).

Selected Bibliography

Alvesson, Mats, and Yvonne Due Billing, *Understanding Gender and Organizations* (1997).

American Bar Association, Commission on Opportunities for Minorities in the Profession, *Miles to Go: Progress of Minorities in the Legal Profession* (2000).

American Bar Association, Commission on Women in the Profession, *A Current Glance of Women in the Law* (2001).

———, Commission on Women in the Profession, *Balanced Lives for Lawyers: Changing the Culture of Legal Practice* (report prepared by Deborah L. Rhode, 2001).

———, Commission on Women in the Profession, *Unfinished Agenda: Women and the Legal Profession* (report prepared by Deborah L. Rhode, 2001).

———, Commission on Women in the Profession, *Fair Measure: Toward Effective Attorney Evaluation* (1997).

———, Commission on Women in the Profession, Multicultural Women's Network, *The Burdens of Both, the Privileges of Neither: A Report* (1994).

ABA, Young Lawyers Division, *The State of the Legal Profession* (1991).

Ashford, Susan J., "Championing Charged Issues: The Case of Gender Equity Within Organizations," in *Power and Influence in Organizations* (Roderick M. Kramer and Margaret A. Neale, eds. 1998).

Astin, Helen S., and Carole Leland, *Women of Influence, Women of Vision: A Cross-Generational Study of Leaders and Social Change* (1991).

Bar Association of San Francisco, *Interim Report: Goals and Timetables for Minority Hiring and Advancement* (2000).

Beiner, Theresa M., "What Will Diversity on the Bench Mean for Justice?" 6 *Mich. J. Gender and L.* 113 (1999).

Bell, Ella L.J. Edmondson, and Stella M. Nkomo, *Our Separate Ways: Black and White Women and the Struggle for Professional Identity* (2001).

Bell, Ella L., Toni Denton, and Stella Nkomo, "Women of Color in Management, Toward an Inclusive Approach," in *Women in Management: Trends, Issues, and Challenges in Managerial Diversity* (Ellen A. Fagenson, ed. 1993).

Boston Bar Association Task Force on Professional Challenges and Family Needs, *Facing the Grail: Confronting the Cost of Work-Family Imbalance* (1999).

Bowman, Cynthia Grant, "Bibliographical Essay: Women and the Legal Profession," 7 *Am. U. J. Gender Soc. Pol'y & L.* 149 (1999).

Braden, Maria, *Women Politicians and the Media* (1996).

Bridge, Diana L., "The Glass Ceiling and Sexual Stereotyping: Historical and Legal Perspectives of Women in the Workplace," 4 *Va. J. Soc. Pol'y & L.* 581 (1997).

Burke, Ronald J., and Marilyn J. Davidson, "Women in Management: Current Research Issues," in *Women in Management: Current Research Issues* (Marilyn J. Davidson and Ronald J. Burke, eds. 1994).

Business and Professional Women Foundation and American Management Association, *Compensation and Benefits: A Focus on Gender* (1999).

Cahill, Stephanie Francis, and Pearl J. Platt, "Bringing Diversity to Partnerships Continues to Be an Elusive Goal," *San Francisco Daily J.*, July 28, 1997, at 1.

Carroll, Susan J., *Representing Women: Congresswomen's Perceptions of Their Representational Roles* (2000).

———, "The Politics of Difference: Women Public Officials as Agents of Change," 5 *Stan. L. & Pol'y Rev.* 11 (1994).

Carter, Terry, "Paths Need Paving," *ABA J.*, Sept. 2000, at 34.

Case, Mary Anne C, "Disaggregating Gender from Sex and Sexual Orientation: The Effeminate Man in the Law and Feminist Jurisprudence," 105 *Yale L. J.* 1 (1995).

Catalyst, *Women of Color in Corporate Management: Three Years Later* (2002).

———, *Women in Law: Making the Case* (2001).

———, *Catalyst Facts: Women in Business* (2000).

———, *Census of Women Corporate Officers and Top Earners* (2000).

———, *Flexible Work Arrangements III: A Ten Year Perspective* (2000).

———, *Creating Women's Networks: A How-to Guide for Women and Companies* (1999).

———, *Minority Women in Management* (1999).

———, *Women of Color in Corporate Management: Dynamics of Career Advancement* 15 (1999).

———, *Advancing Women in Business: The Catalyst Guide to Best Practices from the Corporate Leaders* (1998).

————, *A New Approach to Flexibility: Managing the Work/Time Equation* 16 (1997).

————, *Women in Corporate Leadership: Progress and Prospects* 37 (1996).

Center for American Women in Politics, *Women in Elected Office, 2000 Fact Sheet Summaries* (May 2000).

————, *Voices, Views, and Votes: Women in the 103rd Congress* (1995).

————, *The Impact of Women in Public Office* (1991).

Chanow, Linda B., *Results of Lawyers, Work, and Family: A Study of Alternative Schedule Programs at Law Firms in the District of Columbia* (May 2000).

Clanton, Karen, ed., *Dear Sisters, Dear Daughters: Words of Wisdom from Multicultural Women Attorneys Who've Been There and Done That* (2000).

Cleveland, Jeanette N., Margaret Stockdale, and Kevin R. Murphy, *Women and Men in Organizations: Sex and Gender Issues at Work* (2000).

Clift, Eleanor, and Tom Brazaitis, *Madam President: Shattering the Last Glass Ceiling* (2000).

Davidson, Marilyn J., and Ronald J. Burke, eds., *Women in Management: Current Research Issues* (1994).

Davis, Sue, Susan Haire, and Donald R. Songer, "Voting Behavior and Gender on the U.S. Court of Appeals," 77 *Judicature* 129 (1993).

Dolan, Julie, "Support for Women's Interests in the 103rd Congress: The Distinct Impact of Congressional Women," 18 *Women and Politics* 81 (1997).

Dolan, Kathleen, and Lynne E. Ford, "Women in the State Legislatures: Feminist Identity and Legislative Behaviors," 23 *American Politics Quarterly* 96 (1995).

Duerst-Lahti, Georgia, and Rita Mae Kelly, eds., *Gender, Power, Leadership, and Governance* (1995).

————, "On Governance, Leadership, and Gender," in *Gender, Power, Leadership, and Governance*, at 12.

Eagly, Alice H., and Blair T. Johnson, "Gender and Leadership Style: A Meta-Analysis," 108 *Psychol. Bull.* 233 (1990).

Eagly, Alice H., and S. J. Karau, "Gender and Emergence of Leaders: A Meta-Analysis," 60 *Psychol. Bull.* 685 (1991).

Eagly, Alice H., S. J. Karau, and Mona G. Makhijani, "Gender and the Effectiveness of Leaders: A Meta-Analysis," 117 *Psychol. Bull.* 125 (1995).

Eagly, Alice H., Mona G. Makhijani, and Bruce G. Klonsky, "Gender and the Evaluation of Leaders: A Meta-Analysis," 111 *Psychol. Bull.* 3 (1992).

Eagly, Alice H., and Wendy Wood, "Explaining Sex Differences in Social Behavior: A Meta-Analytic Perspective," 17 *Personality and Social Psychol. Bull.* 306 (1991).

Ely, Robin J., and David A. Thomas, "Making Differences Matter: A New Paradigm for Managing Diversity," *Harvard Business Review*, Sept.–Oct. 1996, at 79.

Epstein, Cynthia Fuchs, *Deceptive Distinctions: Sex, Gender, and the Social Order* (1988).

Epstein, Cynthia Fuchs, et al., "Glass Ceilings and Open Doors: Women's Advancement in the Legal Profession," 64 *Fordham L. Rev.* 291 (1995).

Epstein, Cynthia Fuchs, Carroll Seron, Bonnie Oglensky, and Robert Saute, *The Part-Time Paradox* (1999).

Families and Work Institute, *Business Work-Life Study* (1998).

Federal Glass Ceiling Commission, *Good for Business: Making Full Use of the Nation's Human Capital* (1995).

Final Report and Recommendations of the Eighth Circuit Gender Fairness Task Force, 31 *Creighton L. Rev.* 9 (1997).

Fletcher, Joyce K., *Disappearing Acts: Gender, Power, and Relational Practice at Work* (1999).

Foschi, Martha, "Double Standards in the Evaluation of Men and Women," 59 *Soc. Psychol.* 237 (1996).

Gatland, Laura, "The Top 5 Myths About Part-Time Partners," *Perspectives*, spring 1997, at 11.

Graham, Deborah, "Second to None: Best Practices for Women Lawyers and Their Employers" (ABA Commission on Women in the Profession, unpublished discussion draft 2001).

Gruhl, John, et al., "Women as Policymakers: The Case of Trial Judges," 25 *Am. J. Pol. Science* 308 (1981).

Handlin, Alice, *Whatever Happened to the Year of the Woman? Why Women Still Aren't Making It to the Top in Politics* (1998).

Hartman, Mary S., ed., *Talking Leadership: Conversations with Powerful Women* (1995).

Harvard Women's Law Association, *Presumed Equal: What America's Top Women Lawyers Really Think of Their Firms* 72 (1995).

Heilbrun, Carolyn, and Judith Resnik, "Convergences: Law, Literature, and Feminism," 99 *Yale L. J.* 1913 (1990).

Hochschild, Arlie Russell, *The Time Bind: When Work Becomes Home and Home Becomes Work* (1997).

Jamieson, Kathleen Hall, *Beyond the Double Bind: Women and Leadership* (1995).

Kabacoff, Robert I., *Gender Differences in Organizational Leadership: A Large Sample Study*, available on-line at [www.mrg.com/articles/Gender_Paper_1998.pdf].

Kanter, Rosabeth Moss, *Men and Women of the Corporation* (1977).

Kellerman, Barbara, *Reinventing Leadership: Making the Connection Between Politics and Business* (1999).

Kent, Russell L., and Sherry E. Moss, "Effects of Sex and Gender Role on Leader Emergence," 37 *Academy of Mgmt. J.* 1335 (1994).

Kessler, Gladys, "Women, Justice, and Authority Conference," (unpublished paper 2000).

King, Cherryl Simrell, "Sex Role Identity and Decision Styles: How Gender Helps Explain the Paucity of Women at the Top," in *Gender Power, Leadership and Governance* 67 (Georgia Duerst-Lahti and Rita May Kelly, eds. 1995).

Klenke, Karin, *Women and Leadership: A Contextual Perspective* (1996).

Kolb, Judith A., "The Effect of Gender Role, Attitude Toward Leadership, and Self-Confidence on Leader Emergence: Implications for Leadership Development," 4 *Hum. Resource Dev. Q.* 305 (1999).

————, "Are We Still Stereotyping Leadership? A Look at Gender and Other Predictors of Leader Emergence," 28 *Small Group Research* 370 (1997).

Kramer, Roderick M., and Margaret A. Neale, eds., *Power and Influence in Organizations* (1998).

Krieger, Linda Hamilton, "The Content of Our Categories: A Cognitive Bias Approach to Discrimination and Equal Employment Opportunity," 47 *Stan. L. Rev.* 1161 (1995).

Landau, Jacqueline, "The Relationship of Race and Gender to Managers' Ratings of Promotion Potential," 16 *J. Organizational Behav.* 391 (1995).

Landers, Renee M., James B. Rebitzer, and Lowell J. Taylor, "Rat Race Redux: Adverse Selection in the Determination of Work Hours in Law Firms," 86 *Am. Econ. Rev.* 329 (1996).

Lerner, Melvin J., *The Belief in a Just World: A Fundamental Delusion* (1980).

Lipman-Blumen, Jean, "Connective Leadership: Female Leadership Styles in the 21st Century Workplace," 35 *Soc. Perspectives* 183 (1992).

Lorber, Judith, *Paradoxes of Gender* (1994).

Los Angeles County Bar Association Ad Hoc Committee on Sexual Orientation Bias, "The Los Angeles County Bar Association Report on Sexual Orientation Bias," reprinted in 4 *S. Cal. L. & Women's Stud.* (1995).

Mandel, Ruth B., and Debra L. Dodson, "Do Women Officeholders Make a Difference?" in *The American Women 1992–1993* (Paula Ries and Ann J. Stone, eds. 1992).

Martell, Richard F., "Sex Stereotyping in the Executive Suite: 'Much Ado About Something,'" 13 *J. Soc. Behav. and Personality* 127 (1998).

Martin, Joanne, and Debra Meyerson, "Women and Power: Confronting Resistance and Disorganized Action," in *Power and Influence in Organizations* 311 (Roderick M. Kramer and Margaret A. Neale, eds. 1998).

Mattis, Mary C., "Organizational Initiatives in the USA for Advancing Managerial Women," in *Women in Management: Current Research Issues* (Marilyn J. Davidson and Ronald J. Burke, eds. 1994).

Meyerson, Debra E., and Maureen A. Scully, "Tempered Radicalism and the Politics of Ambivalence and Change," 6 *Org. Science* 585 (1995).

Mezey, Susan Gluck, "Increasing the Numbers of Women in Office: Does It Matter?" in *The Year of the Woman: Myths and Realities* (Elizabeth Adell Cook, Sue Thomas, and Clyde Wilcox, eds. 1994).

Molm, Linda, and Mark Hedley, "Gender, Power and Social Exchange," in *Gender Interaction and Inequality* (Cecilia L. Ridgeway, ed. 1992).

Morris, Betsy, "Executive Women Confront Midlife Crisis," *Fortune,* Sept. 18, 1995.

Morrison, Ann M., et al., *Breaking the Glass Ceiling: Can Women Reach the Top of America's Largest Corporations?* (1987).

Moskal, Brian S., "Women Make Better Managers," *Industry Wk.*, Feb. 3, 1997, at 17.

Nossel, Suzanne, and Elizabeth Westfall, *Presumed Equal: What America's Top Women Lawyers Really Think About Their Firms* (2d ed. 1998).

Pettigrew, Thomas F., and Joanne Martin, "Shaping the Organizational Context for Black American Inclusion," 43 *J. Soc. Issues* 41 (1987).

Platz, Sue, "Sex Differences in Leadership: How Real Are They?" *Acad. of Mgmt. Review* 118 (1986).

Poirier, Mark R., "Gender Stereotypes at Work," 65 *Brook. L. Rev.* 1073 (1999).

Poole, Keith T., and L. Harmon Zeigler, *Women, Public Opinion, and Politics: The Changing Political Opinions of American Women* 8 (1985).

Powell, Gary N., *Women and Men in Management* (1988).

———, "One More Time: Do Female and Male Managers Differ?" 4 *Acad. of Mgmt. Executive* 68 (1990).

Radcliffe Public Policy Institute and The Boston Club, *Suiting Themselves: Women's Leadership Styles in Today's Workplace* (1999), available on-line at: [www.thebostonclub.com/resources/rc.pdf].

Report of the Ninth Circuit Gender Bias Task Force, *The Effects of Gender in the Federal Courts* 60 (discussion draft 1992).

Rhode, Deborah L., "Balanced Lives for Lawyers," 70 *Fordham L. Rev.* 2207 (2002).

———, "Gender and the Profession: The No-Problem Problem," 30 *Hofstra L. Rev.* 1001 (2002).

———, *In the Interests of Justice: Reforming the Legal Profession* (2000).

———, *Speaking of Sex: The Denial of Gender Inequality* (1998).

———, "Myths of Meritocracy," 65 *Fordham L. Rev.* 585 (1996).

———, "Gender and Professional Roles," 63 *Fordham L. Rev.* 39 (1994).

Ridgeway, Cecilia L., and Shelley J. Correl, "Limiting Inequality Through Interaction: The End(s) of Gender," 29 *Contemp. Soc.* 110 (2000).

Rubenstein, William B., "Queer Studies II: Some Reflections on the Study of Sexual Orientation Bias in the Legal Profession," 8 *UCLA Women's L. J.* 379 (1998).

Samborn, Hope Viner, "Higher Hurdles for Women," *ABA J.*, Sept. 2000, at 30.

Schor, Juliet B., *The Overworked American: The Unexpected Decline of Leisure* (1993).

Segal, Jennifer A., "The Decision Making of Clinton's Nontraditional Judicial Appointees," 80 *Judicature* 279 (1997).

Shimanoff, S. B., and M. M. Jenkins, "Leadership and Gender: Challenging Assumptions and Recognizing Resources," in *Small Group Communication* (R. S. Cathcart and L. A. Samovar, eds. 1996).

Spelman, Elizabeth V., *Inessential Woman: Problems of Exclusion in Feminist Thought* (1988).

Stites-Doe, Susan, and James J. Cordiro, "The Impact of Women Managers on Firm Performance: Evidence from Large U.S. Firms," *International Review of Women and Leadership*, July 1997.

Tamerius, Karen L., "Sex, Gender, and Leadership in the Representation of Women," in *Gender, Power, Leadership, and Governance* 93, 108 (Georgia Duerst-Lahti and Rita Mae Kelly, eds. 1995).

Thomas, David A., and Karen L. Proudford, "Making Sense of Race Relations in Organizations," in *Addressing Cultural Issues in Organization, Theory for Practice* (Robert T. Carter, ed. 2000).

Thomas, Sue, *How Women Legislate* (1994).

———, "Women in State Legislatures: One Step at a Time," in *The Year of the Woman: Myths and Realities* (Elizabeth Adell Cook, Sue Thomas, and Clyde Wilcox, eds. 1994).

Valian, Virginia, "The Cognitive Basis of Gender Bias," 65 *Brook. L. Rev.* 1037 (1999).

———, *Why So Slow? The Advancement of Women* (1998).

Wajcman, Judy, *Managing Like a Man: Women and Men in Corporate Management* (1998).

Walker, Thomas G., and Deborah J. Barrow, "Diversification of the Federal Bench: Policy and Process Ramifications," 47 *J. Pol.* 596, 607 (1985).

Wangensteen, Betsy, "Managing Style: What's Gender Got to Do with It?" *Crain's New York Business*, Sept. 29, 1997, at 23.

Whicker, Marcia Lynn, and Lois Duke Whitaker, "Women in Congress," in *Women in Politics: Outsiders or Insiders?* 171 (Lois Duke Whitaker, ed. 1999).

Wilkins, David, and G. Mitu Gulati, "Why Are There So Few Black Lawyers in Corporate Law Firms? An Institutional Analysis," 84 *Cal. L. Rev.* 493, 570 (1996).

Willard, Abbie F., and Paula A. Patton, National Association for Law Placement Foundation, *Perceptions of Partnership: The Allure and Accessibility of the Brass Ring* 99 (1999).

Williams, Joan, *Unbending Gender: Why Family and Work Conflict and What to Do About It* (2000).

Witt, Linda, *Running as a Woman: Gender and Power in American Politics* (1994).

Index